THE ARCHAEOLOGICAL EXPLORATIONS OF RAJASTHAN

A BRIEF HISTORY OF EXPLORATIONS IN RAJASTHAN

ISHWAR SINGH

Made with ♥ on the Notion Press Platform
www.notionpress.com

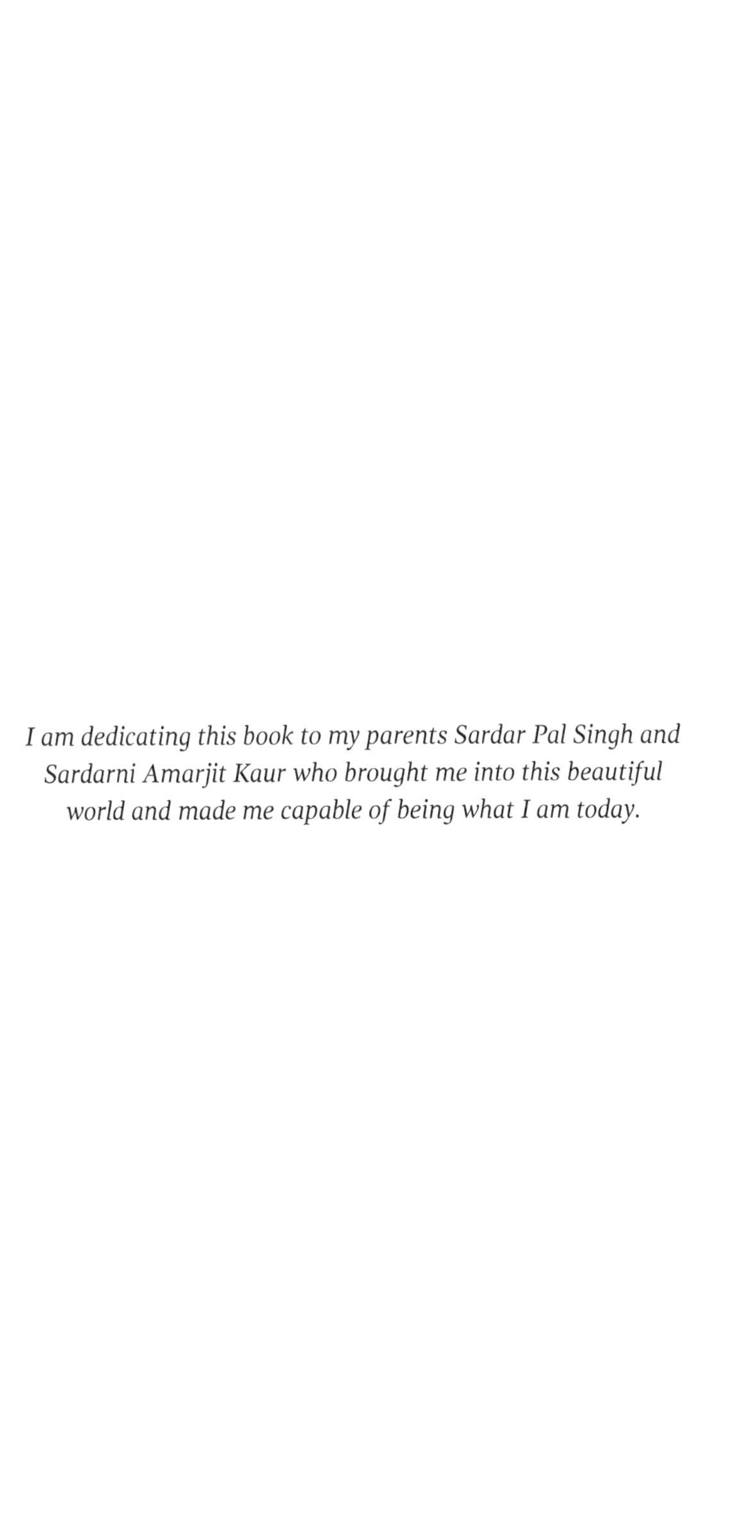

I am dedicating this book to my parents Sardar Pal Singh and Sardarni Amarjit Kaur who brought me into this beautiful world and made me capable of being what I am today.

Contents

Contents

Foreword

Rajasthan, a land of vibrant colors, rich traditions, and a storied past, serves as a remarkable tapestry of human history and culture. From the rugged terrains of the Thar Desert to the majestic forts that dot the skyline, every corner of this region holds secrets waiting to be uncovered. This book, "The Archaeological Explorations of Rajasthan," embarks on a journey to illuminate these secrets, offering readers a comprehensive understanding of the archaeological significance that defines this captivating state.

The history of Rajasthan is one of resilience and adaptability. Ancient civilizations flourished in this arid landscape, crafting intricate societal structures and monumental architecture that speak to their ingenuity and creativity. As we delve into the layers of history embedded in Rajasthan's soil, we encounter stories of the early inhabitants who thrived against the odds, the grand dynasties that rose and fell, and the enduring cultural practices that continue to thrive today.

In an era where technology intersects with traditional methods of exploration, this book highlights the transformative power of modern archaeological techniques. Aerial surveys and remote sensing have revolutionized our understanding of the past, enabling researchers to reveal hidden sites and artifacts without disturbing the delicate historical context. This innovative approach, combined with a rich interdisciplinary perspective, allows for a more nuanced appreciation of

Rajasthan's heritage.

Each section of this book offers insights into the various epochs of Rajasthan's history, from the Stone Age to the medieval period, emphasizing the continuous evolution of its civilizations. By exploring the architectural marvels, the cultural practices, and the environmental adaptations of its people, we come to understand the profound relationship between humans and their surroundings.

As you embark on this exploration, I invite you to immerse yourself in the rich narrative that unfolds within these pages. The stories of Rajasthan are not merely relics of the past; they are the threads that connect us to our shared human experience. This book is a tribute to the archaeologists, historians, and communities who have dedicated themselves to preserving and interpreting Rajasthan's cultural heritage.

May this journey through time inspire curiosity and foster a deeper appreciation for the remarkable history of Rajasthan, reminding us of the enduring legacies that shape our present and guide our future.

Birinder Pal Kaur

Preface

In embarking on the journey of writing *The Archaeological Explorations of Rajasthan*, I have aimed to illuminate the rich tapestry of history, culture, and heritage that defines this remarkable region of India. Rajasthan, known for its stunning landscapes, architectural grandeur, and vibrant traditions, holds within its bounds a wealth of archaeological treasures that reflect the resilience and ingenuity of its people over millennia.

This book serves as a comprehensive exploration of Rajasthan's archaeological landscape, documenting the various civilizations that have thrived in this diverse environment. From prehistoric settlements to the majestic forts and palaces of the Rajput era, each chapter delves into a specific aspect of the region's archaeological significance. My intention is to provide readers with an in-depth understanding of how the geography of Rajasthan has influenced human settlement, cultural development, and architectural styles.

The importance of archaeology in understanding our past cannot be overstated. As we uncover artifacts, structures, and ancient remnants, we piece together the narratives of those who came before us. This book highlights the transformative power of modern techniques such as aerial surveys and remote sensing, which have revolutionized archaeological research and allowed for discoveries that were once thought impossible. These innovations provide a clearer picture of Rajasthan's historical landscape, revealing hidden sites and allowing us to interpret the social and cultural dynamics of ancient civilizations.

Throughout this work, I have sought to integrate interdisciplinary perspectives, drawing from history, anthropology, environmental studies, and folklore. By doing so, I aim to present a holistic view of Rajasthan's past, recognizing the interconnectedness of various cultural influences that have shaped its identity. I believe that understanding the past enriches our appreciation of the present and informs our vision for the future.

I am grateful to the many scholars, archaeologists, and local communities who have contributed to the ongoing exploration and preservation of Rajasthan's heritage. Their dedication and passion for unearthing the stories embedded in the landscape serve as an inspiration for this work.

As you delve into the pages of this book, I hope you will be inspired to explore the wonders of Rajasthan and foster a deeper connection with its rich history. May this exploration ignite a sense of curiosity and appreciation for the incredible journeys of human civilization that continue to shape our world today.

Ishwar Singh

Acknowledgements

I would like to take a moment to express my heartfelt gratitude to my late mother-in-law, Smt. Gurjeet Kaur, and my father-in-law, Justice Narinder Singh. Their unwavering support and encouragement have been instrumental in my journey, both personally and professionally.

Smt. Gurjeet Kaur's wisdom, warmth, and love have left an indelible mark on my life. Her passion for learning and appreciation for culture inspired me to delve deeper into the rich heritage of Rajasthan. Though she is no longer with us, her spirit continues to guide me, and I hope to honor her memory through my work.

Justice Narinder Singh's commitment to justice, integrity, and excellence has been a beacon for me. His insights and guidance have provided me with the strength to pursue my endeavors with confidence. The values he instilled in our family resonate throughout this book, reminding me of the importance of knowledge and heritage.

To both of them, I dedicate this work in gratitude for their love, guidance, and the lasting legacy they have created within our family. Thank you for your unwavering belief in me and for inspiring me to explore and share the stories of Rajasthan's rich archaeological heritage.

Ishwar Singh

Prologue

Rajasthan, a land that resonates with echoes of its storied past, is more than just a geographical entity; it is a vibrant canvas painted with the colors of ancient civilizations, majestic architecture, and rich cultural traditions. As one traverses the undulating sand dunes of the Thar Desert or gazes upon the towering fortresses that dot the skyline, it becomes evident that this region has been a cradle of human ingenuity, resilience, and artistry.

The essence of Rajasthan lies not only in its breathtaking landscapes but also in the myriad stories etched into its soil. From the earliest Stone Age settlements to the grand palaces of the Rajputs, every artifact and architectural marvel tells a tale of adaptation, survival, and cultural evolution. This book seeks to uncover these narratives, diving deep into the archaeological explorations that have revealed the richness of Rajasthan's history.

As we embark on this journey, we will explore the evolution of civilizations that have flourished in this arid landscape, understanding how they adapted to the challenges posed by their environment. We will delve into the profound impact of geography on settlement patterns, agricultural practices, and architectural styles. By examining archaeological findings, we aim to piece together the complex puzzle of human history that has unfolded in Rajasthan over thousands of years.

In a world where technological advancements continually reshape our understanding of the past, modern archaeological methods such as aerial surveys and remote sensing have opened new frontiers in research. These innovations enable us to see Rajasthan's historical landscape in unprecedented detail, uncovering hidden treasures that were previously overlooked. The stories of these discoveries will be woven throughout the pages of this book, illustrating how the past remains a vital part of our present.

This work is not merely an academic exploration; it is a celebration of the rich heritage that defines Rajasthan. It is an invitation to all who read it to appreciate the intricacies of human history, the beauty of cultural diversity, and the importance of preserving our shared legacy. As we delve into the archaeological explorations of this remarkable region, let us embark on a journey that transcends time, connecting us to the echoes of those who walked these lands long before us. Welcome to the world of Rajasthan's archaeological wonders—a realm where the past comes alive, waiting to share its secrets with those willing to listen.

CHAPTER ONE

Introduction to Rajasthan's Archaeological Landscape

1.1 Overview of Rajasthan's Geography and Historical Settlements

Rajasthan, located in the northwestern part of India, is renowned for its diverse geography, rich cultural heritage, and significant historical settlements. The state, which translates to "Land of Kings," is the largest in India by area, covering approximately 342,239 square kilometers. It is bordered by Punjab to the north, Haryana to the northeast, Uttar Pradesh to the east, and Madhya Pradesh to the southeast, while to the west and southwest, it shares an international border with Pakistan. The geographical diversity of Rajasthan encompasses vast deserts, fertile plains, rugged mountains, and significant river systems, contributing to its unique cultural and historical landscape.

1.1.1 Geographic Features of Rajasthan

The geography of Rajasthan is characterized by its striking contrasts. The Aravalli Range, one of the oldest mountain ranges in the world, runs diagonally through the state, stretching from the northeastern part of Rajasthan to its southwestern tip. This mountain range is not only a prominent geographic feature but also plays a crucial role in influencing the climate and biodiversity of the region. To the west of the Aravallis lies the Thar Desert, also known as the Great Indian Desert, which covers a significant portion of western Rajasthan. The Thar Desert is known for its arid landscape, sandy dunes, and extreme temperature variations between day and night.

Rajasthan is also home to several rivers, with the Chambal, Banas, and Sabarmati being the most notable. These rivers, along with their tributaries, provide essential water resources for irrigation and drinking, especially in regions that face water scarcity. The state's geography has not only shaped its environment but has also influenced human settlements and the development of various civilizations throughout history.

1.1.2 Historical Settlements in Rajasthan

Rajasthan boasts a rich tapestry of historical settlements, many of which date back to ancient times. These settlements have been influenced by various dynasties, including the Mauryas, Guptas, Rajputs, and Mughals, each contributing to the cultural and architectural heritage of the region. The historical significance of these settlements is evident in the numerous forts, palaces, temples, and other architectural marvels that dot the landscape.

One of the most famous historical cities is Jaipur, the capital of Rajasthan, known as the "Pink City." Founded in the 18th century by Maharaja Sawai Jai Singh II, Jaipur is renowned for its well-planned streets, stunning palaces, and forts, including the iconic Hawa Mahal and Amber Fort. The city is a UNESCO World Heritage Site and serves as a testament to the grandeur of Rajput architecture and urban planning.

Another notable historical settlement is Udaipur, often referred to as the "City of Lakes." Founded by Maharana Udai Singh II in the 16th century, Udaipur is famous for its beautiful palaces, including the City Palace and Jag Mandir, set against the backdrop of picturesque lakes. The city reflects the cultural richness of Rajasthan and has been a center for art and architecture for centuries.

Jaisalmer, known as the "Golden City," is another significant historical settlement, characterized by its yellow sandstone architecture and the magnificent Jaisalmer Fort, which stands as a UNESCO World Heritage Site. The fort is a living fort with shops, hotels, and residences, showcasing the vibrant culture of the local population.

1.1.3 Archaeological Significance

The archaeological significance of Rajasthan is immense, with numerous sites revealing evidence of ancient civilizations and cultures. Excavations at sites such as Kalibangan and Ahar have uncovered artifacts dating back to the Indus Valley Civilization, providing insights into early urban planning and lifestyle. These sites have revealed a wealth of information about the social, economic, and technological advancements of the time.

The state's historical settlements also provide a glimpse into the lives of the Rajput warriors who ruled the region. The forts and palaces constructed by these rulers not only served as military strongholds but also as symbols of power and prestige. The architectural styles found in Rajasthan, characterized by intricate carvings, frescoes, and majestic structures, reflect the artistic sensibilities of the time and the influence of various cultures that interacted within the region.

1.1.4 Climate and Its Impact on Settlements

The climate of Rajasthan is predominantly arid, with extreme temperatures and limited rainfall. The state experiences three primary seasons: summer, monsoon, and winter. Summers can be scorching, with temperatures soaring above 45°C (113°F), while winters are relatively mild, with temperatures dropping to around 5°C (41°F) in some areas. The monsoon season, though brief, brings much-needed rainfall, which is crucial for agriculture and water supply.

The harsh climatic conditions have significantly influenced settlement patterns in Rajasthan. Historically, people settled near riverbanks and in regions where water was accessible, leading to the development of agricultural communities. The scarcity of water resources has also led to innovative water management practices, such as the construction of stepwells and tanks, which served as vital sources of water for drinking and irrigation. These practices highlight the adaptability of the inhabitants to their environment and their resilience in the face of climatic challenges.

1.1.5 Cultural Heritage and Diversity

Rajasthan's geography and historical settlements have fostered a rich cultural heritage that is evident in its festivals, music, dance, and handicrafts. The diverse communities residing in Rajasthan, including Rajputs, Jats, Meenas, and others, contribute to the state's vibrant cultural fabric. Each community has its own traditions, customs, and art forms, creating a mosaic of cultural expressions.

The state is famous for its folk music and dance forms, such as Ghoomar, Kalbeliya, and Bhavai, which are often performed during festivals and celebrations. Rajasthan is also known for its handicrafts, including block printing, pottery, and jewelry, which reflect the artistic skills passed down through generations. These cultural elements are deeply intertwined with the historical context of the region, offering a glimpse into the lives and traditions of its people.

1.2 Importance of Archaeological Studies in Rajasthan

Archaeological studies in Rajasthan play a pivotal role in understanding the region's rich historical, cultural, and social evolution. As one of the most culturally diverse and historically significant states in India, Rajasthan presents a unique opportunity for archaeologists and researchers to explore the interplay between geography, human settlement, and cultural development. The importance of archaeological studies in Rajasthan can be categorized into several key aspects, each contributing to a more comprehensive understanding of the region's past.

1.2.1 Uncovering Historical Narratives

One of the foremost benefits of archaeological studies in Rajasthan is their capacity to uncover historical narratives that have shaped the state and the broader Indian subcontinent. The region is home to numerous ancient settlements, forts, and temples that hold invaluable artifacts and inscriptions. Excavations at sites like Kalibangan and Ahar have revealed remnants of the Indus Valley Civilization, allowing researchers to piece together insights into early urban planning, trade, and cultural practices. Such discoveries not only enrich our understanding of Rajasthan's history but also contribute to the larger narrative of India's ancient civilizations.

1.2.2 Cultural Heritage Preservation

Archaeological studies are crucial for the preservation of Rajasthan's cultural heritage. The state boasts a wealth of historical monuments, forts, and palaces, many of which face threats from urbanization, tourism, and environmental factors. Systematic archaeological research helps document and assess these sites, ensuring that their historical and cultural significance is recognized and preserved for future generations. Initiatives focused on restoration and conservation, informed by archaeological findings, can protect these irreplaceable cultural assets from degradation and loss.

1.2.3 Understanding Socio-Economic Structures

Archaeological studies provide valuable insights into the socio-economic structures of past societies in Rajasthan. By examining artifacts such as pottery, tools, and remnants of daily life, researchers can infer the economic activities, trade networks, and social hierarchies of ancient communities. For instance, findings from the Harappan sites in Rajasthan highlight advanced agricultural practices and trade relations with other regions, offering a glimpse into the complexity of early economies. Understanding these socio-economic structures is essential for comprehending how communities adapted to their environments and interacted with one another over time.

1.2.4 Enhancing Educational and Research Opportunities

Rajasthan's archaeological wealth creates numerous educational and research opportunities for scholars, students, and enthusiasts alike. Universities and research institutions often engage in archaeological projects that foster collaboration between local and international scholars. These initiatives not only contribute to academic knowledge but also promote public awareness and appreciation of Rajasthan's history. Moreover, educational programs that incorporate archaeological studies can inspire future generations to explore careers in history, archaeology, and heritage conservation, ensuring a continued interest in the region's past.

1.2.5 Promoting Tourism and Economic Development

The archaeological sites of Rajasthan, including forts, palaces, and ancient settlements, attract millions of tourists each year. This influx of visitors has significant implications for the local economy, as tourism generates revenue, creates jobs, and supports local crafts and industries. By promoting archaeological studies and highlighting the historical significance of these sites, the state can enhance its tourism offerings, creating a sustainable economic model that benefits local communities. Additionally, responsible tourism that prioritizes preservation can ensure that these historical sites remain intact for future visitors.

1.2.6 Fostering National Identity and Pride

Archaeological studies in Rajasthan contribute to the understanding of national identity and cultural pride. The discoveries and narratives revealed through archaeology help residents connect with their heritage and history. The rich tapestry of Rajasthan's past, including its valorous Rajput warriors, artistic traditions, and architectural marvels, fosters a sense of belonging and pride among its inhabitants. Celebrating and promoting this heritage can also strengthen regional identity within the broader context of India's diverse cultural landscape.

1.2.7 Interdisciplinary Insights

Finally, archaeological studies in Rajasthan offer interdisciplinary insights that enrich various fields of study, including history, anthropology, geology, and art history. By integrating methods and perspectives from different disciplines, researchers can develop a holistic understanding of the region's past. For example, geological studies can inform archaeological excavations about site formation processes, while art historical analysis can shed light on the aesthetic and symbolic significance of artifacts. Such interdisciplinary collaborations can lead to innovative research approaches and a deeper appreciation of Rajasthan's cultural heritage.

1.3 Chronological Evolution of Civilization in Rajasthan

Rajasthan, with its diverse landscapes and rich history, has been a cradle of civilization since ancient times. The chronological evolution of civilization in this region showcases the interplay of geography, culture, and politics over millennia. From prehistoric settlements to the rise of powerful kingdoms, Rajasthan's history reflects a complex tapestry of human achievement, resilience, and cultural richness.

1.3.1 Prehistoric Era

The journey of civilization in Rajasthan can be traced back to prehistoric times. Archaeological evidence suggests that early humans inhabited the region as far back as the Paleolithic period. Sites such as Bhimbetka and the nearby rock shelters provide evidence of early hunter-gatherer communities, showcasing their artistic expressions through cave paintings that depict hunting scenes, animals, and human figures. These artworks offer valuable insights into the lifestyle, beliefs, and environmental interactions of prehistoric societies.

Moving into the Mesolithic and Neolithic periods, Rajasthan saw the emergence of settled agricultural communities. The discovery of microliths and pottery at various sites indicates a transition from nomadic lifestyles to more settled forms of existence. The Neolithic period is particularly significant, as it marks the advent of agriculture, which laid the foundation for future civilizations. Settlements like Ahar and Kalibangan, located near the Ghaggar-Hakra River, are key archaeological sites that reveal evidence of early urban planning and agricultural practices.

1.3.2 Indus Valley Civilization (c. 3300–1300 BCE)

Rajasthan played a vital role in the Indus Valley Civilization (IVC), one of the world's earliest urban cultures. The IVC, known for its advanced urban planning, sophisticated drainage systems, and extensive trade networks, reached its zenith around 2500 BCE. Sites such as Kalibangan, located in the northern part of Rajasthan, provide crucial insights into this civilization's urban structure, with well-planned streets, public baths, and brick houses.

Kalibangan is notable for its unique layout, which includes a distinctive grid pattern and evidence of fire altars, suggesting religious practices among its inhabitants. The archaeological findings also point to agricultural practices, with the cultivation of wheat, barley, and pulses. The IVC's decline around 1900 BCE, attributed to factors like climate change and shifting trade routes, marked a significant turning point in the region's history.

1.3.3 Early Historical Period (c. 600 BCE – 300 CE)

The early historical period of Rajasthan is characterized by the rise of various kingdoms and the influence of religious philosophies. During this time, the region saw the emergence of several small republics and kingdoms, including the Kshatrapas and the Mauryas. The Mauryan Empire, under the leadership of Emperor Ashoka (c. 268–232 BCE), played a crucial role in spreading Buddhism across the region. Ashoka's edicts, inscribed on pillars and rocks, serve as a testament to his commitment to promoting moral governance and the welfare of his subjects.

The spread of Buddhism and Jainism during this period had a profound impact on the cultural and spiritual landscape of Rajasthan. Important Buddhist sites such as Sarnath and Ajmer reflect the influence of these religions on the socio-political dynamics of the time. The establishment of trade routes, particularly along the Grand Trunk Road, facilitated economic interactions and cultural exchanges with neighboring regions, further enriching Rajasthan's cultural heritage.

1.3.4 Rise of Rajput Kingdoms (c. 6th – 12th centuries)

The rise of the Rajput clans marked a significant phase in Rajasthan's history. From the 6th century onwards, various Rajput clans established powerful kingdoms throughout the region, including the Sisodias of Mewar, the Rathores of Marwar, and the Chauhans of Ajmer. These clans, known for their valor and chivalry, played a crucial role in shaping the political landscape of Rajasthan.

The Rajputs established numerous forts and palaces, many of which stand as architectural marvels today. The iconic Chittorgarh Fort, associated with the Sisodia dynasty, is a symbol of Rajput pride and resilience, featuring a series of palaces, temples, and water bodies. The fort witnessed several heroic tales of bravery and sacrifice, particularly during the sieges by Alauddin Khilji in the early 14th century.

The period also saw cultural advancements, with the flourishing of literature, music, and arts. The Rajput courts became centers of artistic expression, patronizing poets, musicians, and artisans. The development of the Rajput painting style, characterized by vibrant colors and intricate detailing, became an integral part of Rajasthan's artistic heritage.

1.3.5 Mughal Influence and Integration (c. 1526 – 1707)

The arrival of the Mughals in the early 16th century marked a new chapter in Rajasthan's history. The Mughal Empire, under Akbar, sought alliances with the Rajput clans, leading to a unique relationship characterized by mutual respect and cultural exchange. The marriages between Mughal emperors and Rajput princesses, notably the union of Akbar and Jodha Bai, fostered diplomatic ties and cultural integration.

The Mughals introduced new architectural styles, as seen in the construction of magnificent forts and palaces, blending Rajput and Mughal architectural elements. The Amer Fort in Jaipur, which showcases this amalgamation, is a prime example of the architectural grandeur that emerged during this period. Additionally, the Mughals promoted art, literature, and music, leading to a flourishing of cultural expressions in Rajasthan.

However, the later years of the Mughal Empire witnessed growing tensions and resistance from Rajput rulers. The decline of Mughal power in the late 17th century led to the resurgence of Rajput autonomy, as various clans sought to reclaim their sovereignty.

1.3.6 British Colonial Era (c. 1858 – 1947)

The British colonial period brought significant changes to Rajasthan's political landscape. The establishment of British rule in 1858 resulted in the integration of various princely states into the British Empire. The British adopted a policy of indirect rule, allowing local rulers to maintain some degree of autonomy in exchange for loyalty to the crown.

During this period, Rajasthan underwent infrastructural developments, including the construction of railways and roads, which facilitated trade and communication. However, the British policies also led to socio-economic changes, impacting traditional livelihoods and agrarian practices.

The Indian independence movement gained momentum in the early 20th century, with various leaders advocating for the rights of the people. Rajasthan witnessed significant participation in the freedom struggle, with local leaders rallying support for independence. The merging of princely states into the Indian Union post-independence marked a turning point, leading to the formation of modern Rajasthan.

1.3.7 Contemporary Era

In the contemporary era, Rajasthan has emerged as a prominent state in India, known for its rich cultural heritage, tourism, and economic development. The preservation of historical sites and the promotion of tourism have become key priorities, contributing to the state's economy. Rajasthan is recognized for its vibrant festivals, traditional crafts, and diverse cuisine, attracting visitors from across the globe.

The government and various organizations are actively involved in archaeological research and conservation efforts to safeguard the state's historical treasures. The integration of technology in archaeology has enabled more effective excavations, documentation, and preservation of artifacts, enhancing our understanding of the region's past.

Rajasthan's chronological evolution reflects a dynamic interplay of cultural, political, and social factors that have shaped its identity. From prehistoric settlements to the rise of powerful kingdoms and the influence of empires, the history of Rajasthan is a testament to human resilience and creativity. As scholars continue to explore the archaeological and historical landscape of Rajasthan, they unravel layers of history that enrich our understanding of this vibrant region and its contributions to India's diverse cultural heritage.

CHAPTER TWO

Prehistoric Rajasthan: The Early Human Settlements

2.1 Stone Age Tools and Findings

The Stone Age marks the earliest period of human history, characterized by the use of stone tools for hunting, gathering, and daily activities. In Rajasthan, this era holds significant archaeological importance, as it provides insights into the early human settlements and the lifestyle of prehistoric communities in the region. The discoveries of Stone Age tools and artifacts in various parts of Rajasthan offer valuable information about the technological advancements, survival strategies, and environmental adaptations of ancient populations. This section delves into the different phases of the Stone Age in Rajasthan, the types of tools discovered, and their implications for understanding early human history.

2.1.1 Paleolithic Era (c. 2.6 million years ago – 10,000 BCE)

The Paleolithic era, or the Old Stone Age, represents the earliest phase of human tool-making and the longest period of the Stone Age. The tools from this period were primarily made of stone, and early humans used them for hunting, cutting, and processing food. In Rajasthan, several Paleolithic sites have been discovered, shedding light on the presence of early human communities.

One of the most significant Paleolithic sites in Rajasthan is the Didwana region in the Nagaur district. Excavations in Didwana have unearthed a large number of stone tools, including hand axes, cleavers, and choppers. These tools, crafted from locally available materials such as quartzite and sandstone, suggest that early humans in the region had developed basic tool-making techniques. The hand axes, with their sharp edges, were likely used for cutting meat, processing plants, and breaking bones, while the cleavers and choppers were employed for more specific tasks such as skinning animals or cutting through tough materials.

The tools discovered in Didwana resemble those found in other parts of the Indian subcontinent, indicating that early humans in Rajasthan were part of a broader cultural tradition that spanned much of prehistoric India. Moreover, the presence of these tools in various stratigraphic layers suggests that early humans inhabited the region over a long period, adapting to changing environmental conditions and refining their tool making techniques over time.

Another important Paleolithic site in Rajasthan is the Luni River basin, where archaeologists have discovered a wide range of stone tools, including scrapers, points, and blades. These tools indicate that early humans in the region engaged in a variety of activities, from hunting to processing hides and other materials. The scrapers, for example, were likely used to clean animal hides, while the pointed tools may have been used for hunting or fishing.

2.1.2 Mesolithic Era (c. 10,000 BCE – 6,000 BCE)

The Mesolithic era, or the Middle Stone Age, represents a transitional phase between the Paleolithic and Neolithic periods. During this time, humans began to adapt to changing environmental conditions brought about by the end of the last Ice Age. As the climate became warmer and more stable, humans in Rajasthan developed new tools and techniques to exploit their environment more efficiently.

The Mesolithic sites in Rajasthan are particularly notable for the discovery of microliths—small, finely crafted stone tools that represent a significant technological advancement over the larger, cruder tools of the Paleolithic. Microliths were often used as composite tools, meaning they were attached to wooden or bone shafts to create more versatile and efficient implements such as arrows, spears, and knives.

Bagor, located in the Bhilwara district, is one of the most important Mesolithic sites in Rajasthan. Excavations at Bagor have revealed a large number of microliths, including blades, lunates (crescent-shaped tools), and burins (tools used for engraving or carving). The presence of these tools suggests that the inhabitants of Bagor were skilled hunters and gatherers, capable of making sophisticated tools for a variety of purposes. In addition to microliths, archaeologists have also discovered grinding stones at Bagor, indicating that the Mesolithic people of Rajasthan may have begun to process plant materials for consumption.

The Mesolithic era also saw the development of more complex social structures and the establishment of semi-permanent settlements. Evidence from sites like Bagor suggests that Mesolithic communities in Rajasthan may have practiced a form of seasonal migration, moving between different areas depending on the availability of resources. This mobility allowed them to exploit a wide range of environments, from river valleys to arid desert regions, and ensured their survival in a challenging and changing landscape.

2.1.3 Neolithic Era (c. 6,000 BCE – 2,000 BCE)

The Neolithic era, or the New Stone Age, marks a major turning point in human history, as it is associated with the development of agriculture and the transition from a nomadic, hunter-gatherer lifestyle to settled farming communities. In Rajasthan, the Neolithic period is characterized by the use of more advanced stone tools, the domestication of animals, and the cultivation of crops.

One of the most important Neolithic sites in Rajasthan is the Ahar culture, located near the modern city of Udaipur. The Ahar culture, which dates back to around 3,000 BCE, is notable for its use of stone tools, pottery, and agricultural practices. The people of Ahar were among the first in Rajasthan to cultivate crops such as wheat, barley, and pulses, marking the beginning of settled farming communities in the region. The discovery of sickle blades at Ahar suggests that Neolithic farmers used stone tools to harvest their crops, while the presence of grinding stones indicates that they processed grains into flour.

In addition to agricultural tools, Neolithic communities in Rajasthan also developed a wide range of stone implements for other purposes. These included axes, which were used for clearing land and building structures, as well as arrowheads and spear points, which were used for hunting. The Neolithic people of Rajasthan also began to experiment with new materials, such as bone and antler, which they used to make tools and ornaments.

The Neolithic period in Rajasthan also saw the development of more permanent settlements, with evidence of mud-brick houses and granaries at sites like Ahar. These settlements reflect the increasing complexity of Neolithic society, as communities became more sedentary and began to engage in activities such as trade, craft production, and social organization. The domestication of animals, including cattle, sheep, and goats, further contributed to the development of a stable and sustainable way of life.

2.1.4 Chalcolithic Transition (c. 2,000 BCE – 1,500 BCE)

The Chalcolithic period, also known as the Copper-Stone Age, marks the transition from the Stone Age to the use of metal tools. In Rajasthan, this period is represented by the Ahar-Banas culture, which flourished in the southern part of the state. The Ahar-Banas people were among the first in Rajasthan to use copper tools alongside stone implements, marking a significant technological advancement.

Archaeological excavations at Ahar have revealed a wide range of copper objects, including axes, chisels, and ornaments. These copper tools were used in conjunction with traditional stone tools, allowing the Ahar-Banas people to engage in more complex activities such as metalworking, craft production, and long-distance trade. The presence of copper artifacts suggests that Rajasthan was part of a broader trade network that extended across the Indian subcontinent, facilitating the exchange of goods and ideas between different regions.

The Chalcolithic period also saw the development of more sophisticated pottery, with the Ahar-Banas people producing fine red and black ware pottery decorated with intricate designs. This pottery provides valuable insights into the cultural practices of Chalcolithic communities in Rajasthan, as it was used for both everyday activities and ritual purposes.

2.2 Evidence of Early Human Activity in the Aravalli Range

The Aravalli Range, one of the oldest mountain ranges in the world, stretching from Gujarat through Rajasthan and into Delhi, is a site of immense archaeological significance. For millennia, these ancient hills have served as a cradle for human habitation, providing natural resources, shelter, and access to water bodies like the Luni and Sabarmati rivers. The evidence of early human activity in the Aravalli Range offers a fascinating glimpse into the lives of prehistoric populations, their survival strategies, and their technological advancements. This section explores the archaeological findings that reveal the presence of early humans in this region, from the Paleolithic to the Neolithic periods, and their interactions with the environment.

2.2.1 Paleolithic Evidence

The earliest evidence of human activity in the Aravalli Range dates back to the Lower Paleolithic period, roughly 2.6 million years ago. The discovery of stone tools, particularly hand axes and cleavers, suggests that early humans inhabited this region during the Old Stone Age. These tools, made from locally available materials like quartzite and chert, were likely used for hunting, processing animal carcasses, and other daily survival tasks.

Some of the most significant Paleolithic sites in the Aravalli region are located near the cities of Udaipur, Ajmer, and Alwar. At these sites, archaeologists have found evidence of stone tool production and usage, indicating that early humans had developed a rudimentary form of technology to exploit the natural resources available in the area. The tools found here closely resemble those from other parts of the Indian subcontinent, suggesting that the early human populations in the Aravallis were part of a larger cultural tradition that spanned across prehistoric India.

The stone tools discovered at these sites are often crude in design but highly functional. The hand axes, for example, have sharp, bifacial edges and were likely used for cutting and chopping, while the cleavers have broader edges, ideal for splitting bones and other tough materials. The discovery of these tools in stratified layers of sediment suggests that the Aravalli Range was inhabited by successive waves of human populations over a long period, with each generation refining their tool-making techniques to adapt to changing environmental conditions.

2.2.2 Mesolithic Discoveries

As the climate became more stable following the end of the last Ice Age, human populations in the Aravalli Range began to adapt to new environmental conditions. The Mesolithic period, which began around 10,000 BCE, saw the development of more sophisticated stone tools, particularly microliths. These small, finely crafted tools represent a significant technological advancement over the larger, cruder tools of the Paleolithic.

Microliths, often made from flint or chert, were typically used as composite tools, meaning they were affixed to wooden or bone shafts to create spears, arrows, or sickles. These tools were more versatile and efficient than their Paleolithic counterparts, allowing humans to hunt smaller, faster prey and to process plant materials more effectively.

Several Mesolithic sites have been discovered in the Aravalli Range, particularly in the southern part of Rajasthan. One of the most important of these is Bagor, located on the banks of the Kothari River in the Bhilwara district. Excavations at Bagor have revealed a large number of microliths, as well as evidence of animal domestication and early farming activities. The presence of grinding stones at Bagor suggests that the inhabitants of this site were beginning to process wild grains, possibly marking the transition toward more settled, agrarian lifestyles.

The Mesolithic period also saw the development of more complex social structures and the establishment of semi-permanent settlements in the Aravalli region. Evidence from Bagor and other Mesolithic sites suggests that communities moved seasonally between different areas, exploiting a wide range of environments for food and other resources. This mobility allowed them to adapt to the changing climate and to develop a diverse subsistence strategy that included hunting, gathering, fishing, and limited agriculture.

2.2.3 Neolithic Settlements

The Neolithic period (c. 6,000 BCE – 2,000 BCE) marks a significant shift in human activity in the Aravalli Range, as communities began to transition from nomadic hunter-gatherer lifestyles to settled farming practices. This period is characterized by the development of agriculture, animal husbandry, and more permanent forms of habitation.

One of the most significant Neolithic sites in the Aravalli region is Gilund, located near the Banas River in southern Rajasthan. Gilund is part of the Ahar-Banas culture, which flourished in the region during the Neolithic and Chalcolithic periods. Excavations at Gilund have revealed evidence of mud-brick houses, storage facilities, and agricultural tools, indicating that the inhabitants of this site had developed a complex agrarian society.

The discovery of sickle blades and grinding stones at Gilund suggests that the Neolithic people of the Aravalli Range were engaged in farming activities, cultivating crops such as wheat, barley, and pulses. The presence of domesticated animals, including cattle, sheep, and goats, further indicates that animal husbandry was an important part of their subsistence strategy. This combination of farming and animal rearing allowed Neolithic communities in the Aravalli region to establish more permanent settlements and to develop a stable and sustainable way of life.

In addition to agricultural tools, the Neolithic people of the Aravalli Range also produced a variety of stone implements for other purposes. These included axes for clearing land and building houses, as well as arrowheads and spear points for hunting. The development of pottery during this period also marks a significant advancement, as it allowed communities to store food and water more efficiently, further supporting their transition to a more settled way of life.

2.2.4 Chalcolithic Transition

The Chalcolithic period, or the Copper-Stone Age, marks the transition from the Neolithic period to the use of metal tools. In the Aravalli Range, this period is represented by the Ahar-Banas culture, which thrived in the region from around 3,000 BCE to 1,500 BCE. The Ahar-

Banas people were among the first in Rajasthan to use copper tools alongside stone implements, representing a significant technological advancement.

Archaeological excavations at sites such as Ahar and Gilund have revealed a wide range of copper objects, including axes, chisels, and ornaments. These copper tools were used for a variety of purposes, from farming to craft production, and they allowed the Ahar-Banas people to engage in more complex activities such as metalworking and long-distance trade. The presence of copper tools in the Aravalli region suggests that Rajasthan was part of a broader trade network that extended across the Indian subcontinent and possibly into the Middle East.

In addition to copper tools, the Ahar-Banas people continued to use stone implements for everyday tasks. Stone tools, particularly those made from quartzite and chert, were still used for hunting, farming, and crafting, while pottery production reached new levels of sophistication. The fine red and black ware pottery produced by the Ahar-Banas people is decorated with intricate designs, reflecting their artistic and cultural achievements.

2.2.5 Impact of Geography on Early Human Activity

The geographical features of the Aravalli Range played a crucial role in shaping the patterns of early human activity in the region. The range provided a natural barrier against invasions, offering protection to the communities that inhabited its valleys and foothills. At the same time, the rivers and streams that flow through the Aravalli Range, such as the Banas, Luni, and Sabarmati, provided a reliable source of water, enabling early humans to establish settlements and engage in farming.

The Aravalli Range is also rich in natural resources, including stone for tool-making and copper for metalworking. The availability of these resources allowed early human populations to develop complex technologies and to engage in trade with neighboring regions. The discovery of copper artifacts at sites such as Ahar and Gilund suggests that the Aravalli Range was an important center for copper production during the Chalcolithic period, contributing to the region's economic and cultural development.

2.3 Significant Prehistoric Sites: Bagor, Tilwara, etc.

Rajasthan is home to numerous prehistoric sites that provide significant insight into early human civilizations. The state's geographical diversity, ranging from the Thar Desert to fertile plains, has played a crucial role in shaping the patterns of human settlement. Over the centuries, this region witnessed various phases of prehistoric life, with each stage leaving behind valuable archaeological evidence. Key prehistoric sites like Bagor, Tilwara, and others reveal the progression of human activity from hunter-gatherer societies to early agricultural communities. This chapter explores the importance of these sites and their contributions to understanding the evolution of human civilization in Rajasthan.

2.3.1 Bagor: A Mesolithic Settlement

One of the most significant prehistoric sites in Rajasthan is Bagor, located on the banks of the Kothari River in the Bhilwara district. Bagor is renowned for being one of the largest Mesolithic sites in India, providing rich evidence of Mesolithic life, including tools, artifacts, and animal remains. The discovery of microlithic tools at Bagor highlights the technological advancement of the Mesolithic people, who used these small, finely-crafted tools for hunting and gathering.

Bagor is particularly important because it shows evidence of long-term human habitation. Excavations at the site revealed multiple layers of occupation, indicating that the Mesolithic people returned to this area over centuries. The discovery of hearths suggests that these prehistoric people cooked their food, while the presence of grinding stones indicates that they may have processed plant materials for consumption. The tools found at Bagor, such as blades, scrapers, and lunates, demonstrate the versatility and adaptability of the Mesolithic communities.

One of the most intriguing aspects of Bagor is the evidence of domesticated animals. Archaeologists have discovered remains of domesticated cattle, sheep, and goats, suggesting that the people of Bagor were transitioning from a purely hunter-gatherer lifestyle to a more settled form of existence, incorporating animal husbandry. This early domestication of animals marks an important step toward the development of more complex agricultural societies in later periods.

2.3.2 Tilwara: A Paleolithic Site

Tilwara, located in the Barmer district of Rajasthan, is another prominent prehistoric site. It is primarily known for its Paleolithic artifacts, dating back to the Lower Paleolithic period. The tools found at Tilwara, including hand axes, cleavers, and choppers, are typical of the Acheulean tradition, which is characterized by large, bifacially worked stone tools. These tools were used for a variety of tasks, such as hunting, skinning animals, and processing food.

Tilwara holds great significance because it provides evidence of early human occupation in the arid region of western Rajasthan. The tools discovered here suggest that Paleolithic humans were highly adaptable, capable of surviving in a harsh desert environment. The Luni River, which flows near Tilwara, likely provided a vital water source for these early humans, supporting both their subsistence and mobility across the region.

One of the key findings at Tilwara is the presence of large stone tools, which were used by early humans to manipulate their environment and hunt large game. These tools, made from locally available materials like quartzite, show a high degree of craftsmanship, reflecting the ingenuity of Paleolithic communities. The Acheulean hand axes found here are among the oldest known tools in Rajasthan, offering valuable insights into the early stages of human technology and survival strategies.

2.3.3 Gilund: A Chalcolithic Site

Gilund, located near the Banas River in southern Rajasthan, is a significant Chalcolithic site that provides evidence of early agricultural communities. It is closely associated with the Ahar-Banas culture, which flourished in the region during the Chalcolithic period (c. 3000–1500 BCE). The people of Gilund were among the first in Rajasthan to adopt copper tools alongside stone implements, marking a major technological advancement.

Excavations at Gilund have revealed a wide range of artifacts, including copper objects, pottery, and agricultural tools. The presence of copper tools, such as axes and chisels, suggests that the people of Gilund were engaged in metalworking, a craft that would have required significant skill and knowledge. The pottery discovered at the site, known as Black and Red Ware, is finely crafted and often decorated with geometric patterns, reflecting the artistic and cultural practices of the Chalcolithic communities.

Gilund is also notable for its evidence of early urban planning. The settlement is organized into well-defined areas, with houses made of mud-brick and stone. The discovery of granaries suggests that the people of Gilund practiced agriculture on a large scale, storing surplus crops for future use. This level of organization indicates that the Chalcolithic communities of Rajasthan were not only skilled in agriculture but also in managing their resources and maintaining a stable, settled way of life.

2.3.4 Balathal: A Neolithic-Chalcolithic Transition Site

Balathal, situated near Udaipur, is an important site that illustrates the transition from the Neolithic to the Chalcolithic period. The site is significant for its evidence of early agriculture, animal domestication, and the use of both stone and copper tools. The people of Balathal were among the first in Rajasthan to engage in settled farming, cultivating crops such as wheat, barley, and lentils.

One of the key findings at Balathal is the presence of fortified structures, suggesting that the settlement was well-organized and possibly involved in defense or trade. The discovery of copper tools and ornaments indicates that the people of Balathal had access to metal resources, which they used to produce both functional and decorative items.

Balathal is also notable for its burial practices. Excavations have revealed several human burials, often accompanied by grave goods such as pottery and jewelry. These burials provide valuable insights into the social and religious practices of the Neolithic-Chalcolithic communities in Rajasthan. The presence of grave goods suggests that the people of Balathal believed in an afterlife or had developed complex ritualistic practices associated with death.

2.3.5 Pachpadra: A Microlithic Site

Pachpadra, located in the Barmer district, is another important site that has yielded a wealth of microlithic tools. These small, finely crafted stone tools are typical of the Mesolithic period and were used for a variety of purposes, including hunting, cutting, and processing plant materials. The tools found at Pachpadra include blades, lunates, and scrapers, indicating that the Mesolithic people of the region were skilled in producing versatile and efficient tools.

One of the most significant aspects of Pachpadra is the evidence of seasonal habitation. The site appears to have been used by nomadic or semi-nomadic groups who moved between different locations depending on the availability of resources. The tools discovered at Pachpadra suggest that these groups were highly mobile, exploiting a variety of environments, from river valleys to desert areas, in their quest for food and resources.

The discovery of microliths at Pachpadra also indicates that the Mesolithic people of Rajasthan were engaged in hunting small game and gathering plant materials. The small size of the tools suggests that they were used for precision tasks, such as processing hides or preparing food. These tools, often made from locally available stone, reflect the adaptability and resourcefulness of the Mesolithic communities in Rajasthan.

2.3.6 Adamgarh and Akhaj: Early Human Habitation

While not as extensively excavated as Bagor or Tilwara, the sites of Adamgarh and Akhaj in Rajasthan have yielded important prehistoric evidence. These sites contain both Paleolithic and Mesolithic artifacts, offering insights into early human habitation in the region. The tools found at these sites are similar to those discovered at other prehistoric locations, including hand axes, scrapers, and microliths.

Adamgarh and Akhaj are significant because they provide a broader context for understanding the prehistoric landscape of Rajasthan. The presence of similar tools at multiple sites across the state suggests that early humans in Rajasthan were part of a larger cultural and technological tradition that spanned much of the Indian subcontinent. These sites also highlight the continuity of human habitation in Rajasthan, with evidence of occupation stretching from the Paleolithic to the Mesolithic periods.

CHAPTER THREE

Harappan Influence and Chalcolithic Rajasthan

3.1 Sites Showcasing Harappan Influence: Kalibangan, Ahar, Balathal

The Indus Valley Civilization, also known as the Harappan Civilization, is one of the most prominent ancient cultures in South Asia, flourishing between 3300 BCE and 1300 BCE. While the core of the civilization was concentrated in present-day Pakistan and western India, its influence extended far beyond the central urban sites like Harappa and Mohenjo-daro. Several archaeological sites in Rajasthan, particularly Kalibangan, Ahar, and Balathal, exhibit significant evidence of Harappan cultural influences. These sites provide key insights into how Harappan civilization interacted with and influenced the communities in Rajasthan, fostering trade, technological exchange, and cultural assimilation. This section delves into the history and importance of these sites, exploring their connections to the larger Harappan culture.

3.1.1 Kalibangan: Harappan Urbanism on the Ghaggar-Hakra River

Kalibangan, located in the Hanumangarh district of Rajasthan, is one of the most significant sites showcasing direct Harappan influence. Situated on the banks of the now-dry Ghaggar-Hakra River (believed to be the ancient Sarasvati River), Kalibangan is considered a major provincial capital of the Indus Valley Civilization. It was first excavated by archaeologists B.B. Lal and B.K. Thapar in the 1960s, revealing a well-planned urban settlement that mirrored the structural layout and civic organization of major Harappan sites like Harappa and Mohenjo-daro.

One of the most striking features of Kalibangan is its city planning. The settlement was divided into two parts: a fortified citadel and a lower town, both of which exhibit advanced Harappan urbanism. The citadel, located on an elevated platform, was home to the elite or ruling class and contained significant administrative and religious structures. The lower town, where the common populace lived, was laid out in a grid-like pattern with streets intersecting at right angles, similar to the urban layouts found in Harappa and Mohenjo-daro. The uniformity in city planning reflects the influence of Harappan ideas on governance, urban design, and social organization.

Kalibangan also provides crucial evidence of early agriculture, a hallmark of Harappan civilization.

Archaeologists have found remnants of plowed fields, marking it as one of the earliest sites to show signs of organized farming. The distinctive furrows in these fields suggest that the Harappans practiced intensive agriculture, growing crops such as wheat, barley, and pulses. This agricultural system supported the urban population and likely fostered trade with other Harappan settlements.

The pottery, seals, and terracotta figurines discovered at Kalibangan further demonstrate the site's connection to Harappan culture. The pottery, for example, is similar to that found in other Harappan sites, featuring geometric designs, animal motifs, and black-on-red painting. The discovery of seals with the distinctive Harappan script and animal engravings indicates that Kalibangan was integrated into the larger Harappan trade network. The seals may have been used for administrative purposes, possibly to regulate trade or property ownership.

However, Kalibangan also exhibits some unique features that distinguish it from the central Harappan sites. For instance, the site contains evidence of fire altars, suggesting the performance of ritualistic activities. These altars, found in the citadel, point to a complex belief system and possibly the early development of Vedic rituals, as fire sacrifices (yajnas) are central to later Vedic practices. This makes Kalibangan an essential link in understanding the cultural evolution from Harappan to post-Harappan periods.

3.1.2 Ahar: A Chalcolithic Culture with Harappan Links

Ahar, located near Udaipur in southern Rajasthan, is a significant Chalcolithic (Copper-Stone Age) site that reveals Harappan influence through trade and cultural exchange. Although Ahar itself is not a fully Harappan site, it exhibits strong connections to the Indus Valley Civilization, particularly in its material culture, craftsmanship, and settlement patterns.

The Ahar culture, which dates back to around 3000 BCE, is known for its advanced use of copper, making it one of the earliest metallurgical cultures in South Asia. Copper objects, including tools, weapons, and ornaments, have been found in abundance at Ahar, reflecting the community's expertise in metalworking. These copper artifacts, along with the discovery of smelting furnaces, suggest that Ahar may have played a role in the copper trade with Harappan cities, as copper was a valuable commodity for the Indus Valley Civilization. The Harappans, in turn, likely exchanged other goods such as pottery, beads, and textiles with the Ahar culture.

The pottery of the Ahar culture is another element that demonstrates Harappan influence. The red and black ware pottery found at Ahar is similar in design to that of Harappan sites, featuring geometric patterns, animal motifs, and intricate decorations. The pottery suggests that the two cultures were in contact and that the people of Ahar were influenced by Harappan artistic traditions.

Archaeological evidence also points to the existence of organized settlements at Ahar, though on a smaller scale than Harappan cities like Kalibangan. The houses at Ahar were made of mud-bricks, and the settlement was planned around a central area, possibly indicating some form of administrative or religious control. The presence of granaries and storage facilities suggests that the people of Ahar practiced agriculture and stored surplus grain, much like their Harappan counterparts.

While Ahar was not fully urbanized like the Harappan cities, it provides a fascinating example of how Harappan cultural elements were transmitted to and adapted by local communities in Rajasthan. The interactions between Ahar and Harappan traders likely facilitated the exchange of ideas, technologies, and goods, contributing to the development of a distinctive regional culture in southern Rajasthan.

3.1.3 Balathal: A Harappan Outpost in Rajasthan

Balathal, another important Chalcolithic site located near Udaipur, offers further evidence of Harappan influence in Rajasthan. Balathal was first excavated in the 1990s, and it has since emerged as a key site for understanding the spread of Harappan culture into Rajasthan's interior regions. Like Ahar, Balathal is not a core Harappan settlement but shows significant cultural exchange with the Indus Valley Civilization.

One of the most remarkable discoveries at Balathal is the presence of a fortified settlement, indicating a high level of social organization and the need for defense against external threats. The fortifications at Balathal suggest that the site was a regional center of power and may have been involved in controlling trade routes or agricultural resources. The layout of the settlement, with well-planned streets and drainage systems, reflects Harappan urban planning principles, even though Balathal was much smaller in scale compared to Harappan cities.

The material culture of Balathal also reveals Harappan connections. Pottery found at the site is similar to that of

Harappan settlements, featuring red and black ware with geometric patterns and animal designs. Additionally, the discovery of copper artifacts at Balathal, including tools and ornaments, suggests that the site was part of a larger network of trade and resource exchange, possibly linked to the copper mines in the Aravalli Range.

Balathal also provides evidence of early agriculture, with the remains of wheat, barley, and other crops found in the area. The agricultural practices at Balathal appear to have been influenced by Harappan techniques, such as the use of irrigation and plowing. The discovery of granaries at the site further indicates that the people of Balathal were engaged in organized farming and had developed systems for storing surplus produce.

While Balathal was not as large or as urbanized as Kalibangan, it represents a crucial link in the spread of Harappan influence into the interior regions of Rajasthan. The site's fortified settlement, advanced metallurgy, and agricultural practices suggest that Balathal was an important regional center during the Chalcolithic period, interacting with the larger Harappan world through trade and cultural exchange.

3.2 Unique Findings: Pottery, Tools, and Artifacts

Rajasthan, with its rich prehistoric and historical past, has been an epicenter for remarkable archaeological discoveries. The state's varied geography, from the deserts of the west to the fertile plains and hill regions, has provided a unique environment where ancient civilizations flourished. Among the most important aspects of these explorations are the findings of pottery, tools, and artifacts that offer a window into the technological, artistic, and cultural practices of early inhabitants. This chapter explores the significance of these unique findings, their historical context, and what they reveal about the daily lives and social structures of Rajasthan's ancient communities.

3.2.1 Pottery: Cultural Expressions in Clay

Pottery is one of the most ubiquitous artifacts found at archaeological sites across Rajasthan. It provides not only an indication of the lifestyle of past civilizations but also their artistic sensibilities, technological capabilities, and trade networks. The pottery discovered in various prehistoric and early historic sites in Rajasthan ranges from simple utilitarian wares to finely decorated vessels that were likely used in ceremonial or symbolic contexts.

One of the most significant pottery discoveries in Rajasthan comes from the Chalcolithic Ahar-Banas culture, which flourished in southern Rajasthan around 3000 BCE. The Ahar people produced a distinctive type of pottery known as Black and Red Ware (BRW), characterized by its fine craftsmanship and intricate geometric patterns. The black and red colors were achieved through a two-stage firing process, where the vessels were first fired in a reducing atmosphere (lack of oxygen) and then in an oxidizing atmosphere (plenty of oxygen). This technique allowed for the creation of striking visual contrasts between the black and red surfaces.

BRW pottery often features a range of motifs, including zigzag lines, dots, triangles, and wavy lines. These designs are not merely decorative; they may have held symbolic significance, possibly related to religious beliefs or social status. The pottery of the Ahar-Banas culture also suggests that these people were engaged in agricultural activities, as many of the vessels were used for storing grains and other foodstuffs. The discovery of large storage jars and cooking pots indicates that the inhabitants of this region had a well-developed system for food production and storage, which was essential for sustaining settled communities.

Another significant pottery tradition in Rajasthan is associated with the Harappan civilization, which extended into parts of northern Rajasthan, particularly around the site of Kalibangan. Harappan pottery is renowned for its uniformity and high quality, with vessels often decorated with intricate designs, including motifs of animals, plants, and geometric patterns. The pottery from Kalibangan includes large storage jars, dishes, and goblets, suggesting that the people of this region were part of a complex, organized society with specialized craft production. Harappan pottery also reflects the extensive trade networks that existed during this period, as the materials and techniques used to produce the pottery were often exchanged between different regions.

3.2.2 Tools: Technological Advancements Across Eras

The discovery of tools at archaeological sites provides crucial insights into the technological capabilities and subsistence strategies of ancient communities in Rajasthan.

From the earliest stone tools used by Paleolithic hunter-gatherers to the more advanced metal implements of the Chalcolithic and Iron Age societies, these artifacts illustrate the gradual evolution of human ingenuity and adaptation to the environment.

One of the earliest phases of tool-making in Rajasthan is represented by the Paleolithic period, during which early humans crafted large stone tools such as hand axes, cleavers, and choppers. These tools were primarily used for hunting and processing food, as well as for basic tasks such as cutting wood and animal hides. The discovery of Paleolithic tools in the Luni River basin, as well as in sites like Tilwara, reveals that early humans were able to thrive in a variety of environments, from river valleys to arid desert regions.

As human societies in Rajasthan transitioned into the Mesolithic period, they began to develop smaller, more specialized tools known as microliths. These small, finely-crafted stone tools were used in combination with wooden or bone handles to create more efficient implements, such as arrows, spears, and knives. The microlithic tools discovered at sites like Bagor demonstrate the increasing sophistication of tool-making techniques during this period. The ability to produce microliths allowed Mesolithic communities to engage in more efficient hunting and gathering activities, which in turn supported larger, more stable populations.

The Chalcolithic period saw the introduction of metal tools, particularly copper, alongside the continued use of stone implements. This period marks a major technological shift in Rajasthan, as the use of metal tools allowed for more complex agricultural practices, craft production, and trade. Sites like Gilund and Balathal have yielded a wide range of copper tools, including axes, chisels, and knives, which were used for tasks such as clearing land, building structures, and processing food. The introduction of copper tools also suggests that Chalcolithic communities in Rajasthan were engaged in long-distance trade, as copper is not naturally abundant in the region and would have been imported from other areas.

In addition to copper tools, the discovery of grinding stones and sickle blades at Chalcolithic sites indicates that these early agricultural communities had developed specialized tools for harvesting and processing crops. These tools were essential for the development of settled farming communities, as they allowed for the efficient cultivation of crops such as wheat, barley, and pulses.

3.2.3 Artifacts: Insights into Daily Life and Ritual Practices

Artifacts, ranging from household items to ritual objects, offer valuable insights into the daily lives, beliefs, and social structures of ancient communities in Rajasthan. The objects discovered in various archaeological contexts provide clues about how people lived, worked, and interacted with one another, as well as how they understood the world around them.

One of the most important categories of artifacts discovered in Rajasthan is related to personal adornment. Jewelry made from a variety of materials, including beads, shells, and metals, has been found at sites such as Ahar, Kalibangan, and Balathal. These items of personal adornment were not only used for decorative purposes but also likely served as symbols of social status or identity. The discovery of finely crafted beads and pendants made from semi-precious stones, such as carnelian and lapis lazuli, suggests that these items were highly valued and possibly traded over long distances.

Ritual artifacts, such as figurines and ceremonial vessels, provide insights into the religious beliefs and practices of ancient Rajasthan communities. One of the most notable examples is the discovery of terracotta figurines at Harappan sites like Kalibangan. These figurines, often depicting animals or human figures, may have been used in religious rituals or as offerings to deities. The presence of these figurines suggests that the people of Kalibangan practiced some form of organized religion, with specific rituals and ceremonies designed to ensure the prosperity and well-being of the community.

Another significant category of artifacts is related to craft production. The discovery of pottery kilns, metalworking tools, and stone-working implements at sites like Gilund and Ahar indicates that the people of these regions were engaged in specialized crafts. The production of pottery, metal objects, and stone tools would have required a high degree of skill and knowledge, suggesting the presence of specialized artisans within these early communities.

In addition to these artifacts, the discovery of domestic items, such as cooking pots, grinding stones, and storage jars, provides valuable information about the daily activities of ancient communities in Rajasthan. These items were essential for the preparation and storage of food, as well as for other household tasks, such as weaving and textile production. The presence of these domestic artifacts suggests that the inhabitants of Rajasthan's prehistoric and early historic settlements led relatively stable, sedentary lives, supported by agriculture and craft production.

3.2.4 Interpretation of Findings: Cultural and Social Implications

The pottery, tools, and artifacts discovered in Rajasthan offer a wealth of information about the cultural and social dynamics of ancient communities. The technological advancements represented by these artifacts illustrate the gradual evolution of human societies from hunter-gatherers to settled agriculturalists, while the artistic and symbolic elements found in pottery and personal adornments provide clues about the beliefs and values of these early peoples.

One of the key implications of these findings is the evidence of social stratification and specialization. The presence of finely crafted jewelry and ritual objects, as well as specialized tools for agriculture and craft production, suggests that these communities were organized into different social roles, with some individuals engaged in craft production, others in farming, and still others in religious or political leadership.

The discovery of long-distance trade networks, as evidenced by the presence of materials such as copper and semi-precious stones, also suggests that Rajasthan was part of a larger, interconnected world. These trade networks would have facilitated the exchange of goods, ideas, and technologies between different regions, contributing to the development of more complex societies in Rajasthan.

3.3 Chalcolithic Settlements and Trade Routes

The Chalcolithic period, also known as the Copper Age (c. 3000–1500 BCE), marks a significant phase in the history of human civilization in Rajasthan, as it represents the transition from the Stone Age to the Bronze Age. During this time, people began to use copper alongside stone tools, leading to more sophisticated technology and the development of early forms of metallurgy. The Chalcolithic era is also notable for the emergence of settled agricultural communities, the growth of long-distance trade, and the establishment of complex socio-economic structures. In Rajasthan, several Chalcolithic settlements have been discovered, shedding light on the region's early agricultural practices, craft production, and trade routes. This chapter explores the major Chalcolithic settlements in Rajasthan, their economic activities, and the role of trade routes in connecting these communities to the broader Indian subcontinent.

3.3.1 Chalcolithic Settlements in Rajasthan

Rajasthan's Chalcolithic settlements were largely concentrated around the river valleys, particularly those of the Banas, Chambal, and Luni rivers. These water sources provided fertile land for agriculture and served as important conduits for trade and communication. Some of the most significant Chalcolithic sites in Rajasthan include

Ahar, Gilund, Balathal, and Ganeshwar. Each of these settlements played a crucial role in the region's cultural and economic development during the Chalcolithic period.

3.3.1.1 Ahar: A Center of Agriculture and Metallurgy

Ahar, located near Udaipur, is one of the most prominent Chalcolithic settlements in Rajasthan. The site, also known as the Ahar-Banas culture, dates back to around 3000 BCE and is characterized by its use of both stone and copper tools. The people of Ahar were among the first in Rajasthan to engage in settled agriculture, cultivating crops such as wheat, barley, and lentils. The discovery of sickle blades and grinding stones at Ahar indicates that the community had developed advanced agricultural techniques, including harvesting and food processing.

In addition to agriculture, Ahar was a major center of copper production. The presence of copper slag and furnaces suggests that the people of Ahar were skilled metallurgists who produced copper tools and ornaments. These copper objects were likely used for both practical and ceremonial purposes, reflecting the growing complexity of Chalcolithic society. The production of copper at Ahar also suggests that the settlement was part of a broader trade network, as copper ore would have been sourced from nearby regions such as the Aravalli hills.

3.3.1.2 Gilund: A Trade and Craft Production Hub

Another significant Chalcolithic site in Rajasthan is Gilund, located in the Mewar region near the Banas River. Like Ahar, Gilund was an agricultural settlement, but it also played an important role in trade and craft production. Excavations at Gilund have revealed evidence of specialized craft industries, including pottery production and metalworking. The discovery of Black and Red Ware pottery at the site is particularly notable, as this type of pottery is often associated with Chalcolithic cultures across the Indian subcontinent. The finely crafted pottery, decorated with geometric designs, indicates that the people of Gilund had developed advanced artistic and cultural practices.

Gilund's strategic location near the Banas River would have facilitated trade with other settlements in Rajasthan and beyond. The river likely served as a trade route, allowing the people of Gilund to exchange goods such as pottery, metal objects, and agricultural products with neighboring communities. The discovery of copper objects at Gilund further supports the idea that the settlement was involved in long-distance trade, as copper would have been imported from regions with rich copper deposits.

3.3.1.3 Balathal: A Fortified Settlement

Balathal, located near Udaipur, is another key Chalcolithic site in Rajasthan. The settlement is notable for its evidence of fortifications, suggesting that the people of Balathal were concerned with defense and protection. The presence of mud-brick structures and stone walls indicates that the settlement was well-organized and possibly involved in trade or political activities that required the defense of its resources.

In addition to its fortifications, Balathal is significant for its evidence of early urban planning. The site contains a number of houses, granaries, and workshops, suggesting that the community was engaged in a variety of economic activities, including agriculture, craft production, and trade. The discovery of copper tools and ornaments at Balathal indicates that the settlement was part of the broader Chalcolithic trade network, exchanging goods with other settlements in Rajasthan and beyond.

Balathal's location near the Banas River would have made it an ideal hub for trade, as the river provided a natural route for the movement of goods. The settlement's fortifications suggest that it may have played a role in controlling or regulating trade in the region, possibly acting as a center of political or economic power during the Chalcolithic period.

3.3.1.4 Ganeshwar: A Center for Copper Production

Ganeshwar, located near the copper-rich Aravalli hills, is another important Chalcolithic site in Rajasthan. The settlement is particularly notable for its extensive copper production, with excavations revealing large quantities of copper tools, weapons, and ornaments. The people of Ganeshwar were highly skilled metallurgists, using locally sourced copper to produce a wide range of objects. These copper objects were likely traded with other Chalcolithic communities in Rajasthan and beyond, making Ganeshwar a key player in the region's early trade networks.

The discovery of copper hoards at Ganeshwar suggests that the settlement was not only a center of production but also a hub for the storage and distribution of copper objects. The people of Ganeshwar may have controlled access to copper resources, facilitating trade with other settlements in Rajasthan and neighboring regions. The settlement's proximity to the Aravalli hills, which are rich in copper deposits, would have given it a strategic advantage in the Chalcolithic trade network.

3.3.2 Trade Routes in Chalcolithic Rajasthan

The development of trade routes during the Chalcolithic period played a crucial role in connecting Rajasthan's settlements with other regions of the Indian subcontinent. These trade routes facilitated the exchange of goods, ideas, and technologies, contributing to the growth of early Chalcolithic societies. Several factors influenced the establishment of trade routes in Rajasthan, including the availability of natural resources, the presence of navigable rivers, and the strategic location of settlements.

3.3.2.1 Rivers as Trade Routes

The rivers of Rajasthan, particularly the Banas, Chambal, and Luni rivers, served as important trade routes during the Chalcolithic period. These rivers provided a natural means of transportation, allowing goods to be moved over long distances with relative ease. Settlements like Ahar, Gilund, and Balathal, which were located near these rivers, were ideally positioned to engage in trade with other communities in Rajasthan and beyond.

The Banas River, in particular, played a key role in the Chalcolithic trade network. The river connected the fertile plains of southern Rajasthan with the desert regions to the west, allowing for the exchange of agricultural products, pottery, and copper objects. The presence of copper tools and ornaments at sites along the Banas River suggests that the river was used to transport copper from production centers like Ganeshwar to other parts of Rajasthan.

3.3.2.2 Overland Trade Routes

In addition to river-based trade, Rajasthan's Chalcolithic settlements were also connected by overland trade routes. These routes linked the copper-producing regions of the Aravalli hills with the agricultural communities of the Banas and Chambal valleys. The movement of copper objects along these trade routes suggests that metalworking played a central role in the Chalcolithic economy, with copper being one of the most valuable commodities exchanged between settlements.

Overland trade routes also connected Rajasthan's Chalcolithic settlements with other regions of the Indian subcontinent. For example, the discovery of Black and Red Ware pottery at sites like Gilund indicates that Rajasthan's Chalcolithic communities were part of a broader cultural network that extended across northern India. This pottery, which is found at Chalcolithic sites throughout the subcontinent, suggests that trade routes connected

Rajasthan's settlements with other important Chalcolithic centers in the Gangetic plains and beyond.

3.3.2.3 The Role of Camels and Carts

The use of pack animals, such as camels and carts, likely facilitated overland trade during the Chalcolithic period. While direct evidence of camel domestication in Rajasthan during this time is limited, it is possible that camels were used to transport goods across the desert regions of western Rajasthan. The arid landscape of the Thar Desert would have made overland travel difficult, but camels, with their ability to endure harsh conditions, would have been well-suited to this environment.

Carts, pulled by domesticated animals such as cattle, may have also been used to transport goods along overland trade routes. The presence of agricultural tools and granaries at Chalcolithic sites suggests that surplus crops were produced and traded between settlements. Carts would have provided an efficient means of moving these goods over long distances, contributing to the growth of inter-settlement trade during the Chalcolithic period.

CHAPTER FOUR

THE IRON AGE AND THE RISE OF THE EARLY KINGDOMS

4.1 Transition to Iron Usage in Rajasthan

The transition to iron usage marked a pivotal shift in human history, and in Rajasthan, this development led to significant socio-economic, technological, and cultural transformations. The use of iron tools and weapons revolutionized agriculture, warfare, and craftsmanship, laying the foundation for the rise of complex societies and powerful kingdoms in the region. This transition occurred during the late Chalcolithic period and the early Iron Age, roughly between 1200 BCE and 600 BCE, and coincided with the decline of the Harappan civilization and the emergence of new cultural and technological innovations.

This section explores the factors that contributed to the transition to iron usage in Rajasthan, the archaeological evidence of iron production and usage, and its impact on the region's early societies. Key sites, including Ahar, Balathal, and Gilund, provide valuable insights into this transformative period.

4.1.1 Pre-Iron Metallurgy in Rajasthan: The Chalcolithic Period

Before the widespread use of iron, Rajasthan was home to a thriving Chalcolithic (Copper-Stone Age) culture, characterized by the use of copper tools and weapons. The Ahar-Banas culture, which flourished in southern Rajasthan from around 3000 BCE to 1500 BCE, was one of the most prominent Chalcolithic cultures in the region. Copper was mined and smelted in the Aravalli Range, which is rich in copper ores, and the inhabitants of sites like Ahar, Balathal, and Gilund developed advanced metallurgical skills.

Copper tools such as axes, chisels, and knives were used for farming, construction, and crafting. However, copper's relatively soft nature limited its effectiveness, particularly in comparison to iron, which is harder and more durable. While copper was sufficient for basic tasks, its limitations became apparent as societies grew more complex and as agricultural and military needs increased.

The Chalcolithic period in Rajasthan also saw the development of sophisticated pottery, agriculture, and trade networks, with these cultures engaging in exchanges with the Harappan civilization. Despite these advancements, the region remained on the cusp of technological change, with iron soon emerging as a game-changer for the region's development.

4.1.2 The Arrival of Iron in Rajasthan

The transition to iron usage in Rajasthan occurred around 1200 BCE, during the late Chalcolithic and early Iron Age. The exact reasons for the shift from copper to iron are still debated, but several factors likely contributed to this transition:

1. **Resource Availability**: Unlike copper, which was confined to specific regions like the Aravallis, iron ores were more widely available across Rajasthan. The accessibility of iron allowed for broader adoption of iron tools, enabling more communities to access and use this versatile material.

2. **Technological Advancements**: The development of iron smelting techniques allowed humans to extract and forge iron at higher temperatures than copper. Once iron could be smelted and worked into tools and weapons, its superiority over copper became evident. Iron tools were stronger, more durable, and could hold a sharper edge, making them more efficient for agricultural, military, and construction purposes.

3. **Cultural Interactions**: As iron usage spread across northern India, Rajasthan's proximity to major trade routes facilitated the exchange of new technologies and ideas. The Gangetic plains and central Indian regions,

which were early adopters of iron technology, likely influenced the transition in Rajasthan through trade and cultural contact.

4. **Environmental Pressures**: The region's growing population and the need for more intensive agriculture may have driven the demand for more effective tools. Iron plows, for instance, were better suited for clearing and cultivating the dense, hard soils of Rajasthan, making agriculture more productive.

The transition to iron allowed Rajasthan's communities to expand their agricultural output, strengthen their military capabilities, and build more complex infrastructure, all of which laid the groundwork for the region's early kingdoms.

4.1.3 Key Archaeological Evidence of Iron Usage

Several archaeological sites in Rajasthan have provided critical evidence of the transition to iron usage, shedding light on the technological advancements and socio-economic changes that accompanied this shift.

- **Ahar (Udaipur District)**: Excavations at Ahar, a key site of the Ahar-Banas Chalcolithic culture, have revealed a gradual shift from copper to iron tools. While copper remained in use for a considerable time, by the end of the Chalcolithic period, iron tools such as axes, arrowheads, and knives began to appear. This co-existence of copper and iron tools indicates a period of technological transition, where both materials were used based on availability and purpose.

- **Balathal (Udaipur District)**: Balathal, another important Chalcolithic site, provides valuable insights into the introduction of iron technology. Excavations have unearthed iron artifacts alongside the more traditional copper tools, suggesting that iron became increasingly integrated into daily life. The presence of smelting furnaces at Balathal indicates that iron production was taking place locally, likely using ore from the nearby Aravalli Range.

- **Gilund (Rajsamand District)**: Gilund, a large Ahar-Banas settlement, has also yielded evidence of early iron usage. The discovery of iron slag, furnaces, and tools suggests that the inhabitants of Gilund were among the early adopters of iron technology in Rajasthan. Iron tools were likely used in agriculture, which would have significantly increased productivity, and in construction, allowing for the development of more durable buildings.

The presence of iron at these sites marks a critical turning point in Rajasthan's prehistory, signaling the end of the Chalcolithic era and the beginning of the Iron Age.

4.1.4 Impact of Iron on Agriculture and Society

The introduction of iron tools had a profound impact on agriculture in Rajasthan. Iron plows, sickles, and hoes allowed for more efficient cultivation of land, particularly in the hard, dry soils of the region. Iron tools were better suited for clearing forests and tilling large tracts of land, enabling the expansion of agriculture and supporting larger populations.

With improved agricultural productivity, societies in Rajasthan became more complex and hierarchical. The surplus of food produced by iron-based agriculture allowed for the development of specialized professions, such as artisans, traders, and soldiers. This economic diversification, in turn, contributed to the rise of early states and kingdoms in the region, laying the foundation for the powerful Rajput dynasties that would emerge in later centuries.

Iron also transformed warfare in Rajasthan. The introduction of iron weapons, such as swords, spears, and arrowheads, gave local communities a significant advantage in combat. Iron weapons were stronger, more lethal, and more durable than their copper counterparts, making them the preferred choice for warriors. This military advantage likely played a role in the consolidation of power by early rulers, as control over iron production and the ability to equip armies with iron weapons would have been a key factor in regional dominance.

4.1.5 Ironworking and Trade Networks

Iron production in Rajasthan not only supported local communities but also became an important part of regional trade networks. The Aravalli Range, with its rich deposits of iron ore, became a center for iron smelting and tool production. Iron artifacts from Rajasthan have been found at distant sites, indicating that iron products were traded across northern and central India.

This trade in iron contributed to the growth of Rajasthan's economy and connected it to other parts of the Indian subcontinent. The diffusion of iron technology and products facilitated the exchange of ideas, goods, and cultural practices, further integrating Rajasthan into the broader South Asian cultural sphere.

4.1.6 Cultural and Religious Impact of Iron

The transition to iron usage in Rajasthan also had cultural and religious implications. The use of iron tools in religious rituals and ceremonies became more common, as iron was associated with strength, power, and transformation. In later Vedic texts, iron weapons were linked to gods such as Indra, the warrior deity, and iron came to symbolize military prowess and divine protection.

The development of iron technology also influenced artistic and architectural practices. Iron tools allowed for more precise craftsmanship, enabling the construction of temples, fortifications, and other monumental structures that would become hallmarks of Rajasthan's cultural heritage.

4.1.7 The Legacy of Iron in Rajasthan's History

The transition to iron usage in Rajasthan marked the beginning of a new era in the region's history, one characterized by increased agricultural productivity, technological innovation, and the rise of complex societies. Iron tools and weapons played a crucial role in the development of early kingdoms and laid the groundwork for the rich cultural and political history of Rajasthan.

As iron technology spread across the region, it became a defining feature of Rajasthan's identity, influencing everything from agriculture to warfare, trade, and religion. The mastery of ironworking and the strategic control of iron resources helped shape Rajasthan's political landscape, paving the way for the emergence of the powerful Rajput clans who would dominate the region for centuries.

4.2 Early Tribal Kingdoms: Matsya, Malwa

Rajasthan, with its expansive landscapes and strategic geographic position, has been home to several ancient tribes and kingdoms. Among these, the Matsya and Malwa tribal kingdoms stand out as significant entities in the early history of the region. These early kingdoms, which emerged before the rise of more prominent dynasties, were instrumental in laying the foundations for political organization, social structures, and cultural practices that would later define Rajasthan's historical legacy. In this chapter, we will delve into the origins, development, and significance of the Matsya and Malwa kingdoms, and how they shaped the early history of Rajasthan.

4.2.1 The Matsya Kingdom: Historical Context and Origins

The Matsya Kingdom, one of the earliest tribal polities in ancient Rajasthan, is believed to have existed during the Vedic period (c. 1500–500 BCE). It was one of the sixteen Mahajanapadas (great kingdoms) mentioned in ancient Indian texts such as the Mahabharata and the Puranas. The Matsya people, a branch of the Indo-Aryan tribes, are thought to have migrated to the region during the early Vedic period, settling in the areas around present-day Alwar, Bharatpur, and Jaipur.

The kingdom of Matsya, centered around its capital at Viratnagar (modern-day Bairat), played a crucial role in the early political landscape of northern India. Viratnagar was strategically located near the Aravalli Range, which provided natural defense against invasions while also facilitating trade and communication with other regions. The Matsya people were primarily pastoralists and agriculturalists, relying on the fertile plains of the region for sustenance.

According to the Mahabharata, the Matsya Kingdom was ruled by King Virata, who played a significant role in the epic's narrative. The Pandavas, during their period of exile, are said to have lived in disguise in King Virata's court, where they found refuge from their enemies. This association with the Pandavas elevated the status of the Matsya Kingdom in Indian mythology, linking it to the broader narrative of the Mahabharata and the Kurukshetra

War.

4.2.2 Social and Political Organization of the Matsya Kingdom

The Matsya Kingdom was organized as a tribal polity, with a decentralized form of governance. The king, while holding supreme authority, was supported by a council of tribal elders and chieftains who played an essential role in decision-making. This tribal council helped maintain law and order, resolved disputes, and oversaw the administration of justice. The king was also responsible for leading the kingdom's military forces, defending the territory from external threats, and expanding its influence through alliances and warfare.

The society in the Matsya Kingdom was primarily agrarian, with agriculture forming the backbone of the economy. The fertile plains of the region, irrigated by rivers such as the Chambal and Banganga, supported the cultivation of crops like wheat, barley, and millet. Animal husbandry was also an important economic activity, with cattle, sheep, and goats playing a vital role in the pastoral economy of the Matsya people.

The Matsya people practiced Vedic rituals and worshipped a pantheon of gods, including Indra, Agni, and Varuna. The religious practices of the kingdom were closely tied to nature and the agrarian lifestyle, with rituals aimed at ensuring bountiful harvests and protecting livestock. The presence of sacred groves and temples dedicated to various deities in the region suggests that religion played a central role in the lives of the Matsya people.

4.2.3 Decline of the Matsya Kingdom and Its Legacy

The Matsya Kingdom, like many other early tribal polities, eventually declined due to external pressures and internal conflicts. The rise of more powerful kingdoms, such as the Magadha and Kuru, in northern India led to the subjugation of smaller tribal kingdoms like Matsya. By the time of the Mauryan Empire (c. 322–185 BCE), the Matsya Kingdom had been absorbed into the expanding Mauryan realm.

Despite its decline, the legacy of the Matsya Kingdom continued to influence the region. The city of Viratnagar remained an important cultural and religious center during the Mauryan and Gupta periods. The discovery of Buddhist stupas and Ashokan edicts in Viratnagar suggests that the region continued to play a significant role in the religious and political life of northern India long after the decline of the Matsya Kingdom.

The Matsya people's contributions to the cultural and political history of Rajasthan are also evident in the region's folklore and traditions. The memory of King Virata and his association with the Pandavas has been preserved in local legends and festivals, reinforcing the kingdom's place in Rajasthan's historical consciousness.

4.2.4 The Malwa Kingdom: Geographic and Cultural Context

The Malwa Kingdom, like Matsya, was another significant tribal kingdom that existed in the early history of Rajasthan. The Malwa region, which lies to the south of Rajasthan and extends into present-day Madhya Pradesh, was home to the Malwa tribe, an Indo-Aryan group that settled in the region during the Vedic period. The Malwa Kingdom's territory was centered around the city of Ujjain, which later became a major political and cultural hub in ancient India.

The Malwa region, known for its fertile black soil, was well-suited for agriculture, and the Malwa people practiced both farming and animal husbandry. The kingdom's strategic location along important trade routes, such as the Ujjain-Delhi and Ujjain-Kanauj routes, allowed it to flourish as a center of commerce and culture. The Malwa Kingdom was known for its production of textiles, pottery, and metalwork, which were traded with neighboring regions.

The Malwa people, like their Matsya counterparts, were deeply influenced by Vedic culture and religion. They practiced rituals associated with the worship of deities like Surya (the Sun God) and Varuna (the God of Water). The Malwa region is also associated with the early development of astronomy and mathematics, particularly through its connections with the city of Ujjain, which later became a renowned center for learning during the Gupta period.

4.2.5 Political Structure and Military Conflicts in the Malwa Kingdom

The political structure of the Malwa Kingdom was similar to other early tribal polities, with a king or tribal chief exercising authority over a confederation of clans. The kingdom's military forces were organized into small tribal units, with each clan contributing warriors to the defense of the kingdom. The Malwa Kingdom, due to its location along key trade routes, was often involved in conflicts with neighboring tribes and kingdoms over control of resources and territory.

One of the most significant military conflicts involving the Malwa Kingdom occurred during the period of Alexander the Great's invasion of India (c. 326 BCE). The Malwa people, along with other tribes from the region, resisted the advance of Alexander's forces, leading to skirmishes in the areas around the Malwa plateau. Although Alexander's campaign did not reach deep into Malwa territory, the kingdom's resistance demonstrated its military capabilities and strategic importance.

The Malwa Kingdom also played a role in the larger geopolitical conflicts of northern India during the Vedic and post-Vedic periods. Its position as a border state between the northern kingdoms of the Gangetic plains and the southern Deccan regions made it a key player in regional politics. The kingdom's alliances with neighboring states, as well as its military strength, allowed it to maintain its independence for several centuries.

4.2.6 Decline and Integration into Larger Empires

Like the Matsya Kingdom, the Malwa Kingdom eventually declined due to the rise of more powerful empires in northern India. The expansion of the Magadha Kingdom and the Mauryan Empire brought the Malwa region under the control of larger political entities. By the time of the Gupta Empire (c. 320–550 CE), the Malwa region had become fully integrated into the imperial structure, with Ujjain serving as an important administrative and cultural center for the Guptas.

The decline of the Malwa Kingdom did not mark the end of the region's significance. Ujjain, the former capital of the Malwa Kingdom, continued to flourish as a center of learning, culture, and religion during the Gupta period and beyond. The region's association with the development of astronomy, mathematics, and literature ensured that the legacy of the Malwa Kingdom endured long after its political decline.

4.3 Key Discoveries from the Iron Age: Weapons, Inscriptions, Architecture

The Iron Age (c. 1500 BCE – 200 BCE) marked a transformative period in Rajasthan's history, as iron became the dominant material for tools, weapons, and other utilitarian objects. This period saw significant developments in warfare, agriculture, metallurgy, and cultural expression, as communities in Rajasthan evolved into more complex, stratified societies. The Iron Age in Rajasthan is particularly notable for the archaeological discoveries related to iron weapons, inscriptions that reveal important aspects of governance and religion, and architecture that reflects new building techniques and urban planning. In this section, we will explore the key discoveries from the Iron Age in Rajasthan, examining how these findings have helped historians and archaeologists understand the region's historical and cultural landscape during this critical period.

4.3.1 Iron Weapons and Warfare

One of the most important aspects of the Iron Age was the widespread use of iron for weapons and tools. In Rajasthan, the discovery of iron swords, spearheads, arrowheads, and axes has provided valuable insights into the region's military practices and the role of warfare in shaping its societies. Iron, being more durable and abundant than bronze, revolutionized combat, allowing for the production of stronger and more efficient weapons. This technological advancement had a profound impact on both defensive and offensive strategies, as communities competed for resources and territory.

4.3.1.1 Weapons of War: Swords, Spears, and Arrowheads

The excavation of several Iron Age sites in Rajasthan, including those at Atranjikhera and Nagari, has revealed a variety of iron weapons. Swords made from iron were longer and more durable than their bronze predecessors, giving warriors an advantage in hand-to-hand combat. The blades were often double-edged and designed for both slashing and thrusting. Archaeologists have also uncovered iron spearheads, which were likely used by infantry soldiers. The spears were versatile, functioning as both close-range and long-range weapons when thrown.

Arrowheads made of iron were another common discovery at Iron Age sites. These arrowheads, often triangular in shape, were attached to wooden shafts and used by archers in both hunting and warfare. The durability of iron allowed for the creation of more effective projectiles, which could penetrate armor and shields more easily than those made from stone or bronze. The use of iron weapons, therefore, played a critical role in the military conflicts of the time, contributing to the rise of warrior elites who controlled large territories through force.

4.3.1.2 Defensive Armament: Shields and Armor

While offensive weapons like swords and spears were essential, Iron Age warriors in Rajasthan also employed defensive gear to protect themselves in battle. Although few examples of iron armor have been discovered in Rajasthan, there is evidence to suggest that warriors used iron-plated shields to defend against enemy attacks. These shields were often round and reinforced with metal to withstand blows from swords and arrows. The use of iron in defensive equipment reflects the increasing sophistication of warfare during the Iron Age, as communities sought to protect their soldiers while also improving their offensive capabilities.

4.3.2 Inscriptions: Political Power and Religious Beliefs

Inscriptions from the Iron Age provide valuable information about the political, social, and religious life of the people in Rajasthan. These inscriptions, often engraved on stone or metal, served as official records of rulers, laws, and religious practices. They provide insight into the governance structures of Iron Age societies and the role of kingship in maintaining order and control over large territories. Additionally, many inscriptions are religious in nature, offering clues about the spiritual beliefs and rituals that were important to the people of Rajasthan during this period.

4.3.2.1 Royal Inscriptions: Authority and Governance

One of the most significant types of Iron Age inscriptions in Rajasthan are those that document the achievements and authority of rulers. These royal inscriptions were typically engraved on stone pillars or rock faces and often included the names of kings, their military conquests, and their contributions to the construction of temples and other public works. Inscriptions from this period frequently mention the granting of land or resources to loyal subjects or religious institutions, indicating the ways in which rulers maintained power and legitimacy.

For example, the inscriptions found at the Nagari site near Chittorgarh include references to the rule of ancient monarchs who governed parts of Rajasthan during the later Iron Age. These inscriptions offer a glimpse into the administrative practices of Iron Age Rajasthan, including the use of taxation, the distribution of land, and the support of religious institutions as a means of consolidating political power.

4.3.2.2 Religious Inscriptions: Spiritual Practices and Beliefs

Religious inscriptions from the Iron Age reveal the importance of spirituality and ritual in the lives of the people of Rajasthan. Many of these inscriptions are dedicated to deities and include invocations, prayers, or records of offerings made to temples. These inscriptions provide evidence of the early forms of religious practices that would later evolve into the more organized religions of the historical period, such as Hinduism and Jainism.

One notable example is the discovery of inscriptions dedicated to the worship of fertility deities and nature gods, reflecting the agrarian-based society of the time. These inscriptions, often found near rivers or sacred groves, suggest that the people of Rajasthan saw a strong connection between the natural world and the divine. The practice of inscribing prayers or dedications on stone is indicative of the deep religious devotion that characterized Iron Age communities in Rajasthan.

4.3.3 Architectural Discoveries: Fortifications and Urban Planning

The Iron Age in Rajasthan also witnessed significant advancements in architecture, particularly in the construction of fortifications and urban settlements. As societies became more complex and warfare more prevalent, the need for defensible structures and organized urban spaces grew. Archaeological excavations have uncovered the remains of fortifications, large public buildings, and well-planned urban layouts that reflect the increasing social and political complexity of Iron Age societies in Rajasthan.

4.3.3.1 Fortifications: Protecting Settlements

One of the most important architectural discoveries from the Iron Age in Rajasthan is the remains of fortified settlements. These fortifications, often built on elevated ground or natural hilltops, were designed to protect communities from external threats. The construction of stone walls, ramparts, and gates provided defense against invading forces, while also symbolizing the power and wealth of the ruling elite.

The site of Nagari near Chittorgarh, for example, contains the remains of a fortified settlement that dates back to the Iron Age. The stone walls of this settlement, which were built to withstand sieges, indicate the growing importance of defense in Iron Age society. Fortifications not only protected the inhabitants from external threats but also served as centers of political power, where rulers could govern and control their territories.

4.3.3.2 Urban Planning and Public Architecture

In addition to fortifications, the Iron Age saw the emergence of well-planned urban settlements in Rajasthan. These settlements often featured public buildings, such as granaries and assembly halls, that served the needs of the community. The development of organized urban spaces reflects the increasing complexity of Iron Age societies, as populations grew and social hierarchies became more defined.

One notable example of Iron Age urban planning is the layout of the settlement at Ahar, which includes evidence of streets, public spaces, and residential areas. The presence of large storage facilities suggests that the people of Ahar engaged in surplus agricultural production, which would have supported a growing population. The organization of space within the settlement indicates that Iron Age societies in Rajasthan had developed systems of governance and resource management that allowed for the coordination of large-scale building projects.

CHAPTER FIVE

Buddhism and Jainism: Early Religious Influences

5.1 Buddhist Archaeological Sites in Rajasthan

Rajasthan, known for its rich cultural heritage and historical significance, is home to numerous archaeological sites that reveal the profound impact of Buddhism on the region. Buddhism, which emerged in the 6th century BCE with the teachings of Siddhartha Gautama (the Buddha), spread across India and reached Rajasthan through various routes and patronage. The Buddhist sites in Rajasthan offer valuable insights into the history of the religion, its architectural styles, monastic practices, and its role in shaping the socio-political landscape of the region.

This section explores some of the most significant Buddhist archaeological sites in Rajasthan, including Sarnath, Ajmer, Rani Sati Dadi, and Dhank, highlighting their historical context, architectural features, and cultural importance.

5.1.1 Ajmer: A Center of Buddhist Learning

Ajmer, located in the Aravalli range, is one of the most prominent Buddhist sites in Rajasthan. The region holds historical significance as a center of learning and pilgrimage during the Mauryan period and later. One of the key archaeological findings in Ajmer is the **Ajmer Jain Temple**, which, although primarily a Jain site, reveals evidence of early Buddhist influence in its architectural design and artistic motifs.

Not far from Ajmer lies the famous **Anasagar Lake**, where ancient inscriptions and remnants of monastic complexes have been discovered. The **Ajmer inscriptions** highlight the patronage of various kings, including the Mauryan emperor Ashoka, who played a pivotal role in promoting Buddhism throughout his empire. Ashoka's edicts, which emphasize moral governance and the spread of Dharma, were inscribed on pillars and rocks near Ajmer, showcasing the region's importance in Buddhist history.

The presence of several stupas, monastic complexes, and rock-cut caves in and around Ajmer indicates that it was a significant center for Buddhist monks and scholars. The **Kankali Devi Temple**, located in the nearby **Kankal village**, features remnants of ancient stupas that further attest to the region's rich Buddhist heritage.

5.1.2 Sarnath: The Cradle of Buddhism

While Sarnath is primarily associated with Uttar Pradesh, its historical significance extends into Rajasthan due to the extensive interactions between Buddhist monks and the local populace. The Sarnath stupa, where the Buddha delivered his first sermon after attaining enlightenment, symbolizes the teachings of Buddhism and serves as a pilgrimage site for devotees.

The influence of Sarnath can be observed in the architectural style and layout of Buddhist stupas in Rajasthan. The design principles of the **Sarnath stupa** were adopted by local builders, leading to the construction of stupas in Rajasthan that reflected similar architectural elements. The stupa's hemispherical shape, surrounded by a square base, became a common motif in the construction of later stupas throughout the region.

The legacy of Sarnath in Rajasthan can also be seen in the proliferation of monastic communities that emerged in response to the teachings propagated by the Buddha. As monks traveled across the region, they established monasteries that became vital centers for learning and spiritual practice. These monasteries served as hubs for the exchange of ideas and culture, allowing Buddhism to flourish in Rajasthan.

5.1.3 Dhank: The Ancient Monastic Complex

Dhank, located near the town of **Churu**, is one of the most significant archaeological sites showcasing the impact of Buddhism in Rajasthan. The site features a series of rock-cut caves and monastic complexes dating back to the 1st century BCE to the 5th century CE. Dhank was an important center for Buddhist learning and practice, attracting monks and scholars from various regions.

The rock-cut caves at Dhank demonstrate remarkable architectural ingenuity. The caves feature intricately carved pillars, stupas, and viharas (monasteries) that provide insights into the monastic lifestyle of early Buddhists. The **Dhank cave complex** consists of several chambers used for meditation, prayer, and community gatherings, highlighting the communal aspect of Buddhist practice.

One of the most notable features of Dhank is the **Viharas**, where monks lived and engaged in spiritual practices. The layout of these monastic complexes reflects the principles of Buddhist architecture, with separate areas for meditation, communal activities, and teaching. The presence of stupas within the complex served as focal points for worship and reflection.

The murals and carvings found in Dhank's caves depict various scenes from the life of the Buddha, as well as Jataka tales—stories of the Buddha's previous lives. These artistic representations not only provide insights into the spiritual narratives of Buddhism but also reflect the socio-cultural dynamics of the time.

5.1.4 Rani Sati Dadi: A Unique Blend of Buddhism and Local Traditions

The **Rani Sati Dadi temple**, located near **Jhunjhunu**, represents a unique intersection of Buddhist and local traditions. While primarily a site of worship for the Hindu goddess Rani Sati, the temple complex contains remnants of earlier Buddhist structures, indicating the coexistence and adaptation of religious practices in the region.

Archaeological findings at Rani Sati Dadi suggest that the site was once a thriving Buddhist monastery before it was transformed into a Hindu pilgrimage center. The presence of stupas, rock-cut caves, and ancient inscriptions demonstrates the layered history of the site, reflecting the ebb and flow of religious practices over the centuries.

The fusion of Buddhist and local traditions is evident in the architectural elements of the Rani Sati Dadi temple. The temple features carvings and motifs reminiscent of Buddhist art, showcasing the influence of Buddhist iconography on later Hindu religious practices. This blending of traditions highlights the syncretic nature of religious practices in Rajasthan, where various beliefs coexisted and influenced one another.

5.1.5 The Influence of Buddhism on Art and Culture in Rajasthan

The Buddhist archaeological sites in Rajasthan not only provide insights into the religious practices of the time but also highlight the influence of Buddhism on the region's art and culture. The intricate carvings, sculptures, and frescoes found at these sites reflect the artistic traditions of the period, showcasing a blend of local styles with Buddhist iconography.

Buddhist art in Rajasthan often features motifs such as lotus flowers, stupas, and representations of the Buddha, emphasizing the spiritual themes central to Buddhism. The craftsmanship involved in creating these artworks reflects the high level of skill possessed by local artisans, who were likely influenced by Buddhist artistic traditions from other regions.

Moreover, the spread of Buddhism contributed to the establishment of trade networks across Rajasthan, facilitating cultural exchanges and the dissemination of artistic ideas. As monks traveled between regions, they brought with them not only religious teachings but also artistic styles and techniques that enriched the local culture.

5.2 Jain Heritage: Temples and Monasteries

Rajasthan, renowned for its rich cultural and religious diversity, is home to a significant legacy of Jain heritage that manifests itself in numerous temples, monasteries, and other architectural marvels. Jainism, one of the oldest religions in India, promotes a philosophy of non-violence, truth, and asceticism. The state's historical and geographical context has contributed to the flourishing of Jain communities, leading to the establishment of impressive temples and monastic institutions that are emblematic of Jain art, architecture, and spirituality. This chapter explores the historical significance, architectural features, and cultural contributions of Jain temples and monasteries in Rajasthan.

5.2.1 Historical Context of Jainism in Rajasthan

Jainism is believed to have originated in India around the same time as Buddhism, around the 6th century BCE. The Tirthankaras, revered teachers in Jainism, played a significant role in shaping its principles and philosophies. Lord Mahavira, the 24th Tirthankara, is particularly associated with the establishment of Jain doctrines and practices. His teachings emphasized the importance of ahimsa (non-violence), aparigraha (non-possessiveness), and the pursuit of spiritual enlightenment through self-discipline and asceticism.

Rajasthan, with its arid landscapes and rugged terrain, became a sanctuary for Jain communities seeking refuge from external conflicts and persecution. During the medieval period, particularly from the 9th century onwards, Jainism gained prominence in Rajasthan as several Jain merchants, traders, and artisans settled in the region, contributing to its economic and cultural development. The flourishing of trade routes facilitated the spread of Jain ideals, leading to the establishment of vibrant Jain communities across various towns and cities in Rajasthan.

The political patronage from various ruling dynasties, including the Rajputs, also played a crucial role in the promotion of Jainism in Rajasthan. The Rajput kings, known for their chivalry and valor, often sought the support of Jain merchants and used their financial resources for building temples and supporting religious institutions. This symbiotic relationship between the Jain community and the ruling elite resulted in the construction of exquisite temples that reflect the architectural grandeur and spiritual significance of Jainism.

5.2.2 Architectural Marvels: Temples in Rajasthan

Jain temples in Rajasthan are celebrated for their intricate craftsmanship, exquisite marble work, and stunning architectural designs. The temples serve as places of worship, meditation, and community gathering, reflecting the values and beliefs of Jainism. Among the most notable Jain temples in Rajasthan are the following:

1. **Dilwara Temples** (Mount Abu): The Dilwara Temples, built between the 11th and 13th centuries, are a prime example of Jain architecture and artistry. Renowned for their exceptional marble craftsmanship, the temples feature intricately carved pillars, ornate ceilings, and elaborate doorways. The most famous among the Dilwara temples is the Vimal Vasahi Temple, dedicated to Lord Adinath, which showcases exquisite relief work depicting celestial beings, floral motifs, and geometric patterns. The Luna Vasahi Temple, dedicated to Lord Neminath, is another architectural marvel adorned with intricate carvings that tell stories from Jain mythology.

2. **Ranakpur Temple**: Located in the Pali district, the Ranakpur Temple is dedicated to Tirthankara Adinath and is one of the largest Jain temples in India. Built in the 15th century, the temple features over 1,400 intricately carved pillars, each uniquely designed, showcasing the skill of the artisans of the time. The temple's main hall is adorned with stunning sculptures depicting scenes from Jain cosmology and mythology, creating an ethereal atmosphere that invites

contemplation and reverence.

3. **Sammet Shikhar** (Parasnath Hills): Sammet Shikhar, located in Jharkhand, is a significant pilgrimage site for Jains and is known for its temples dedicated to various Tirthankaras. However, it holds historical significance for the Jain community in Rajasthan, as many pilgrims from Rajasthan visit this site. The temples are situated atop a hill and offer breathtaking views of the surrounding landscape, making it a popular destination for spiritual seekers.

4. **Sambhar Lake Temples**: The Sambhar Lake region is home to several ancient Jain temples that date back to the 10th century. These temples, though lesser-known, are significant for their historical value and architectural features. The temples are often adorned with intricate carvings and inscriptions that provide insights into the religious practices and beliefs of the Jain community in Rajasthan.

5. **Jain Temples in Jaipur**: The capital city of Jaipur boasts several noteworthy Jain temples, including the Shri Adinath Temple in the Chandpole area and the Jain Mandir in the nearby town of Sanganer. These temples reflect the influence of Mughal and Rajput architectural styles, featuring elegant domes, minarets, and intricately carved marble screens.

5.2.3 Monastic Traditions and Institutions

In addition to temples, Rajasthan is home to several Jain monasteries (known as "Gumtis" or "Panchayats") that serve as centers of learning, spiritual practice, and community life. These monasteries have played a crucial role in preserving Jain teachings, rituals, and traditions over the centuries. Some notable monastic institutions include:

1. **Kshullak Sangh**: This monastic order, established in the 19th century, has made significant contributions to the propagation of Jain philosophy and ethics. The Kshullak Sangh operates several educational institutions and community service projects aimed at promoting Jain values and ethics in contemporary society.

2. **Brahma Kumaris**: While primarily known for its spiritual teachings, the Brahma Kumaris movement has been influenced by Jain principles, particularly the emphasis on non-violence and self-discipline. The organization has established various centers in Rajasthan that promote spiritual growth and community service.

3. **Shvetambar and Digambar Monasteries**: Rajasthan is home to both Shvetambar and Digambar sects of Jainism, each with its own monastic traditions and practices. Shvetambar monasteries often feature community living arrangements, where monks and nuns engage in meditation, study, and community service. Digambar monasteries, on the other hand, emphasize ascetic practices and often have a more austere lifestyle.

These monastic institutions serve as repositories of knowledge, preserving ancient texts, manuscripts, and scriptures that embody the teachings of Jainism. The monks and nuns residing in these monasteries often engage in scholarly pursuits, studying and interpreting Jain philosophy, and passing down their knowledge to future generations.

5.2.4 Cultural Contributions of Jain Heritage

The Jain community in Rajasthan has made significant contributions to the state's cultural landscape, influencing art, literature, and social practices. Jainism's principles of non-violence and compassion have permeated the cultural ethos of Rajasthan, fostering a sense of harmony and coexistence among diverse communities.

1. **Art and Sculpture**: Jain art and sculpture, particularly in the form of temple carvings and idols, have had a profound impact on the artistic traditions of Rajasthan. The intricate carvings found in Jain temples reflect a unique fusion of artistic styles, often incorporating elements from local and regional artistic practices. Jain artisans have played a crucial role in preserving traditional craftsmanship, passing down their skills from generation to generation.

2. **Literature**: Jain literature, including scriptures, commentaries, and philosophical treatises, has contributed significantly to the intellectual heritage of

Rajasthan. The writings of Jain scholars, such as Hemachandra and Jinaprabha Suri, have provided insights into the philosophy, ethics, and practices of Jainism. Many Jain texts are composed in regional languages, contributing to the development of literary traditions in Rajasthan.

3. **Festivals and Rituals**: Jain festivals, such as Paryushana and Mahavir Jayanti, are celebrated with great fervor in Rajasthan. These festivals not only serve as occasions for religious observance but also foster a sense of community and cultural identity among Jains. The rituals associated with these festivals often include prayers, fasting, and charitable acts, reinforcing the core values of Jainism.

4. **Social Responsibility**: The Jain community in Rajasthan is known for its philanthropic activities, supporting various charitable initiatives, educational institutions, and healthcare projects. The principles of non-violence and compassion drive these efforts, reflecting the community's commitment to social responsibility and welfare.

5.2.5 Preservation and Challenges

Despite the rich heritage of Jain temples and monasteries in Rajasthan, several challenges threaten their preservation. Urbanization, tourism, and environmental factors pose risks to the integrity of these historical sites.

The increasing influx of visitors can lead to wear and tear on the structures, while inadequate maintenance and conservation efforts can exacerbate the situation.

Efforts to preserve Jain heritage are underway, with various organizations and communities working to safeguard these temples and monasteries. Restoration projects, awareness campaigns, and educational initiatives aim to promote the importance of preserving this cultural heritage for future generations.

5.3 Inscriptions and Stupas at Key Locations: Sarnath, Bairat

The spread of Buddhism across India from the 6th century BCE marked a significant cultural and religious transformation in the region. Among the many sites that witnessed the flourishing of Buddhism, Sarnath and Bairat stand out due to their historical significance, monumental architecture, and rich inscriptions. This chapter explores the key inscriptions and stupas at these locations, highlighting their importance in understanding the propagation of Buddhist teachings, the patronage of emperors, and the socio-religious landscape of ancient India.

5.3.1 Sarnath: The Cradle of Buddhist Teachings

Sarnath, located near Varanasi in Uttar Pradesh, holds a special place in Buddhist history as the site where

Siddhartha Gautama, after attaining enlightenment, delivered his first sermon to his five former companions. This moment marked the foundation of the Buddhist Sangha and the dissemination of the Four Noble Truths. The archaeological remains of Sarnath include stupas, monasteries, and inscriptions that illuminate the early development of Buddhism and its institutional framework.

5.3.1.1 The Dhamek Stupa: A Symbol of Enlightenment

The Dhamek Stupa is the most prominent structure at Sarnath and is believed to date back to the 5th century CE, although earlier versions of the stupa existed. This massive circular mound, made of brick and stone, is a significant pilgrimage site for Buddhists worldwide. It is said to mark the spot where Buddha delivered his first sermon, making it a symbol of his teachings and the establishment of the Buddhist community.

The architectural design of the Dhamek Stupa reflects the artistic and architectural styles prevalent during its construction. The stupa is adorned with intricate carvings and floral motifs, showcasing the craftsmanship of ancient artisans. Inscriptions found on the stupa's base provide insight into the patronage and devotion of various kings and rulers, who contributed to its construction and renovation. The inscriptions, written in Brahmi script, often record the names of donors, their intentions for building, and blessings for the community, thereby serving as historical records of Buddhist patronage.

5.3.1.2 Inscriptions of Ashoka: A Testament to Royal Patronage

One of the most significant aspects of Sarnath is its connection to Emperor Ashoka, who reigned during the 3rd century BCE. Ashoka is renowned for his role in promoting Buddhism after his conversion following the Kalinga War. At Sarnath, he erected a pillar known as the Lion Capital, which is now recognized as the national emblem of India.

The inscriptions on Ashoka's pillar at Sarnath contain edicts that promote the principles of Dharma, emphasizing moral conduct, compassion, and the importance of non-violence. These edicts serve as an early expression of the integration of Buddhist philosophy into statecraft, reflecting Ashoka's commitment to spreading the teachings of the Buddha. The inscriptions advocate for the welfare of all living beings, encourage religious tolerance, and promote the establishment of monasteries and stupas, thus demonstrating the emperor's vision of a moral and just society.

The edicts also emphasize the need for monks and laity to engage in spiritual practices, illustrating the interconnectedness of the monastic community and the lay population. Ashoka's inscriptions at Sarnath stand as a testament to the impact of royal patronage on the growth of Buddhism, as well as the broader socio-political context of the time.

5.3.1.3 The Archaeological Significance of Sarnath

Excavations at Sarnath have uncovered various artifacts, including pottery, coins, and relics associated with monastic life. These findings provide insight into the daily lives of monks and laypersons, highlighting the vibrant community that thrived in this religious center. The ruins of monasteries and monastic complexes, such as the Mulagandhakuti Vihara, reveal the architectural layout and spatial organization of early Buddhist institutions.

In addition to its religious significance, Sarnath has become an important site for archaeological research. Scholars continue to study the inscriptions and artifacts found at the site, contributing to a deeper understanding of the socio-economic conditions of the period, the interactions between various religious communities, and the role of Sarnath as a pilgrimage destination.

5.3.2 Bairat: An Archaeological Gem

Bairat, located in the Jaipur district of Rajasthan, is another significant site for understanding the spread of Buddhism in India. While it may not be as well-known as Sarnath, Bairat boasts remarkable archaeological remains, including stupas, inscriptions, and ancient monasteries. The site dates back to the 3rd century BCE and provides valuable insights into the early phases of Buddhist architecture and inscriptions.

5.3.2.1 The Bairat Stupa: Architectural Marvel

The Bairat Stupa, also known as the Bairat Chetiya Stupa, is one of the oldest stupas in Rajasthan. Constructed around the 3rd century BCE, it showcases the early architectural style of stupas, characterized by its hemispherical dome and square base. The stupa is built with locally sourced stone and brick, reflecting the regional craftsmanship of the time.

The Bairat Stupa is significant for its historical context, as it is believed to have been constructed during the reign of Ashoka. Like the Dhamek Stupa at Sarnath, the Bairat Stupa serves as a monumental representation of Buddhist beliefs and practices. Its design and structure reflect the principles of Buddhism, symbolizing the path to enlightenment.

5.3.2.2 Inscriptions and Their Historical Context

The inscriptions found at Bairat are crucial for understanding the spread of Buddhism in Rajasthan and the patronage it received from local rulers. The inscriptions, written in Brahmi script, often contain references to the donations made by individuals and kings for the construction and maintenance of the stupa and associated monasteries. These inscriptions serve as vital records of the social and political dynamics of the time.

One of the most important inscriptions at Bairat is attributed to Ashoka, which emphasizes the significance of the stupa as a sacred site for Buddhist practice. The inscriptions also highlight the role of the community in supporting the monastic order, showcasing the interdependence between monks and laypersons in the practice of Buddhism. By examining these inscriptions, scholars can gain insights into the motivations behind the construction of stupas and the broader cultural context of Buddhist patronage.

5.3.2.3 The Role of Bairat in Buddhist Heritage

Bairat's archaeological significance extends beyond its stupas and inscriptions. The site features remnants of monastic complexes, meditation halls, and other structures associated with early Buddhist practices. These architectural remains illustrate the organization of monastic life and the communal aspects of Buddhist worship.

Moreover, Bairat is believed to have been an important trade route during the ancient period, facilitating interactions between various cultures and communities. The location of Bairat along trade routes would have contributed to its role as a center for the dissemination of Buddhist teachings, allowing for the exchange of ideas and cultural practices between different regions.

The site has also attracted considerable attention from archaeologists and historians seeking to understand the interplay between religion, politics, and trade in ancient India. The discoveries at Bairat, combined with the inscriptions and stupas, contribute to a richer understanding of the development of Buddhism and its impact on the cultural landscape of Rajasthan.

CHAPTER SIX

Medieval Rajasthan: Rajput Kingdoms and Fortifications

6.1 Architectural Grandeur of Rajput Forts: Chittorgarh, Jaisalmer, Mehrangarh

The Rajput forts of Rajasthan are a testament to the architectural prowess, cultural richness, and historical significance of the region. Among these, Chittorgarh, Jaisalmer, and Mehrangarh stand out as iconic representations of Rajputana's heritage. Each fort reflects the unique history, architectural style, and strategic importance that characterized the era of Rajput rule. This section delves into the architectural grandeur of these three forts, highlighting their historical contexts, structural features, and cultural significance.

6.1.1 Chittorgarh Fort: A Symbol of Valor and Sacrifice

Chittorgarh Fort, one of the largest and most majestic forts in India, sprawls over a hilltop in the Mewar region. Its historical significance is closely tied to the valor and sacrifice of the Rajputs, particularly the legendary tales of Rani Padmini and the siege by Alauddin Khilji. The fort's architectural design is a blend of Rajput and Mughal influences, showcasing intricate carvings, expansive courtyards, and majestic palaces.

The fort, covering an area of approximately 700 acres, is enclosed by massive walls that rise to a height of about 1,500 meters. The **entrances to the fort** are adorned with beautiful gateways, including the **Ram Pol** and **Suraj Pol**, which lead into the fort complex. These gates, built with strategic foresight, served as defensive structures against invasions.

At the heart of the fort lies the **Vijay Stambh (Victory Tower)**, built by Maharaja Rana Kumbha in the 15th century to commemorate his victory over the Muslims. The tower, standing at 37 meters high, is adorned with intricate carvings depicting Hindu deities and scenes from Hindu epics. Climbing to the top of the tower offers a panoramic view of the surrounding landscape, symbolizing the Rajputs' connection to their land.

The **Padmini Palace**, another architectural marvel within Chittorgarh, is famously associated with the tragic tale of Rani Padmini. The palace, located by a serene lake, features beautiful lattice work and mirror-studded walls that reflect the elegance of Rajput architecture. It is believed that Rani Padmini performed Jauhar (self-immolation) along with other women of the palace to protect their honor from the invading forces.

Chittorgarh Fort is not just an architectural marvel; it embodies the spirit of bravery and sacrifice that defines the Rajput ethos. The fort's ruins, temples, and palaces narrate tales of valor and resilience, making it a UNESCO World Heritage Site and a prominent attraction for history enthusiasts and travelers alike.

6.1.2 Jaisalmer Fort: The Golden Citadel

Jaisalmer Fort, also known as the **Sonar Quila (Golden Fort)**, is one of the most stunning examples of fort architecture in Rajasthan. Built in 1156 AD by Maharawal Jaisal Singh, the fort is renowned for its golden-yellow sandstone, which shimmers like gold, particularly during sunrise and sunset. Perched on Trikuta Hill, Jaisalmer Fort is a living fort, with a bustling community residing within its walls.

The fort's **architecture is characterized by intricate jali work (lattice screens), elaborate facades, and beautifully carved balconies**. The use of local sandstone not only enhances its aesthetic appeal but also reflects the region's climatic adaptation, as the thick walls provide insulation against the desert heat. The fort's **entrances**, including the **Patwon Ki Haveli** and **Salim Singh Ki Haveli**, showcase stunning architectural details, with their ornate carvings and decorative motifs.

Inside the fort, visitors can explore a labyrinth of narrow alleys, temples, and havelis that highlight the rich cultural tapestry of Jaisalmer. The **Jaisalmer Fort Palace**, which served as the royal residence, features a blend of Hindu and Islamic architectural styles. Its intricately carved pillars and ceilings reflect the artistic excellence of the craftsmen of that era.

The fort's strategic location along the ancient Silk Route facilitated trade and cultural exchanges between India and Central Asia. The wealth generated from trade is evident in the opulent havelis built by merchants within the fort. These havelis, such as **Patwon Ki Haveli**, are adorned with exquisite carvings and frescoes, showcasing the prosperity of Jaisalmer's merchant class.

Jaisalmer Fort, with its golden facade and rich history, stands as a testament to the Rajput legacy and the cultural vibrancy of the desert region. It was declared a UNESCO World Heritage Site in 2013, acknowledging its architectural and historical significance.

6.1.3 Mehrangarh Fort: The Majestic Stronghold

Mehrangarh Fort, located in Jodhpur, is one of the largest and most impressive forts in India. Founded by Rao Jodha in 1459, the fort is situated on a steep hill, offering breathtaking views of the surrounding landscape. The fort's architecture is characterized by its massive walls, towering ramparts, and intricate palaces, making it a prime example of Rajput military architecture.

The fort's **walls, which are about 36 meters high and 21 meters thick**, provide a formidable defense against potential invaders. The fort complex houses several palaces, temples, and courtyards, showcasing the architectural brilliance of the Rajput era. The **Maan Singh Palace** and **Jaswant Thada** are two notable structures within the fort, each with its own unique architectural features.

The **Maan Singh Palace**, built in the 17th century, is adorned with intricately carved stone screens and painted ceilings that depict scenes from Rajput history and mythology. The palace also features lavish courtyards that served as spaces for royal gatherings and ceremonies. The craftsmanship exhibited in the palace reflects the artistic sensibilities of the time and the patronage of the royal family.

Jaswant Thada, a stunning marble cenotaph built in memory of Maharaja Jaswant Singh II, is another architectural gem located near Mehrangarh Fort. The exquisite marble screens and intricate carvings make it a serene and picturesque site for visitors. The cenotaph is surrounded by lush gardens, providing a tranquil space for reflection and remembrance.

Mehrangarh Fort also houses a museum that showcases a rich collection of artifacts, including weapons, textiles, and paintings, reflecting the history and culture of the Rajputs. The fort's museums serve as a repository of Rajput heritage, offering visitors a glimpse into the opulent lifestyle and traditions of the royal family.

The fort's strategic location played a crucial role in the military history of Rajasthan. It served as a stronghold for the Rathore clan and witnessed numerous battles and sieges throughout its history. The fort's resilience against invasions and its ability to adapt to changing political landscapes are a testament to the strategic foresight of its builders.

6.1.4 Cultural Significance and Legacy

The architectural grandeur of Chittorgarh, Jaisalmer, and Mehrangarh forts goes beyond mere aesthetics; it embodies the cultural identity and historical legacy of the Rajput community. These forts served as centers of power, administration, and culture during the Rajput era, playing a vital role in shaping the socio-political landscape of Rajasthan.

Each fort is steeped in stories of bravery, sacrifice, and resilience, encapsulating the spirit of the Rajputs. The legends associated with these forts, such as the tale of Rani Padmini's Jauhar at Chittorgarh or the valorous defense of Mehrangarh, have become integral to Rajasthan's cultural heritage and folklore.

Moreover, the forts attract thousands of tourists and historians each year, contributing significantly to Rajasthan's economy. They serve as venues for cultural festivals, traditional performances, and heritage walks, fostering a deeper appreciation for Rajasthan's architectural and cultural legacy.

6.1.5 Preservation and Conservation Efforts

The preservation of these architectural marvels is crucial for maintaining the cultural heritage of Rajasthan. Various organizations and government bodies are actively involved in the conservation and restoration of the forts to ensure their longevity for future generations. Efforts include regular maintenance, structural repairs, and promoting sustainable tourism practices to mitigate the impact of visitor traffic.

Educational programs and workshops aimed at raising awareness about the historical significance of these forts are also being implemented. Engaging local communities in preservation efforts ensures that the knowledge and skills required for maintaining these heritage sites are passed down through generations.

6.2 Military Architecture and Fort Designs

Rajasthan, often referred to as the "Land of Kings," is renowned for its majestic forts and palaces that exemplify the state's rich military history and architectural prowess. The military architecture and fort designs of Rajasthan are not merely defensive structures; they are symbolic representations of power, strategy, and cultural identity. Built during various periods, particularly during the medieval era, these forts served as crucial bastions for rulers against invasions and played a pivotal role in shaping the political landscape of the region. This chapter delves into the unique features of military architecture and the design elements that characterize Rajasthan's forts, exploring their historical significance, architectural styles, and the socio-political context that influenced their construction.

6.2.1 Historical Context of Military Architecture in Rajasthan

The historical evolution of military architecture in Rajasthan can be traced back to the early medieval period when regional powers began to establish themselves against the backdrop of political instability and external invasions. The state's strategic geographical location, characterized by rugged terrains, deserts, and mountain ranges, made it a crucial area for establishing defensive fortifications. The Rajput clans, known for their valor and warrior ethos, constructed numerous forts to secure their territories and assert their dominance.

The onset of the Mughal Empire in the 16th century further influenced military architecture in Rajasthan. The Mughals brought advanced techniques and styles, resulting in a fusion of Rajput and Mughal architectural elements. As a result, many forts were constructed or renovated during this period, reflecting a blend of military functionality and aesthetic appeal. The historical context of military architecture in Rajasthan is not just a tale of defense; it is also a narrative of power dynamics, cultural exchanges, and the evolution of architectural styles.

6.2.2 Architectural Features of Forts

The forts of Rajasthan are distinguished by their impressive architectural features, which include fortified walls, intricate gateways, bastions, and living quarters for soldiers and their families. Some of the key elements of military architecture in Rajasthan are as follows:

1. **Fortified Walls**: The first line of defense, the fortified walls of Rajasthan's forts are often constructed with thick stones, bricks, and laterite, designed to withstand sieges and attacks. The walls are typically several meters high and often feature battlements for archers and soldiers to defend against enemies. The walls' strategic placement on elevated ground or rocky outcrops further enhanced their defensive capabilities.

2. **Gates and Entrances**: The entrances to these forts are often grand and elaborately designed, serving as both functional and decorative elements. They are typically constructed as multi-tiered gateways, sometimes featuring intricate carvings and reliefs that reflect the artistic sensibilities of the time. Gates like the "Suraj Pol" (Sun Gate) at the Amer Fort and "Bhagwa Pol" (Colorful Gate) at the Mehrangarh Fort exemplify this architectural style.

3. **Bastions and Towers**: Bastions and watchtowers are prominent features of military architecture in Rajasthan, providing vantage points for surveillance and defense. These structures were strategically placed to enhance the fort's defensive capabilities, allowing defenders to monitor approaching threats. The towering bastions, often embellished with intricate motifs, served both military and symbolic purposes, reflecting the power of the ruling elite.

4. **Water Storage Systems**: The harsh arid climate of Rajasthan necessitated innovative water management

solutions within forts. Many fort complexes incorporated extensive water storage systems, including stepwells, reservoirs, and cisterns, ensuring a sustainable water supply during sieges. The intricate design of these systems demonstrates the foresight and ingenuity of the architects and engineers of the time.

5. **Residential Quarters**: Inside the forts, residential quarters for soldiers, their families, and the ruling elite were often designed to accommodate both military and domestic needs. These living spaces, while functional, also reflected the cultural and artistic traditions of the time. Intricate frescoes, stone carvings, and ornamental motifs adorned the walls of palaces and living quarters, creating an atmosphere of luxury amidst military functionality.

6.2.3 Notable Forts of Rajasthan

Several forts in Rajasthan stand out for their historical significance, architectural brilliance, and military prowess. Each fort tells a unique story of the region's past and reflects the evolution of military architecture over time.

1. **Amber Fort**: Located near Jaipur, Amber Fort is a prime example of the fusion of Rajput and Mughal architectural styles. Built in the late 16th century, the fort features a series of gates, extensive fortified walls, and elaborate courtyards. The fort's strategic location on a hilltop provides stunning views of the surrounding

landscape, while its intricate designs and beautiful gardens reflect the opulence of the ruling Kachwaha dynasty.

2. **Mehrangarh Fort**: Perched on a rocky hill in Jodhpur, Mehrangarh Fort is one of the largest forts in India. Built in the 15th century by Rao Jodha, the fort is characterized by its massive walls, imposing gates, and a series of palaces adorned with intricate carvings and artwork. The fort's museum houses a rich collection of artifacts, weapons, and textiles, offering insights into the military history of the region.

3. **Chittorgarh Fort**: A UNESCO World Heritage Site, Chittorgarh Fort is steeped in history and legend. It was the capital of the Mewar kingdom and witnessed numerous sieges and battles. The fort features a series of palaces, temples, and towers, all connected by a network of walls and gates. The iconic Vijay Stambha (Victory Tower) stands tall within the fort, symbolizing the valor of the Rajput kings.

4. **Kumbhalgarh Fort**: Known for its extensive walls, Kumbhalgarh Fort is often referred to as the "Great Wall of India." The fort, built in the 15th century, features a series of bastions and watchtowers that provide panoramic views of the Aravalli Range. The fort's architectural design incorporates defensive strategies and reflects the ingenuity of Rajput military architecture.

5. **Jaigarh Fort**: Overlooking the Amber Fort, Jaigarh Fort was constructed in the 18th century to protect the Amer

Fort and its inhabitants. The fort is renowned for its impressive arsenal, including the world's largest cannon on wheels, "Jaivana." The fort's strategic location and fortified walls made it a formidable military stronghold, and its architectural design showcases the military ingenuity of the time.

6.2.4 The Socio-Political Significance of Forts

The forts of Rajasthan are not merely military structures; they are integral to understanding the socio-political dynamics of the region. These fortifications served as symbols of power and authority for the ruling elites, reflecting their military strength and political stability. The forts also played a crucial role in the administration and governance of the territories, serving as centers for collecting taxes, maintaining law and order, and organizing military campaigns.

The construction of forts often resulted in the establishment of towns and settlements around them, leading to the growth of trade and commerce. Many forts served as hubs for artisans, traders, and soldiers, fostering economic development in the region. The presence of these forts also attracted artisans and craftsmen, leading to the flourishing of local art and culture.

Furthermore, the forts became sites of historical events, battles, and royal ceremonies. They witnessed the rise and fall of dynasties, the valor of warriors, and the sacrifices made for sovereignty. The narratives of honor, bravery, and loyalty associated with these forts are deeply embedded in the cultural consciousness of Rajasthan, contributing to the region's rich folklore and traditions.

6.2.5 Challenges in Preservation and Conservation

Despite their historical and architectural significance, many forts in Rajasthan face challenges related to preservation and conservation. Factors such as urbanization, tourism, and natural degradation pose threats to the structural integrity of these ancient edifices. Inadequate maintenance and funding for restoration projects further exacerbate the situation.

Efforts to conserve Rajasthan's forts are underway, with various organizations and government initiatives aimed at preserving these cultural heritage sites. Restoration projects, public awareness campaigns, and community involvement are crucial for ensuring the longevity of these architectural marvels. It is essential to strike a balance between promoting tourism and preserving the historical authenticity of the forts.

6.3 Inscriptions, Manuscripts, and Royal Decrees from the Rajput Era

The Rajput Era, spanning from the 6th century to the 18th century CE, was a pivotal period in the history of Rajasthan. It was marked by the rise of the Rajput clans, who established powerful kingdoms characterized by a rich cultural heritage, martial valor, and a profound commitment to honor and chivalry. During this time, inscriptions, manuscripts, and royal decrees played a crucial role in documenting political authority, religious patronage, and social customs. This chapter explores the significance of these primary sources from the Rajput Era, providing insights into the administrative practices, cultural expressions, and historical narratives of the time.

6.3.1 Inscriptions: Chronicling Power and Patronage

Inscriptions from the Rajput Era are invaluable for understanding the political and social dynamics of the time. These inscriptions, often carved on stone pillars, temple walls, and memorials, serve as records of royal achievements, religious donations, and administrative directives. They provide insights into the governance structures of Rajput kingdoms, their alliances, and the patronage of the arts and culture.

6.3.1.1 Royal Inscriptions: Celebrating Kingship

Many inscriptions from the Rajput Era are dedicated to the glorification of kings and their accomplishments. These royal inscriptions frequently highlight the military victories of Rajput rulers, celebrating their valor and heroism in battle. For example, the inscriptions found at the Kumbhalgarh Fort commemorate the achievements of Maharana Kumbha, a notable Rajput king of the Mewar dynasty. These inscriptions document his victories, territorial expansions, and contributions to architecture, showcasing the ways in which kings sought to establish their legacy.

Additionally, royal inscriptions often include references to the construction of temples, palaces, and fortifications, underscoring the importance of architecture in asserting power. The inscriptions typically outline the patronage of these projects, detailing the resources allocated and the craftsmen involved. By commissioning grand structures, Rajput kings aimed to demonstrate their wealth, authority, and commitment to their subjects and deities.

6.3.1.2 Inscriptions as Historical Records

Inscriptions also serve as vital historical records, providing dates, names, and events that help historians reconstruct the chronology of the Rajput Era. For instance, the inscriptions found at the famous Chittorgarh Fort contain valuable information about the rulers of the Sisodia clan, including their lineage and the timeline of their reigns. These inscriptions not only document the ruling dynasties but also highlight important events such as battles, treaties, and the construction of significant structures.

Moreover, the use of different scripts, such as Brahmi, Nagari, and Devanagari, in these inscriptions reflects the linguistic diversity of the region and the evolution of writing systems over time. The study of these scripts allows scholars to trace the development of language and literature in Rajasthan, contributing to a broader understanding of cultural continuity and change during the Rajput Era.

6.3.2 Manuscripts: A Repository of Knowledge and Culture

Manuscripts from the Rajput Era provide a wealth of information about the cultural, literary, and artistic traditions of the time. These manuscripts, written on palm leaves, paper, and cloth, encompass a wide range of subjects, including history, poetry, philosophy, and religion. They serve as a testament to the intellectual achievements of Rajput society and the patronage of literature by royal families.

6.3.2.1 Historical Manuscripts: Documenting the Past

Historical manuscripts, such as the "Rajatarangini" by Kalhana, are invaluable sources for understanding the political landscape of Rajasthan during the Rajput Era. Although originally written about Kashmir, the themes and narratives of Rajput history resonate with the broader context of Rajputana. These texts often include genealogies of kings, accounts of battles, and descriptions of court life, providing a rich tapestry of historical events and personalities.

Additionally, manuscripts like the "Prithviraj Raso," an epic poem narrating the life of the legendary king Prithviraj Chauhan, highlight the valor and heroism of Rajput warriors. Such texts not only celebrate individual accomplishments but also reflect the collective identity and ethos of the Rajput clans. The stories of loyalty, honor, and bravery contained in these manuscripts continue to resonate in the cultural memory of Rajasthan.

6.3.2.2 Religious and Literary Manuscripts

In addition to historical accounts, religious manuscripts from the Rajput Era shed light on the spiritual practices and beliefs of the time. Texts such as the "Bhagavad Gita," "Ramayana," and various Puranas were often copied and disseminated in Rajput courts, showcasing the integration of spirituality and governance. Rajput rulers frequently commissioned translations and commentaries on these texts, reflecting their role as patrons of religious scholarship.

Moreover, the literary traditions of Rajasthan flourished during this period, with poets and writers receiving patronage from Rajput kings. Manuscripts of poetry, including works by renowned poets like Jayadeva and Surdas, illustrate the rich cultural landscape of the Rajput Era. These literary works not only celebrated the valor of Rajput heroes but also exprcssed devotion to deities, encapsulating the intersection of art, spirituality, and power.

6.3.3 Royal Decrees: Governance and Administrative Practices

Royal decrees, often inscribed on stone or metal plates, played a significant role in the governance of Rajput kingdoms. These decrees outlined laws, regulations, and administrative directives, serving as official documents that communicated the will of the king to his subjects.

6.3.3.1 Administrative Decrees: Law and Order

The administrative decrees issued by Rajput rulers addressed various aspects of governance, including land revenue, trade regulations, and social customs. These decrees often sought to maintain law and order within the kingdom, outlining penalties for offenses and procedures for dispute resolution. The emphasis on justice and the welfare of subjects reflects the responsibilities of Rajput kings as protectors and upholders of dharma (righteousness).

One notable example is the revenue regulations enacted by Maharaja Sawai Jai Singh II of Amber, who introduced systematic taxation policies that streamlined the collection of revenue. His decrees outlined the responsibilities of local officials, the rights of peasants, and the allocation of resources for public works. Such administrative reforms not only enhanced the efficiency of governance but also fostered loyalty among the subjects.

6.3.3.2 Cultural and Ceremonial Decrees

In addition to administrative matters, royal decrees also addressed cultural and ceremonial aspects of Rajput life. These decrees often regulated festivals, rituals, and public celebrations, reflecting the intertwining of politics and culture in Rajput society. Rulers would issue edicts that mandated the observance of specific rituals, reinforced social hierarchies, and ensured the participation of the populace in ceremonial events.

For instance, the royal decrees of the Sisodia dynasty often included directives related to the celebration of festivals such as Diwali, Holi, and Teej, which were crucial for fostering communal bonds and cultural identity. These decrees would outline the roles of various social groups, including priests, artisans, and commoners, in the execution of rituals, thereby reinforcing the social fabric of Rajput society.

CHAPTER SEVEN

Temple Architecture and Religious Structures

7.1 Evolution of Temple Architecture in Rajasthan

Rajasthan, a state renowned for its rich cultural heritage, has a long and fascinating history of temple architecture that reflects the artistic, religious, and socio-political dynamics of the region. The evolution of temple architecture in Rajasthan can be traced from ancient times through various dynasties, each contributing unique styles, motifs, and innovations that have defined the architectural landscape of the state. This section delves into the various phases of temple architecture in Rajasthan, exploring key periods, architectural features, and the cultural significance of temples.

7.1.1 Ancient Beginnings: Prehistoric and Early Temples

The earliest evidence of religious architecture in Rajasthan dates back to the **Indus Valley Civilization**, around 2500 BCE, where findings suggest the presence of fire altars and possibly proto-temples. Sites like **Kalibangan** reveal a rudimentary understanding of sacred spaces, although the structures are not temples in the traditional sense. The evolution of temple architecture began to take shape during the **Mauryan Empire (circa 322-185 BCE)**, influenced by the spread of Buddhism.

The **rock-cut caves at Ajanta and Ellora**, although primarily in Maharashtra, inspired similar cave architecture in Rajasthan. The **Uparkot Caves** and the **Buddhist caves in the Aravalli range** show the early Indian tradition of carving religious spaces out of rock, which laid the groundwork for later temple construction. This period marked the emergence of sacred spaces dedicated to deities, though they were often simple and unadorned compared to later structures.

7.1.2 The Gupta Period: Flourishing of Hindu Temples

The Gupta period (circa 320-550 CE) is often considered a golden age of Indian art and architecture. The influence of Gupta architecture is evident in several temples in Rajasthan, which began to take on more complex forms and elaborate designs. The **Sas-Bahu Temples** at **Udaipur**, dedicated to Vishnu and Shiva, are prime examples of early medieval temple architecture that flourished during this period. The temples are characterized by intricately carved exteriors, detailed sculptures, and ornate pillars.

The **Shikhara** (spire) became a defining feature of temple architecture during the Gupta period. This architectural style reflects the influence of both local and imperial traditions, leading to a distinct Rajasthani style that combined grandeur with intricate artistry. Temples constructed during this period not only served as places of worship but also became centers for art, culture, and community life.

7.1.3 The Rise of Rajput Architecture: 6th to 16th Century

The Rajput era (circa 6th to 16th century) marked a significant transformation in temple architecture, characterized by regional diversity and the establishment of distinctive styles. The **Rajput clans**, known for their valor and patronage of the arts, commissioned many temples that showcased their artistic sensibilities.

One of the most notable temple complexes from this period is the **Dilwara Temples** near **Mount Abu**, built in the 11th century. These Jain temples exemplify the pinnacle of intricate marble craftsmanship, with detailed carvings, ornate ceilings, and exquisite jali work (lattice screens). The **Vimal Vasahi Temple** and **Luna Vasahi Temple** are particularly renowned for their architectural elegance and artistic finesse.

In addition to Jain temples, Hindu temples flourished during this period, with a focus on deities like Shiva and Vishnu. The **Shiv temple at **Rani Sati Dadi** and the

Brahma Temple at Pushkar showcase the evolution of temple architecture with their towering shikharas and intricately carved pillars. The influence of regional styles, along with the incorporation of local materials, gave rise to unique temple designs that varied from one region to another.

7.1.4 The Mughal Influence: Synthesis of Styles

The arrival of the Mughal Empire in the 16th century brought about significant changes in temple architecture in Rajasthan. While the Mughals are primarily known for their Islamic architecture, their rule also led to a synthesis of styles that influenced Hindu temple designs. The Mughal emperors patronized various forms of art, leading to the construction of several temples characterized by a blend of Hindu and Islamic architectural elements.

The **Kankroli Temple**, also known as the **Rajiv Lochan Temple**, exemplifies this synthesis. Built during the Mughal period, the temple incorporates elements of Mughal architecture, such as domes and intricate tile work, while retaining traditional Hindu architectural features. This blending of styles reflects the cultural exchanges that occurred during the Mughal era.

Moreover, the construction of temples during this time often included elaborate gardens, reflecting the Mughal emphasis on aesthetics and symmetry. The gardens surrounding temples served as serene spaces for worship and contemplation, enhancing the overall experience for devotees.

7.1.5 Post-Mughal Revival: 18th Century and Beyond

The 18th century saw a revival of temple architecture in Rajasthan, characterized by a return to traditional styles and an emphasis on intricate craftsmanship. With the decline of Mughal power, local rulers and feudal lords commissioned new temples, often reflecting a renewed interest in regional artistic traditions.

The **Mehandipur Balaji Temple**, dedicated to the Hindu deity Hanuman, is an example of this revival. Built in the late 18th century, the temple showcases elaborate sculptures and vibrant frescoes that narrate stories from Hindu mythology. The emphasis on storytelling through art became a prominent feature of temple architecture during this period.

The **Khatu Shyamji Temple**, located near **Sikar**, further exemplifies the revival of temple architecture. The temple features stunning carvings, intricate marble work, and elaborate gateways, showcasing the skills of local artisans. The architecture reflects the local cultural identity while adhering to traditional temple designs.

7.1.6 Contemporary Developments: Preservation and Innovation

In recent years, there has been a growing awareness of the need to preserve Rajasthan's rich architectural heritage. Restoration and conservation efforts have been initiated to protect ancient temples from the ravages of time and environmental factors. Organizations and government bodies are working to ensure that these historical sites are maintained for future generations.

Contemporary architects and artisans are also exploring innovative ways to blend traditional architectural styles with modern sensibilities. New temples, such as the **Birla Mandir** in Jaipur, reflect a contemporary approach to temple architecture while drawing inspiration from traditional designs. These structures often incorporate modern materials and techniques while preserving the essence of traditional craftsmanship.

The integration of sustainable practices in temple construction has also gained traction, with a focus on using local materials and eco-friendly techniques. This approach not only honors the historical significance of the temples but also addresses contemporary environmental concerns.

7.2 Key Temples: Dilwara, Ranakpur, Eklingji

Rajasthan is home to numerous temples that not only serve as places of worship but also as architectural masterpieces, showcasing the rich cultural and spiritual heritage of the region. Among these, the **Dilwara Temples**, **Ranakpur Temple**, and **Eklingji Temple** stand out for their exquisite craftsmanship, historical significance, and spiritual importance. This section delves into the unique features and historical contexts of these key temples, highlighting their role in Rajasthan's religious and architectural landscape.

7.2.1 Dilwara Temples: Marvels of Jain Architecture

The **Dilwara Temples**, located near **Mount Abu**, are considered one of the finest examples of Jain architecture in India. Built between the 11th and 13th centuries, these temples are renowned for their intricate marble carvings and architectural brilliance. The temples were commissioned by wealthy Jain merchants and reflect the opulence and artistic sensibilities of the time.

The complex comprises five main temples: **Vimal Vasahi**, **Luna Vasahi**, **Pitalia**, **Khartar Vasahi**, and **Parshvanath**. The **Vimal Vasahi Temple**, dedicated to the first Tirthankara, Adinath, is particularly notable for its stunning entrance adorned with elaborate carvings of floral motifs, dancers, and deities. The ceiling of the temple features intricate domes and carvings, resembling a celestial garden, that mesmerize visitors upon entry.

The **Luna Vasahi Temple**, dedicated to Neminath, showcases equally stunning artistry with its richly decorated pillars and walls. The temple's ceilings are adorned with exquisitely carved motifs depicting scenes from Jain mythology. What sets the Dilwara Temples apart is the meticulous attention to detail in every carving, which reflects the skilled craftsmanship of the artisans.

The use of white marble not only enhances the aesthetic appeal of the temples but also contributes to their spiritual ambiance. The Dilwara Temples are often considered a pilgrimage site for Jains, attracting devotees and tourists alike who come to admire the architectural splendor and immerse themselves in the tranquil atmosphere.

7.2.2 Ranakpur Temple: A Gem of Jain Heritage

The **Ranakpur Temple**, located in the Aravalli Range between Udaipur and Jodhpur, is another remarkable example of Jain architecture. Built in the 15th century, the temple is dedicated to **Tirthankara Adinath** and is one of the largest and most intricately designed Jain temples in India.

The architectural layout of the Ranakpur Temple is unique, featuring 1,444 intricately carved marble pillars, each with a distinct design. The pillars support a stunning array of domes and intricately carved ceilings, showcasing exquisite artwork that reflects the devotion and creativity of the craftsmen. The temple is built in a double-storied layout, with the main shrine located at the upper level, enhancing its grandeur.

One of the most striking features of the Ranakpur Temple is the **main dome**, which is adorned with an elaborate lotus motif and is surrounded by smaller domes, creating a mesmerizing effect. The play of light and shadow in the temple enhances the visual experience, making it a captivating space for worship and contemplation.

The intricate carvings on the walls and pillars depict various scenes from Jain mythology, celestial beings, and floral motifs. The level of detail in the carvings is astonishing, showcasing the artisans' dedication to their craft. Visitors often spend hours admiring the artistry and tranquility of the temple.

Ranakpur Temple not only serves as a significant religious site for Jains but also as a symbol of architectural brilliance. Its serene location amidst the hills and the beautiful surroundings further enhance its appeal, making it a must-visit destination for tourists exploring Rajasthan's rich heritage.

7.2.3 Eklingji Temple: The Abode of Lord Shiva

The **Eklingji Temple**, located about 22 kilometers from Udaipur, is one of the most revered Hindu temples in Rajasthan, dedicated to **Lord Shiva**. Believed to have been built in the 8th century, the temple is a significant pilgrimage site for devotees of Shiva and a fine example of medieval Indian temple architecture.

The Eklingji Temple complex is enclosed by a high wall and features a series of temples dedicated to different forms of Shiva. The primary temple houses a four-faced black stone idol of Eklingji, representing Lord Shiva in his aspect as the supreme being. The idol is adorned with a silver crown and jewels, and the ambiance inside the temple is filled with a sense of devotion and spirituality.

The architectural style of Eklingji Temple reflects the typical **Rajasthani temple design**, with intricately carved pillars, domes, and courtyards. The temple's exterior is adorned with beautiful sculptures and motifs that narrate stories from Hindu mythology. The combination of intricate carvings and serene surroundings creates a peaceful atmosphere for worship and meditation.

The temple complex also includes several smaller shrines, each dedicated to different deities, such as **Goddess Parvati** and **Ganesha**. The complex is surrounded by lush greenery and scenic landscapes, making it a popular destination for pilgrims and tourists seeking solace and spiritual rejuvenation.

The Eklingji Temple holds significant cultural and historical importance, as it has been a center of Shiva worship for centuries. The temple is particularly busy during the Maha Shivaratri festival, attracting thousands of devotees who come to pay their respects and seek blessings from the deity.

7.3 Sculptural Styles and Religious Symbolism in Temples

Rajasthan's temples are not merely architectural wonders; they are repositories of art and culture, reflecting the socio-political and spiritual ethos of their time. Central to the architectural beauty of these temples is their sculptural ornamentation, which plays a crucial role in conveying religious symbolism and narratives. This section delves into the diverse sculptural styles found in Rajasthan's temples, exploring their artistic significance and the religious symbolism embedded within them.

7.3.1 Historical Context of Sculptural Styles

The evolution of sculptural styles in Rajasthan can be traced back to ancient times, with influences from various dynasties, including the Mauryas, Guptas, and Rajputs. Each era contributed distinct styles and techniques, which were further enriched by regional influences. The early period, particularly during the Mauryan and Gupta empires, witnessed the emergence of **narrative reliefs** and **iconography** that laid the foundation for later developments in temple sculpture.

During the **medieval period**, with the rise of the Rajput clans, sculptural art flourished as temples became prominent centers of worship and artistic expression. Rajput rulers commissioned grand temples adorned with intricate carvings and sculptures, depicting deities, celestial beings, and mythological narratives. The sculptural styles evolved, integrating local artistic traditions with broader influences from other parts of India.

7.3.2 Key Sculptural Styles in Rajasthan's Temples

7.3.2.1 Jain Temples: Elegance and Intricacy

The **Dilwara Temples** and **Ranakpur Temple** are prime examples of Jain architectural splendor, characterized by their intricate carvings and delicate sculptures. Jain art is known for its meticulous attention to detail and the use of **white marble**, which enhances the luminosity of the carvings.

In Jain temples, sculptures predominantly depict **Tirthankaras** (spiritual teachers) and celestial beings, illustrating the Jain philosophy of non-violence and compassion. The **Dilwara Temples**, for instance, feature exquisite reliefs of floral motifs, animals, and celestial dancers, symbolizing the soul's journey toward liberation. The use of **aerial perspective** in these carvings creates depth, allowing for a dynamic representation of figures and scenes.

The narrative reliefs often depict stories from Jain texts, showcasing the teachings of Tirthankaras and the significance of righteous living. The delicate and intricate craftsmanship of these sculptures reflects the dedication of the artisans and their spiritual devotion to the Jain faith.

7.3.2.2 Hindu Temples: Rich Iconography and Mythological Themes

Hindu temples in Rajasthan are replete with sculptures that embody a rich tapestry of iconography and mythological themes. The temples dedicated to deities like **Shiva**, **Vishnu**, and **Devi** often feature intricate carvings of these gods, accompanied by a host of attendants, animals, and divine figures. The **Eklingji Temple**, for example, showcases an iconic four-faced image of Lord Shiva, symbolizing his omnipresence.

The sculptures in Hindu temples are often narrative-driven, illustrating various episodes from epics such as the **Ramayana** and **Mahabharata**. The depiction of mythological battles, divine marriages, and the manifestations of deities serve to educate devotees about their religious beliefs. The **Khatu Shyamji Temple** is renowned for its vibrant frescoes and carvings that narrate stories of the divine.

Another significant aspect of Hindu temple sculpture is the representation of **Yogic postures** and **cosmic symbolism**. The sculptures often illustrate the interconnectedness of the divine with the universe, highlighting themes of creation, preservation, and destruction. This symbolic representation serves as a reminder of the cyclical nature of life and the eternal presence of the divine.

7.3.2.3 The Influence of Mughal Art

The Mughal era also left an indelible mark on the sculptural styles in Rajasthan, particularly in the temples constructed during or after this period. The influence of Mughal art is evident in the incorporation of floral motifs, geometric patterns, and the use of **red sandstone** and **white marble** in temple construction.

The **Birla Mandir** in Jaipur exemplifies this synthesis of styles, featuring intricate carvings that reflect Mughal influences while adhering to traditional Hindu themes. The blending of Hindu and Mughal artistic elements symbolizes the cultural exchanges that occurred during this time, resulting in a unique aesthetic that transcends religious boundaries.

7.3.3 Symbolism in Sculptural Art

Sculptures in Rajasthan's temples are laden with religious symbolism, serving not only as decorative elements but also as conduits of spiritual teachings. The intricate carvings often convey complex themes and narratives that resonate deeply with devotees.

7.3.3.1 Deities and Divine Manifestations

The representation of deities in temple sculptures is central to their religious significance. Each deity's physical attributes, gestures (mudras), and accompanying symbols convey specific meanings. For instance, the depiction of **Goddess Durga** with her multiple arms symbolizes her power to vanquish evil, while the serene posture of **Buddha** reflects peace and enlightenment.

The **Shiva Lingam**, a representation of Lord Shiva, is often accompanied by sculptures of **Nandi** (the sacred bull) and various symbols that denote fertility, regeneration, and the cosmic cycle. The arrangement of these sculptures in the temple space enhances the spiritual experience, guiding devotees in their worship and contemplation.

7.3.3.2 Mythological Narratives and Moral Lessons

Many sculptures depict scenes from Hindu and Jain mythologies, serving to educate devotees about moral values and spiritual teachings. The **Ramayana**, for instance, is often represented through reliefs depicting key events such as **Rama's exile**, **Sita's abduction**, and **Hanuman's devotion**. These narratives inspire devotees to embody the virtues of righteousness, courage, and devotion.

The use of sculptural narratives in Jain temples often revolves around the lives and teachings of Tirthankaras, emphasizing values such as **ahimsa** (non-violence) and **truthfulness**. The visual representation of these teachings in stone serves as a reminder of the path to liberation.

7.3.3.3 Cosmic Symbolism and Philosophical Concepts

In addition to depicting deities and narratives, temple sculptures often incorporate cosmic symbolism and philosophical concepts. The representation of the **universe** through geometric patterns, the **lotus** symbolizing purity and spiritual awakening, and the depiction of **Yogic postures** convey profound philosophical ideas.

For example, the depiction of the cosmic dance of **Shiva (Nataraja)** symbolizes the cyclical nature of creation and destruction, reflecting the interconnectedness of all existence. This representation serves as a reminder for devotees to embrace the transient nature of life while seeking spiritual enlightenment.

7.3.4 Contemporary Perspectives on Temple Sculpture

As society evolves, so does the understanding and appreciation of temple sculptures. Contemporary artists and architects draw inspiration from traditional sculptural styles while experimenting with new forms and materials. This fusion of traditional and modern techniques reflects the dynamic nature of art and spirituality.

In recent years, there has been a resurgence of interest in preserving and promoting traditional sculptural techniques. Workshops and cultural initiatives aim to revive ancient practices, ensuring that the skills of artisans are passed down through generations. This effort not only preserves the rich heritage of Rajasthan's sculptural art but also provides opportunities for artisans to showcase their craftsmanship.

CHAPTER EIGHT

TRADE ROUTES AND DESERT CITIES

8.1 Importance of Rajasthan in Medieval Trade Networks

Rajasthan, historically known as Rajputana, was a pivotal region in the medieval trade networks of India and beyond. Its geographical location, lying at the crossroads of significant trade routes connecting the Indian subcontinent with Central Asia, the Middle East, and parts of Europe, made it a crucial hub for commerce and cultural exchanges. This section delves into the factors that contributed to Rajasthan's prominence in medieval trade, the types of goods that flowed through its markets, and how the trade networks influenced the socio-political and economic development of the region.

8.1.1 Strategic Geographical Location

Rajasthan's importance in medieval trade networks can be largely attributed to its **strategic geographical location**. Situated between the fertile plains of the Ganges River and the Thar Desert, Rajasthan provided an essential link between the northern Indian cities and the ports of Gujarat, which were key for maritime trade. Major towns such as **Jodhpur**, **Jaipur**, **Ajmer**, and **Bikaner** became central to these trade routes, offering a transit point for caravans carrying goods across regions.

Additionally, Rajasthan's proximity to the **Silk Road**, one of the most famous trade routes in history, enhanced its role in facilitating the movement of goods between **China**, **Persia**, and the **Arab world**. Caravans passing through Rajasthan would carry luxury items such as silk, spices, gems, and precious metals, connecting the east and west in a vibrant exchange of goods and cultures. The importance of Rajasthan's location also extended to its connection with **Afghanistan**, **Iran**, and the **Arabian Peninsula**, making it a thriving inland trade hub in medieval times.

8.1.2 Major Trade Routes and Caravan Networks

Rajasthan's cities were interconnected by a series of **trade routes** that crisscrossed the desert, facilitating commerce across different regions. These routes were critical for the movement of goods, particularly overland, as they connected major cities and kingdoms not only within Rajasthan but also with the wider world. Two key trade routes that passed through Rajasthan were the **Grand**

Trunk Road and the **ancient Uttarapatha route**.

The **Grand Trunk Road**, established during the Mauryan period and further developed under the **Mughals**, served as a major artery for trade and communication. Rajasthan's cities acted as vital stops along this route, where traders from Central Asia, Persia, and Europe would exchange goods with Indian merchants. The **Thar Desert**, while seemingly inhospitable, was navigable by expert camel riders who guided caravans through the arid landscape, contributing to the establishment of key trading centers in Rajasthan.

Moreover, Rajasthan's cities acted as **caravanserai**, offering rest stops and marketplaces where traders could barter their goods. Towns like **Jaisalmer**, with its golden fort, became known as "the gateway to the west" due to its role as a major hub in this trans-regional trade. Merchants and travelers passing through Jaisalmer would bring goods such as **silk, textiles, spices, and salt**, which were then redistributed throughout northern India and beyond.

8.1.3 Types of Goods Traded in Rajasthan

The diversity of goods traded through Rajasthan reflected the region's wealth and connectivity in the medieval period. Rajasthan's cities were particularly known for the exchange of **luxury items**, such as **gems**, **precious metals**, **spices**, and **silks**. These items were highly valued both in Indian markets and by international traders. The region's abundant supply of **salt** from the **Sambhar Salt Lake** also made it an essential item for trade. Salt was in great demand for both culinary and preservative purposes and was traded extensively across India and into Central Asia.

Rajasthan also became a significant player in the trade of **textiles**, particularly those produced in local textile centers such as **Bikaner** and **Jaipur**. The intricate designs and fine quality of Rajasthani textiles, including **block-printed fabrics**, **tie-dye textiles** (Bandhani), and **embroidered cloth**, were highly sought after in markets as far as Persia and the Mediterranean.

Additionally, **camels**, an integral part of trade through the desert, were bred in Rajasthan and traded widely. The **Pushkar Camel Fair**, which still takes place today, has its origins in these medieval trade networks, where thousands of camels were bought and sold for use in caravans traversing the desert.

Beyond physical goods, Rajasthan also played a key role in the exchange of **cultural and intellectual knowledge**. Trade routes facilitated the movement of ideas, including religious beliefs, art, and architectural styles, between India and Central Asia. This cultural diffusion enriched the region's diversity, bringing new artistic forms and influencing the local **Rajput architecture** and traditions.

8.1.4 Role of Rajput Rulers in Facilitating Trade

The **Rajput rulers** of Rajasthan understood the importance of trade for the prosperity and development of their kingdoms. They actively promoted commerce by maintaining the security of the trade routes and ensuring safe passage for merchants through their territories. The **Rajput warrior clans**, known for their martial prowess, played a dual role as protectors of trade routes and as patrons of commerce.

Rulers like **Rao Jodha of Jodhpur** and **Maharaja Jai Singh II of Jaipur** took measures to fortify their cities, building impressive forts such as **Mehrangarh Fort** and **Amber Fort**, which not only served as military bastions but also protected trade interests. These rulers imposed relatively low tariffs on goods passing through their territories, encouraging merchants from far-off regions to conduct trade in Rajasthan.

Additionally, the construction of **trade bazaars** and **marketplaces** within these cities facilitated commerce. **Jaipur**, under the visionary leadership of Jai Singh II, was designed with wide streets and specialized markets to accommodate merchants and traders from different parts of the world. These bazaars became vibrant centers of exchange, where everything from textiles to spices and jewelry could be bought and sold.

The Rajput rulers also formed alliances with other kingdoms and empires, such as the **Mughals**, who further boosted Rajasthan's involvement in transcontinental trade networks. The political stability provided by the Mughal-Rajput alliances allowed merchants to conduct trade without fear of attack or disruption, making Rajasthan a safer and more attractive region for commerce.

8.1.5 Influence of Trade on Rajasthan's Economy and Culture

The bustling trade networks that passed through Rajasthan had a profound impact on the region's **economy** and **culture**. Trade brought immense wealth to the Rajput kingdoms, which in turn fueled the construction of grand palaces, forts, and temples. The flourishing of arts and architecture in cities like **Jodhpur**, **Jaipur**, and **Udaipur** can be attributed to the wealth generated through trade.

The influx of foreign merchants and travelers also led to the exchange of ideas, artistic styles, and technologies. This cross-cultural interaction enriched Rajasthan's cultural landscape, as can be seen in its **art**, **music**, and **cuisine**. The **fusion of Mughal and Rajput styles** in architecture, the introduction of new musical instruments, and the use of exotic spices in Rajasthani cuisine are all testaments to the influence of trade on the region's cultural evolution.

The wealth generated through trade also allowed the Rajput rulers to maintain large standing armies and support a courtly culture of **patronage for the arts**, including **miniature painting**, **jewelry-making**, and **textile crafts**. Many of the beautiful palaces and forts that survive today were funded by the prosperity that trade brought to Rajasthan during the medieval period.

8.1.6 Decline of Rajasthan's Role in Trade Networks

While Rajasthan thrived as a center of trade during the medieval period, its prominence began to wane with the rise of **European maritime trade** in the 16th and 17th centuries. The Portuguese, Dutch, and British established direct sea routes to India, bypassing the traditional overland routes that had passed through Rajasthan. The opening of these maritime routes reduced the importance of overland trade, leading to a decline in the economic significance of Rajasthan's cities.

Nevertheless, Rajasthan's role in medieval trade networks left a lasting legacy on its culture, economy, and architecture. The region's history as a bustling trade hub continues to be reflected in its vibrant markets, stunning palaces, and rich cultural traditions.

8.2 Archaeological Findings from Desert Cities: Bikaner, Jodhpur

The desert cities of **Bikaner** and **Jodhpur**, located in the arid expanse of the Thar Desert in Rajasthan, hold a significant place in the historical and archaeological record of the region. These cities, known for their splendid forts, palaces, and bustling medieval trade routes, have also revealed a treasure trove of archaeological findings that shed light on their ancient and medieval pasts. Through systematic excavations and explorations, historians and archaeologists have uncovered evidence of early settlements, trade activities, and the material culture of the people who lived in these regions. This section explores the key archaeological findings from the cities of Bikaner and Jodhpur and their importance in understanding Rajasthan's historical and cultural development.

8.2.1 Archaeological Importance of Bikaner

Bikaner, founded by **Rao Bika** in the 15th century, has emerged as an important site for archaeological studies, particularly due to its strategic location near ancient trade routes that connected Rajasthan with the rest of India and Central Asia. Bikaner's history, however, predates its medieval origins, with archaeological evidence pointing to earlier habitation.

8.2.1.1 Early Settlements and Prehistoric Finds

One of the key archaeological findings in Bikaner has been the discovery of **prehistoric artifacts**, including **tools** and **pottery**. These findings suggest that the region was inhabited by early humans, potentially dating back to the **Harappan era**. The excavations near the **Ghaggar-Hakra River** bed, believed to be part of the Sarasvati River system mentioned in ancient Indian texts, have revealed evidence of early human activity and settlement patterns.

Prehistoric tools such as **microliths** (small stone tools used by hunter-gatherer societies) and pottery fragments have been found in the surrounding desert areas, indicating the presence of early human settlements that may have relied on the seasonal flow of the river for survival. These findings are crucial in understanding the early phases of human habitation in the arid regions of Rajasthan and how ancient populations adapted to the harsh desert environment.

8.2.1.2 Findings from Medieval Period

The medieval history of Bikaner is closely tied to its role as a **trade and military center** under the Rajputs. Archaeological excavations in the old parts of Bikaner city, particularly around **Junagarh Fort**, have uncovered a variety of artifacts from the medieval period. **Ceramics**, **coins**, and **weaponry** have been found in abundance, indicating Bikaner's active participation in regional trade and its military significance.

One of the notable findings in Bikaner is the **remnants of ancient stepwells** (baoris) and water storage systems, which demonstrate the advanced water management techniques developed to sustain life in the desert. These stepwells were essential for the survival of both the local population and the traders who passed through the city. The intricate carvings found on these stepwells also provide insights into the architectural and artistic styles prevalent during the medieval period.

8.2.2 Archaeological Significance of Jodhpur

Jodhpur, often referred to as the "Blue City" because of its blue-painted houses, was founded by **Rao Jodha** in the 15th century and has been an important center of Rajput power and culture. Archaeological studies in Jodhpur have revealed layers of historical occupation, from prehistoric times to the medieval period.

8.2.2.1 Prehistoric Evidence and Early Settlements

Like Bikaner, Jodhpur has yielded evidence of **prehistoric human activity**, particularly in the form of stone tools and pottery shards found in the surrounding areas. Excavations in nearby regions such as **Osian** and **Mandore** have revealed the presence of early settlements that may date back to the **Harappan** and **Chalcolithic** periods.

These early settlements are believed to have been part of the extensive trading networks that crisscrossed the Thar Desert. The discovery of **terracotta figurines**, **beads**, and **pottery** indicates that Jodhpur was likely involved in long-distance trade with other regions, possibly exchanging goods such as textiles, spices, and metals.

8.2.2.2 Excavations Around Mehrangarh Fort

The **Mehrangarh Fort**, one of the largest and most imposing forts in India, dominates the landscape of Jodhpur and has been a focal point of archaeological interest. Excavations around the fort have uncovered numerous artifacts, including **weaponry**, **ceramics**, and **coins**, which provide insights into the fort's role as a military stronghold and its connection to the broader trade networks.

One of the most interesting findings from the excavations around Mehrangarh Fort is the discovery of **storage rooms** and **granaries**, indicating the fort's role in safeguarding not only the city's military power but also its economic resources. These findings underscore the strategic importance of Jodhpur in controlling the desert trade routes and its ability to withstand long sieges during times of conflict.

8.2.2.3 Water Management Systems

Jodhpur, like Bikaner, developed sophisticated water management systems to deal with the arid conditions of the desert. The city's famous **stepwells** (baolis) and **tanks** (kunds) have been subjects of archaeological study, revealing the advanced engineering techniques used to ensure a steady supply of water in the harsh desert environment.

The **Toorji ka Jhalra**, a stepwell located in the heart of Jodhpur, is a prime example of this ingenuity. Archaeological studies of the stepwell have uncovered evidence of intricate carvings and inscriptions that highlight the religious and cultural significance of water in the region. The discovery of ancient water channels connected to the stepwell system indicates that Jodhpur had a well-organized network of water storage and distribution, which played a crucial role in sustaining the city's population and enabling trade activities.

8.2.3 Role of Trade in Desert Cities

The desert cities of Bikaner and Jodhpur were integral to the **medieval trade networks** that crisscrossed Rajasthan, linking India with Central Asia, Persia, and beyond. The archaeological findings from both cities provide ample evidence of their roles as key trade hubs.

The discovery of **coins** from different regions, **ceramics** of varied origins, and **trade goods** such as textiles and spices indicates that Bikaner and Jodhpur were connected to long-distance trade routes. Bikaner, in particular, benefited from its proximity to the **Sambhar Salt Lake**, which was a major source of salt—a highly valuable commodity in medieval times. Salt from Bikaner was traded across Rajasthan and into neighboring regions, making the city a key player in the desert economy.

Jodhpur's location at the edge of the Thar Desert also positioned it as a gateway for caravans traveling to and from **Gujarat**, **Delhi**, and **Sindh**. The city's fortifications and strategic location allowed it to control and protect trade routes, ensuring its prosperity.

8.2.4 Cultural and Religious Insights

In addition to trade and military artifacts, the archaeological findings from Bikaner and Jodhpur have revealed important cultural and religious artifacts. Temples, shrines, and religious icons found in these cities provide a window into the spiritual life of their inhabitants.

The discovery of **Hindu**, **Jain**, and **Buddhist artifacts** in Bikaner and Jodhpur reflects the religious diversity of the region during the medieval period. In Bikaner, archaeological studies have unearthed **Jain temples** and **carvings**, which point to the influence of Jainism in the city's cultural and religious life. Similarly, Jodhpur's **Mandore Gardens**, which house ancient temples and cenotaphs, offer insights into the religious practices and architectural styles that flourished under the Rajput rulers.

8.3 Caravanserais, Stepwells, and Market Structures

Rajasthan's historical architecture offers a unique glimpse into the socio-economic and cultural life of its past inhabitants. Among the most significant structures that highlight the region's commercial and logistical prowess are **caravanserais** (inns for traders and travelers), **stepwells** (water storage systems), and **market structures** that played a pivotal role in sustaining trade, commerce, and the daily life of desert cities. These constructions were not only functional but also integral to the survival and prosperity of trade routes that passed through the harsh terrain of the **Thar Desert**.

In this section, we explore the architectural, social, and economic importance of caravanserais, stepwells, and market structures, focusing on how they facilitated trade, water management, and community interactions during medieval and pre-modern periods in Rajasthan.

8.3.1 Caravanserais: Inns for Desert Travelers

The caravanserais of Rajasthan were architectural wonders built along trade routes to provide shelter, food, and rest for travelers and merchants. These structures were crucial for the success of trade routes, particularly those passing through the **Thar Desert**, where resources were scarce, and long journeys could be perilous.

8.3.1.1 Purpose and Structure of Caravanserais

Caravanserais were strategically located at regular intervals along major trade routes and were designed to accommodate large groups of travelers, including merchants, their caravans, and animals such as camels and horses. These inns were typically fortified to provide protection from bandits and wild animals, ensuring the safety of goods and people.

The design of caravanserais was often rectangular or square, with a large central courtyard where animals could be kept, surrounded by rooms for travelers to rest. The walls were typically thick and high, serving as a defense mechanism. In addition to lodging, caravanserais often had facilities for the storage of goods, making them hubs of trade and commerce. Many caravanserais were located near water sources, with stepwells often integrated into their design to provide a reliable supply of water for both travelers and animals.

8.3.1.2 Notable Caravanserais in Rajasthan

Several caravanserais across Rajasthan have stood the test of time, offering insight into the state's historic trade networks. Among the most well-known are those found in **Bikaner**, **Jaisalmer**, and **Jodhpur**. These inns were frequented by traders moving goods such as textiles, spices, and precious metals across the desert and into larger markets in **Gujarat**, **Delhi**, and **Sindh**.

One significant example is the **Lohawat Caravanserai** near Jodhpur, an ancient site that was a key stop for traders. The inn's robust structure and large water reservoir made it an important resting point for caravans traveling to **Delhi** or **Sindh**. Similarly, **Khimsar Fort**, built in the 16th century, served not only as a fortification but also as a caravanserai, providing a safe haven for traders on the Jodhpur-Nagaur route.

8.3.2 Stepwells: Ingenious Water Management

In Rajasthan's desert climate, the availability of water is crucial for survival. The stepwells, or **baoris** (also known as **baolis**), are among the most distinctive features of Rajasthani architecture, serving as critical water storage systems. These structures are not just functional, but often architecturally impressive, reflecting the region's engineering ingenuity and cultural significance.

8.3.2.1 Structure and Purpose of Stepwells

Stepwells were designed to harvest and store water, with steps leading down to the water source. They allowed for easy access to water even as the water table fluctuated seasonally. These wells were often dug deep into the earth and lined with stone to prevent collapse. The descending steps provided an efficient way for people to retrieve water without the need for sophisticated pulleys or other mechanisms.

In addition to their practical purpose, stepwells often became social hubs for local communities. People gathered here to collect water, exchange news, and hold religious ceremonies. The architecture of many stepwells included elaborate carvings and inscriptions, highlighting their cultural importance beyond just water collection.

8.3.2.2 Iconic Stepwells in Rajasthan

Rajasthan is home to several renowned stepwells that have been the subject of archaeological and historical interest. The **Chand Baori** in **Abhaneri**, one of the deepest and largest stepwells in India, is a masterpiece of geometry and symmetry. Built during the **9th century** by King **Chanda** of the **Nikloma Dynasty**, this stepwell is known for its intricate carvings and the sheer scale of its construction. It provided water to the local population as well as to the passing caravans and travelers, reinforcing its importance in regional trade.

In **Patan**, another important stepwell, the **Raniji ki Baori**, built by **Rani Nathavati Ji** in the **17th century**, stands as an architectural marvel, adorned with sculptures and pillars. This stepwell was not only a source of water but also a place for religious and cultural gatherings. It illustrates how the need for water led to the creation of spaces that became focal points of community life.

8.3.3 Market Structures: Hubs of Trade and Commerce

Market structures in Rajasthan, particularly in its medieval desert cities, were essential for facilitating trade and commerce. These markets were often located near caravanserais, forts, and water sources, ensuring easy access for traders and local buyers. The architecture of these markets reflects their dual function as commercial and social spaces.

8.3.3.1 Market Design and Layout

The traditional **bazaar** or market in Rajasthan was usually a bustling, open-air space, often organized around a main street or central square. Stalls and shops were arranged in a grid pattern, allowing traders to display their goods, which ranged from textiles and jewelry to spices and metalware. The markets were strategically positioned near water sources or along major trade routes, ensuring a constant flow of goods and people.

In some cities, markets were also built near temples and religious centers, turning them into places not just for trade but also for cultural exchange. Religious festivals and temple ceremonies would attract large crowds, boosting trade activities.

8.3.3.2 Famous Markets in Desert Cities

The cities of Bikaner and Jodhpur were home to some of the most famous medieval markets. **Sardar Market** in

Jodhpur, located near the **Mehrangarh Fort**, is an iconic example of a historic market that still functions as a trading hub today. The market was established in the **18th century** and is known for its array of textiles, handicrafts, and spices. The **Clock Tower**, located in the center of the market, serves as a landmark that has been used by traders and locals alike to navigate the busy space.

Similarly, the **Manek Chowk** market in **Udaipur** was historically a center for the sale of agricultural goods, handicrafts, and textiles. Its location near the royal palaces and temples ensured a steady stream of customers, including nobility and commoners.

8.3.4 Socio-Economic and Cultural Role of Caravanserais, Stepwells, and Markets

These structures—caravanserais, stepwells, and market spaces—were more than just functional; they were central to the socio-economic life of medieval Rajasthan. **Caravanserais** served as hubs where traders from different parts of the world interacted, exchanged ideas, and spread culture. **Stepwells** became gathering places for communities, where social interactions and religious rituals took place. **Markets** were not only spaces for trade but also arenas for cultural exchange, where the traditions of Rajasthan met with influences from far-off lands through trade.

CHAPTER NINE

Mughal Influence in Rajasthan's Architecture

9.1 Mughal-Rajput Architectural Fusion

The **Mughal-Rajput architectural fusion** stands as one of the most significant cultural and artistic legacies in Indian history, particularly evident in the majestic forts, palaces, and public buildings across Rajasthan. The intermingling of **Mughal** and **Rajput** styles began in the 16th century and continued into the 18th century, producing a hybrid form of architecture that blended the grandiosity and opulence of Mughal design with the intricacy and elegance of Rajput structures. This fusion was not just limited to buildings but extended to art, culture, and politics, reflecting the complex relationship between the Mughal Empire and the Rajput kingdoms.

This section delves into the origins, characteristics, and key examples of the Mughal-Rajput architectural synthesis, emphasizing how this unique blend influenced Rajasthan's landscape and contributed to India's architectural heritage.

9.1.1 Historical Context: Mughal-Rajput Relations

The Mughal-Rajput architectural fusion arose from a unique socio-political environment. The Rajputs, warrior kings who ruled over the **thikanas** (feudal estates) of Rajasthan, engaged with the expanding Mughal Empire through both warfare and diplomacy. Over time, several prominent Rajput rulers, including those of **Amber (Jaipur)**, **Marwar (Jodhpur)**, and **Mewar (Udaipur)**, allied with the Mughal emperors. These alliances, often solidified through strategic marriages, created a cultural exchange between the two powers.

This relationship allowed for the blending of artistic traditions, with Rajput architects adopting Mughal features such as symmetrical layouts, grand domes, and gardens, while Mughal builders incorporated the local craftsmanship and distinct decorative elements of Rajasthan.

9.1.2 Key Characteristics of Mughal-Rajput Architecture

The architectural fusion that emerged from this relationship is marked by several defining characteristics:

9.1.2.1 Symmetry and Geometry

Mughal architecture is renowned for its emphasis on symmetry and geometric precision, a feature that became prevalent in Rajput constructions during the fusion period. Buildings were often planned around central courtyards or axes, creating harmonious and balanced layouts. Rajput forts and palaces that were traditionally more organic in structure began to adopt these symmetrical designs, resulting in a more ordered and aesthetically cohesive architectural style.

9.1.2.2 Ornate Carvings and Intricate Jali Work

One of the hallmarks of Rajput architecture is the intricate **jali** (latticework) and stone carvings that adorn windows, doors, and walls. These designs, featuring floral patterns, religious symbols, and geometric shapes, became integrated with the Mughal use of **marble inlay** and **pietra dura** (stone inlay work), creating a distinct decorative style. The fusion of Mughal motifs like **arabesques** and **calligraphy** with Rajput's local traditions resulted in highly detailed and ornate exteriors and interiors.

9.1.2.3 Use of Domes and Chhatris

The Mughal love for large, prominent **domes** found its way into Rajput architecture, but with a distinctive local twist. Instead of the large, singular domes seen in Mughal structures like the **Taj Mahal**, Rajput architects incorporated smaller domes and **chhatris** (elevated, dome-shaped pavilions) into their forts and palaces. Chhatris, traditionally a Rajput feature, became more pronounced and were often placed symmetrically on terraces, fortifications, and palace roofs, blending Mughal grandeur with Rajput aesthetics.

9.1.2.4 Mughal Gardens and Water Systems

The Mughal fascination with **Persian gardens**, featuring intricate water channels and fountains, greatly influenced Rajput palatial complexes. The **charbagh** (four-part garden) layout became a popular feature in Rajput palaces, reflecting a Mughal desire for paradise-like surroundings. In Rajasthan, where water was scarce, these gardens were ingeniously adapted to the local environment, creating lush oases within desert landscapes. The palaces often featured elaborately planned **baolis** (stepwells) and cisterns to ensure a steady water supply.

9.1.3 Prominent Examples of Mughal-Rajput Architectural Fusion

Several iconic buildings across Rajasthan exemplify the Mughal-Rajput architectural synthesis. These structures not only highlight the collaboration between the two powers but also stand as lasting testaments to the artistic achievements of the period.

9.1.3.1 Amber Fort (Jaipur)

The **Amber Fort**, located in **Jaipur**, is one of the most striking examples of Mughal-Rajput architectural fusion. Originally built by **Raja Man Singh** in the late 16th century, the fort was later expanded by his successors, incorporating both traditional Rajput elements and Mughal influences. The **Diwan-i-Aam** (Hall of Public Audience) and **Sheesh Mahal** (Mirror Palace) are perfect representations of this fusion, with intricate mirrorwork, carved marble panels, and Mughal-style arches blending with the fort's Rajput defensive architecture.

The **Ganesh Pol**, an elaborate gateway within the fort, is another example of the synthesis, showcasing a combination of Rajput frescoes with Mughal floral motifs. The symmetrical layout of the courtyards and the extensive use of **pietra dura** in the fort's decoration also bear the Mughal imprint.

9.1.3.2 City Palace (Jaipur)

The **City Palace** in **Jaipur**, constructed by **Sawai Jai Singh II** in the early 18th century, is a prime example of the Mughal-Rajput blend. The palace complex, with its multiple courtyards, gardens, and temples, showcases Mughal architectural elements such as ornate gateways, expansive courtyards, and Mughal-style **jharokhas** (overhanging enclosed balconies).

The **Mubarak Mahal** within the City Palace complex reflects this architectural fusion with its grand arches, Mughal-inspired gardens, and Rajput-style decorations. The fusion continues in the **Chandra Mahal**, where traditional Rajput decorative styles, including mirror and glasswork, coexist with Mughal-style interiors.

9.1.3.3 Mehrangarh Fort (Jodhpur)

The **Mehrangarh Fort** in **Jodhpur**, one of the largest forts in India, is another outstanding example of the architectural amalgamation. Built by **Rao Jodha** in the 15th century and expanded over several centuries, the fort features both traditional Rajput and Mughal elements. The **Phool Mahal** (Flower Hall) within the fort is adorned with Mughal-style frescoes, paintings, and gold filigree work, reflecting the artistic exchange between the two cultures.

The fort's massive gateways, defensive bastions, and expansive courtyards embody Rajput military architecture, while the delicate stone latticework, grand arches, and painted ceilings within the royal quarters show clear Mughal influence.

9.1.3.4 Fatehpur Sikri's Rajput Architecture

Interestingly, the Mughal-Rajput fusion is not confined to Rajasthan. The influence of Rajput architecture is visible in Mughal constructions outside Rajasthan, such as in

Fatehpur Sikri, the capital city built by **Emperor Akbar**. Akbar, who formed alliances with several Rajput kingdoms, incorporated Rajput architectural styles into the construction of **Jodha Bai's Palace** and the **Panch Mahal**. These buildings feature **chhatris**, jalis, and traditional Rajput ornamentation, symbolizing the cultural exchange that defined Mughal-Rajput relations.

9.1.4 Cultural and Political Significance of Architectural Fusion

The architectural fusion between the Mughals and Rajputs is not just a reflection of artistic collaboration but also symbolizes the broader cultural and political ties between the two powers. For the Mughals, incorporating Rajput elements into their architecture demonstrated their acceptance of regional diversity and helped solidify alliances with the powerful Rajput states. For the Rajputs, adopting Mughal architectural styles allowed them to maintain their identity while participating in the broader imperial culture, thereby enhancing their prestige and influence within the Mughal court.

The fusion of Mughal and Rajput styles also reflects the syncretic nature of Indian society during this period, where cultural and artistic boundaries were fluid, and new forms of expression emerged through mutual respect and exchange.

9.2 Notable Mughal-Era Structures: Amber Fort, City Palace

The **Amber Fort** and **City Palace** are two iconic architectural marvels in Rajasthan that exemplify the influence of **Mughal-era architecture** intertwined with the local **Rajput** style. Both of these structures stand as a testament to the cultural and political dynamics between the Mughal rulers and the Rajput kings, whose alliances and interactions led to a fusion of architectural styles that blended the grandeur of Mughal design with the ornate and intricate details characteristic of Rajput craftsmanship. These structures are not only important for their historical significance but also for their artistic achievements, representing a rich confluence of cultures in Rajasthan.

9.2.1 Amber Fort: A Blend of Mughal and Rajput Grandeur

Amber Fort, located in the town of **Amer**, just outside Jaipur, is one of the most celebrated examples of Mughal-Rajput architecture. Built primarily by **Raja Man Singh I** in the late 16th century and expanded by his successors, Amber Fort combines the strategic fortifications typical of Rajput defense systems with the lavish interior designs that characterize Mughal palaces.

9.2.1.1 Architectural Layout and Features

The fort is constructed with a unique blend of **red sandstone** and **white marble**, materials that symbolize both strength and elegance. The layout of the fort follows a traditional **Rajput hill fort** style, built on a high ridge overlooking the **Maota Lake**, which provided a natural defense. However, the Mughal influence is immediately evident in the symmetrical planning of the courtyards, gateways, and gardens.

One of the most famous features of the Amber Fort is the **Ganesh Pol**, a large gateway leading into the private palaces of the Rajput kings. The gateway is ornately decorated with frescoes and mosaics, blending Mughal floral motifs with Rajput religious themes. Mughal influences are also apparent in the extensive use of arches and domes, which are seamlessly integrated into the traditional Rajput architectural framework of thick walls and narrow passageways designed for defense.

9.2.1.2 Sheesh Mahal: The Mirror Palace

The **Sheesh Mahal** (Mirror Palace), located within Amber Fort, is a prime example of Mughal-inspired luxury in Rajput architecture. The palace is adorned with thousands of tiny mirrors set into the walls and ceilings, creating a dazzling effect when lit by candlelight. This type of intricate **mirrorwork** is a hallmark of Mughal decorative arts, inspired by Persian aesthetics and adapted by local artisans under the Rajput kings.

The Sheesh Mahal's opulence stands in contrast to the fort's otherwise robust exterior, reflecting the dual priorities of defense and luxury that defined Rajput royal life during the Mughal era. The **Diwan-i-Aam** (Hall of Public Audience) and **Diwan-i-Khas** (Hall of Private Audience) within the fort further illustrate this blending of functional and decorative elements, with their grand arches and pillared halls reminiscent of Mughal courtly architecture.

9.2.2 City Palace, Jaipur: A Regal Mughal-Rajput Fusion

The **City Palace** in **Jaipur** is another stunning example of Mughal-Rajput architectural fusion, embodying the elegance and splendor of both styles in one complex. Built by **Sawai Jai Singh II** in the 18th century, the City Palace served as the main residence of the Jaipur royal family and remains a symbol of their historical prominence. The palace complex is an extensive network of courtyards, gardens, and buildings, each reflecting a different aspect of Rajput and Mughal architectural influences.

9.2.2.1 Mubarak Mahal and Chandra Mahal

The **Mubarak Mahal**, built in the late 19th century, is a classic example of the fusion of **Islamic**, **Rajput**, and **European** styles that became popular during the later Mughal period. The building features intricate **jharokhas** (overhanging enclosed balconies), **jali work** (lattice screens), and Mughal-style arches, all designed to create a sense of regal grandeur. The intricate stone carving and latticework reflect Rajput craftsmanship, while the symmetry and layout of the building are distinctly Mughal.

The **Chandra Mahal**, the main palace within the City Palace complex, is another striking example of Mughal-Rajput fusion. The seven-story building combines Mughal decorative styles, such as **floral patterns** and **frescoes**, with traditional Rajput architectural features like chhatris and curved roofs. The interior of the Chandra Mahal is richly decorated with paintings, mirrors, and tiles, reminiscent of the **Shah Jahan period** of Mughal architecture.

9.2.2.2 Peacock Gate and Other Decorative Elements

The **Peacock Gate** within the City Palace is a masterpiece of design that showcases the synthesis of Mughal and Rajput decorative elements. The gate is adorned with intricate peacock motifs, a common theme in Rajput art, but the layout and use of color echo the Mughal tradition of using **nature-inspired designs** to enhance the beauty of architectural spaces. This blending of natural symbolism with geometric precision is a hallmark of Mughal-Rajput architectural fusion, creating an aesthetic that is both majestic and serene.

9.2.3 Cultural and Artistic Exchange

The construction of these iconic structures was part of a broader cultural exchange between the Mughals and Rajputs that went beyond architecture. The Mughal court's appreciation for Rajput bravery and loyalty resulted in the elevation of Rajput kings to high positions within the Mughal administration, which in turn allowed for greater artistic collaboration. Rajput painters, for instance, were heavily influenced by the **Mughal miniature painting** style, incorporating its realistic portraits and attention to detail into their own works.

Similarly, Mughal architects adopted several aspects of Rajput design, particularly in their approach to fortifications and defensive structures. The **Zanana Mahal** (women's quarters) and harem architecture in both Amber Fort and City Palace reflect this blend, with private spaces designed for the comfort of royal women that also embody the grandiose aesthetics of Mughal palaces.

9.2.4 The Significance of Amber Fort and City Palace in Modern Rajasthan

Today, both **Amber Fort** and **City Palace** are among the most popular tourist destinations in Rajasthan, attracting visitors from around the world. Their architectural beauty, combined with their historical significance as symbols of Mughal-Rajput cooperation, makes them essential landmarks in the understanding of India's rich cultural heritage.

These structures are not only architectural achievements but also represent a time of political alliances and cultural synthesis. They stand as reminders of how two distinct traditions—the martial, independent Rajput culture and the expansive, cosmopolitan Mughal Empire—came together to produce a style that remains unparalleled in its beauty and sophistication.

Amber Fort and City Palace remain symbols of Rajasthan's royal past and the lasting legacy of Mughal-Rajput relations. Through their preservation, these monuments continue to inspire admiration for the artistic and cultural achievements of a bygone era, providing invaluable insights into the history and architecture of medieval India.

9.3 Influence of Mughal Art and Architecture on Local Artisans

The **Mughal Empire's** arrival in Rajasthan during the 16th century brought about significant cultural and artistic exchanges that left a lasting imprint on the region's craftsmanship. The **Mughal style** of art and architecture, known for its opulence, precision, and aesthetic appeal, deeply influenced local artisans in Rajasthan, leading to the creation of a unique hybrid style that combined the finesse of Mughal craftsmanship with the distinctive traditions of Rajput artistry. This fusion not only transformed the architectural landscape but also had a profound impact on various forms of **decorative arts**, including painting, metalwork, textiles, and jewelry making.

The influence of Mughal art and architecture on local artisans extended far beyond physical structures. It played a crucial role in shaping the identity of Rajasthani art, giving rise to new techniques, motifs, and methods of artistic expression. This section explores how Mughal artistry permeated local craftsmanship and redefined the artistic traditions of Rajasthan.

9.3.1 Introduction of New Techniques and Materials

One of the most significant ways in which Mughal art influenced local artisans was through the introduction of new techniques and materials. Mughal builders and craftsmen brought with them advanced methods of stone carving, metal inlay, and decorative painting, which had been perfected in their capital cities, such as **Agra** and **Delhi**. Local artisans, skilled in their own right, quickly adopted these methods, leading to the emergence of a new form of craftsmanship that combined Mughal elegance with traditional Rajasthani boldness.

9.3.1.1 Pietra Dura and Marble Inlay

The Mughal technique of **pietra dura** (stone inlay) became particularly influential in Rajasthan. Mughal artisans used this technique extensively in the decoration of **Taj Mahal** and other imperial buildings, where semi-precious stones were inlaid into white marble to create intricate floral and geometric patterns. This technique was soon adopted by local artisans, who began to use it in temples, palaces, and cenotaphs across Rajasthan. The delicate **floral motifs**, often derived from Persian designs, were a hallmark of Mughal artistry, and local artisans adapted them to suit their own preferences and religious iconography.

The city of **Udaipur**, in particular, became known for its marble inlay work, as seen in structures such as the **City Palace** and **Jagdish Temple**. Artisans from Udaipur incorporated pietra dura into the walls and floors of these buildings, combining Mughal-inspired motifs with traditional Hindu symbols like the **lotus flower** and **elephant**.

9.3.1.2 Jali (Latticework)

The Mughal art of **jali work** (latticework) also had a profound influence on local craftsmanship in Rajasthan. Mughal buildings were often adorned with intricately carved stone lattices, which allowed for ventilation while also providing privacy. Local Rajput artisans, particularly those in **Jaisalmer** and **Jodhpur**, took this technique and adapted it to their own aesthetic, creating some of the most intricate and elaborate **jali designs** seen anywhere in India.

These lattice screens were used extensively in the palaces and havelis of Rajasthan, especially in the women's quarters, known as the **zenana**, where they allowed the royal women to observe events outside without being seen. Rajput artisans also incorporated local motifs, such as **peacocks**, **horses**, and **religious symbols**, into the jali patterns, giving the screens a distinctly Rajasthani flavor while maintaining the delicate craftsmanship associated with Mughal design.

9.3.2 Influence on Local Painting Styles

Mughal influence on Rajasthani painting was equally profound, particularly in the development of the region's famed **miniature painting** traditions. The Mughal school of painting, known for its attention to detail, use of vibrant colors, and realistic depiction of human figures, greatly influenced the **Rajput courts**, where painting was already an important art form.

9.3.2.1 Rajput Miniature Paintings

The Mughal style introduced new techniques, such as the use of **perspective** and **shading**, which were previously absent in Rajput paintings. Mughal painters, who often depicted court scenes, battles, and royal hunts, inspired local artists to refine their own techniques and adopt similar subjects. Rajput paintings, which had traditionally focused on religious and mythological themes, began to incorporate more **secular subjects**, including portraits of kings, queens, and courtiers, as well as depictions of nature and animals.

The schools of **Kishangarh**, **Bundi**, and **Udaipur** became particularly well-known for their miniature paintings, which blended Mughal realism with the **vibrant colors** and **ornamental details** characteristic of Rajput art. For example, the **Kishangarh school** is renowned for its portraits of **Radha and Krishna**, which exhibit a delicate Mughal-style attention to facial features and expressions, while maintaining the mystical and romantic spirit of Rajput painting.

9.3.2.2 Mughal Influence on Wall Paintings

Mughal influence also extended to large-scale wall paintings, especially in the palaces and havelis of Rajasthan. Mughal painters had perfected the art of mural painting, using rich pigments and intricate details to decorate the interiors of palaces and public buildings. Local artisans in Rajasthan adopted this technique and adapted it to their own narrative styles, often depicting scenes from the **Mahabharata**, **Ramayana**, or the lives of local heroes and deities.

These wall paintings, found in places like the **City Palace of Jaipur** and the **Bundi Palace**, showcase the Mughal mastery of **composition and realism** combined with the bright colors and bold compositions of Rajput art. The resulting murals are a visual feast, blending the **grandeur of Mughal imperialism** with the **spiritual and heroic themes** dear to the Rajputs.

9.3.3 Impact on Textiles, Metalwork, and Jewelry

Beyond architecture and painting, Mughal influence also transformed the local industries of **textiles**, **metalwork**, and **jewelry making** in Rajasthan. The Mughals, known for their love of luxury, brought new techniques and styles to the region, which were eagerly adopted by local artisans.

9.3.3.1 Textiles and Embroidery

The Mughal court's preference for luxurious textiles, including **silk**, **brocade**, and **velvet**, had a significant impact on the textile industry of Rajasthan. Mughal designs, featuring **floral patterns**, **paisleys**, and **intricate embroidery**, were soon replicated by Rajasthani weavers and embroiderers. Cities like **Jaipur** and **Jodhpur** became renowned for their **zari** (gold and silver thread) work, which adorned royal garments, tapestries, and accessories.

Local artisans incorporated Mughal motifs into traditional Rajasthani textiles, creating a blend of styles that reflected both imperial grandeur and local craftsmanship. The introduction of new dyeing techniques, such as **ikat** and **bandhani** (tie-dye), further enriched the textile traditions of the region, resulting in fabrics that were both visually stunning and highly prized by the royal courts.

9.3.3.2 Metalwork and Jewelry

Mughal artisans were also masters of **metalwork**, and their influence extended to the creation of **jewelry** and **decorative objects** in Rajasthan. Mughal jewelry, known for its use of **precious gemstones**, intricate settings, and **enamel work**, became highly sought after by the Rajput elite. Local jewelers adopted these techniques, producing ornate pieces that combined Mughal design elements, such as **floral motifs** and **Arabic calligraphy**, with traditional Rajasthani symbols of power and fertility, such as the **sun** and **elephant**.

Cities like **Jaipur** and **Udaipur** became centers of jewelry making, where local craftsmen used **kundan** (gold foil setting) and **meenakari** (enamel work) to create stunning necklaces, earrings, and crowns for the royal family. The fusion of Mughal and Rajput styles in jewelry resulted in some of the most exquisite pieces of adornment seen in Indian history.

9.3.4 Lasting Legacy of Mughal Influence on Rajasthan's Artisans

The legacy of Mughal influence on local artisans in Rajasthan is evident in the region's continued reputation for excellence in craftsmanship. Whether in the majestic **palaces** and **forts**, the detailed **miniature paintings**, or the finely crafted **jewelry** and **textiles**, the artistic fusion that began during the Mughal era has left an indelible mark on Rajasthani art.

The synthesis of Mughal and Rajput styles has produced a distinct artistic identity for Rajasthan, one that is both a reflection of its royal past and a testament to the rich cultural exchanges that defined medieval India. Local artisans, through their adaptability and creativity, were able to take the finest elements of Mughal artistry and make them their own, resulting in a hybrid tradition that continues to captivate the world today.

CHAPTER TEN

Royal Palaces and Mansions: Architectural Brilliance

10.1 Palaces of Jaipur, Udaipur, and Jodhpur

Rajasthan, known for its regal past and the legacy of powerful Rajput kingdoms, is home to some of the most magnificent palaces in India. The cities of **Jaipur**, **Udaipur**, and **Jodhpur** are particularly famous for their opulent palaces, which showcase the grandeur, architectural brilliance, and cultural richness of the Rajput rulers. These palaces, often serving as royal residences and administrative centers, are not only architectural marvels but also symbols of the kingdoms' political and cultural significance. Each palace reflects a unique blend of **Rajput, Mughal, and sometimes European architectural styles**, narrating the history of Rajasthan's royal past.

10.1.1 Palaces of Jaipur

The **City of Jaipur**, the capital of Rajasthan, is dotted with royal palaces that serve as testimony to its rich cultural heritage and architectural sophistication. Founded in 1727 by **Sawai Jai Singh II**, Jaipur's architecture combines Rajput traditions with the influence of Mughal and European elements, giving it a distinct character.

10.1.1.1 City Palace

The **City Palace** is one of the most iconic palaces in Jaipur, situated at the heart of the city. Built by Sawai Jai Singh II, the palace complex consists of courtyards, gardens, and buildings, combining the Rajput architectural style with Mughal influences. The **Chandra Mahal**, the residence of the royal family, is the most prominent building within the City Palace complex. Its architecture is a blend of Mughal-style floral decorations, latticework, and Rajput-style balconies and towers. Each floor of the seven-storied Chandra Mahal is uniquely designed, with the **Sukh Niwas** featuring blue decorations and the **Shobha Niwas** displaying intricate mirror work.

Other notable parts of the City Palace include the **Diwan-i-Aam** (Hall of Public Audience) and **Diwan-i-Khas** (Hall of Private Audience), both showcasing exquisite Rajput and Mughal elements. The **Mubarak Mahal**, built in the late 19th century, is another architectural gem within the complex, combining Mughal, Rajput, and European styles. Today, the palace serves as a museum, displaying the royal family's collection of textiles, costumes, and weapons.

10.1.1.2 Hawa Mahal

The **Hawa Mahal** (Palace of Winds) is another famous palace in Jaipur, known for its distinctive **honeycomb façade** with 953 small windows (jharokhas). Built in 1799 by **Maharaja Sawai Pratap Singh**, the Hawa Mahal was designed as an extension of the City Palace to allow royal women to observe street festivities without being seen. The intricate jharokhas, decorated with latticework, are an excellent example of the Rajput style's fusion with Mughal aesthetics. Despite its towering appearance, the palace is only five stories high and remarkably thin, reflecting the traditional **zenana** (women's quarters) architectural style.

10.1.2 Palaces of Udaipur

Udaipur, often called the **City of Lakes**, is known for its romantic palaces that seem to float on water or blend into the surrounding Aravalli hills. Founded in 1559 by **Maharana Udai Singh II**, Udaipur became the capital of the **Mewar Kingdom**, and its palaces reflect the grandeur and legacy of the Sisodia Rajput dynasty.

10.1.2.1 City Palace, Udaipur

The **City Palace of Udaipur** is the largest palace complex in Rajasthan, overlooking the **Lake Pichola**. Built over several centuries by successive rulers, the City Palace showcases a blend of **Rajput**, **Mughal**, and **European architecture**. The palace complex consists of several interconnected palaces, courtyards, terraces, and corridors, all of which offer stunning views of the lake and the surrounding landscape.

The palace is adorned with delicate **glasswork**, **inlaid tile work**, **mirror work**, and **paintings**, reflecting the luxurious lifestyle of the Mewar rulers. Notable parts of the complex include the **Badi Mahal** (Garden Palace), a garden located on a 27-meter-high natural rock formation, and the **Mor Chowk** (Peacock Courtyard), famous for its mosaics of peacocks created with glass and tiles. The palace also houses several museums displaying royal artifacts, weapons, and costumes.

10.1.2.2 Lake Palace

Perhaps the most iconic of Udaipur's palaces is the **Lake Palace**, located on **Jag Niwas Island** in the middle of Lake Pichola. Built in 1746 by **Maharana Jagat Singh II**, the palace was originally intended as a summer retreat for the royal family. Constructed entirely out of **white marble**, the palace appears to float on the lake's surface, creating an ethereal sight. The Lake Palace is an exquisite example of **Mughal-Rajput architecture**, featuring intricately carved columns, domes, and arches. Today, the palace has been converted into a luxury hotel, but its regal charm remains, attracting visitors from around the world.

10.1.3 Palaces of Jodhpur

Jodhpur, known as the **Blue City** due to its blue-painted houses, is home to some of the most awe-inspiring palaces in Rajasthan. Founded in 1459 by **Rao Jodha**, the city is dominated by the towering **Mehrangarh Fort**, which houses a palace within its walls. Jodhpur's palaces reflect the strength and wealth of the **Marwar Kingdom**.

10.1.3.1 Mehrangarh Fort and Palaces

The **Mehrangarh Fort**, perched on a high rocky hill, is one of the largest forts in India and contains within it several palaces that showcase the splendor of the Marwar rulers. The fort was originally built by Rao Jodha and later expanded by his successors. The palaces within the fort are adorned with intricate stone carvings, latticed windows, and spacious courtyards, blending Rajput and Mughal architectural elements.

The **Moti Mahal** (Pearl Palace) is one of the most famous palaces within Mehrangarh Fort. It features beautiful **polished lime plasterwork** that gives the walls a pearl-like sheen. The **Phool Mahal** (Palace of Flowers) is another exquisite palace, known for its **gold-plated ceiling** and **elaborate paintings**. The **Sheesh Mahal** (Mirror Palace) is adorned with intricate mirror work, reflecting the Mughal influence on Jodhpur's architecture. Each of these palaces represents the **opulence** and **grandeur** of Jodhpur's rulers.

10.1.3.2 Umaid Bhawan Palace

The **Umaid Bhawan Palace** is one of the most recent palaces built in India, commissioned by **Maharaja Umaid Singh** in 1929. Designed by British architect **Henry Lanchester**, the palace combines **Indo-Saracenic** and **Art Deco** styles, making it unique among Rajasthan's palaces. Constructed with **yellow sandstone**, the palace features **massive domes, pillars**, and **colonnades** that give it a grand and modern appearance while still retaining traditional Rajasthani elements. Today, a part of the palace is a **luxury hotel**, while another part is a museum showcasing the royal family's history and heritage.

10.1.4 Legacy of Rajasthan's Palaces

The palaces of **Jaipur**, **Udaipur**, and **Jodhpur** are not only architectural masterpieces but also cultural symbols that reflect Rajasthan's **rich history**, **artistic achievements**, and **political significance**. Each palace has its own unique story, yet all share a common thread of grandeur, blending influences from **Rajput**, **Mughal**, and sometimes **European architecture**. These palaces, with their intricate carvings, lavish decorations, and stunning landscapes, continue to captivate visitors and stand as testaments to the artistic and architectural prowess of Rajasthan's royal heritage.

10.2 Archaeological Studies of Royal Lifestyles

Rajasthan, renowned for its majestic forts and palaces, has a rich royal history that extends beyond its architecture. Archaeological studies focusing on **royal lifestyles** provide invaluable insights into the daily lives, customs, and societal structures of the Rajput rulers and their courts. These studies not only emphasize the grandeur and opulence associated with royal life but also shed light on aspects such as **food culture**, **clothing**, **artistic preferences**, and **administrative systems**. Archaeological excavations and historical records, including artifacts, paintings, inscriptions, and structures, have allowed researchers to reconstruct how the rulers of Rajasthan lived, governed, and interacted with their environment and people.

10.2.1 Courtly Life and Administrative Structures

One of the central aspects of royal lifestyles in Rajasthan was the functioning of the **court**, where rulers made decisions, interacted with nobles, and presided over important events. Archaeological findings, such as inscriptions and manuscripts, have provided details about the **hierarchical structure** of the royal courts. The **Diwan-i-Aam** (Hall of Public Audience) and **Diwan-i-Khas** (Hall of Private Audience), found in palaces such as **Jaipur's City**

Palace and **Udaipur's City Palace**, reflect the **administrative and diplomatic roles** of the Rajput rulers. These halls served as spaces where the ruler would engage in matters of governance, address issues of justice, and meet foreign dignitaries, as indicated by the inscriptions and royal decrees discovered at these sites.

Additionally, **archaeological excavations** in and around palace complexes have revealed artifacts such as **official seals**, **coins**, and **inscribed tablets**, offering clues about the bureaucratic systems that supported royal governance. These studies have helped to illustrate how the administration functioned, with **nobles** and **ministers** assisting in various domains like revenue collection, military affairs, and law enforcement.

10.2.2 Royal Residences and Luxury

The palaces of Rajasthan were not only symbols of power but also spaces designed for comfort and luxury, befitting the stature of the ruling class. Archaeological studies have unearthed remnants of **ornate living quarters**, including intricately designed **furniture**, **fabrics**, and **decorative items**. The opulence of **royal bedrooms**, **private chambers**, and **lavish gardens** has been revealed through artifacts such as **finely carved stone ornaments**, **marble inlays**, and **mirror work**, like that found in the **Sheesh Mahal** (Mirror Palace) in Jaipur and Jodhpur.

Studies of **water management systems** within palace complexes, particularly **stepwells** and **fountains**, show how luxury extended to environmental control. The palaces had sophisticated **cooling systems**, and archaeologists have uncovered evidence of complex **water channels** and **storage systems**, demonstrating the rulers' ability to manipulate their surroundings for comfort even in the arid climate of Rajasthan.

10.2.3 Royal Cuisine and Dining Rituals

One of the most fascinating aspects of royal life in Rajasthan is the **cuisine** and dining culture. The **royal kitchens**, or **rasoighars**, were known for their extravagant feasts, and archaeological findings provide insights into the food culture of the Rajput courts. **Excavations of kitchens** in palaces like **Amber Fort** and **Jaisalmer Fort** have revealed artifacts such as **cooking utensils**, **grinding stones**, and **storage vessels**, some of which were used to prepare elaborate meals for royal banquets.

Manuscripts and paintings from the era, found in royal archives, depict scenes of **lavish dining halls** where kings and nobles enjoyed feasts of **meats**, **spices**, and **local produce**. These studies also highlight the **symbolic importance of food** in reinforcing status, as the finest ingredients, including exotic imports, were reserved for the royal family and their esteemed guests. **Herbs and spices** commonly used in Rajasthani cuisine, such as saffron and cardamom, have been identified through **botanical studies** conducted on archaeological remains of food storage facilities.

10.2.4 Clothing and Jewelry

Clothing and jewelry played a critical role in defining royal status and power in Rajasthan. **Textile fragments** and **clothing artifacts** found during archaeological digs provide evidence of the **fabrics**, **designs**, and **embroidery techniques** favored by the royal families. Rajput kings and queens were known for their rich attire, which included **silks**, **brocades**, and **cotton fabrics** dyed in vibrant colors. Studies of **royal garments** preserved in palace museums, along with archaeological findings of **dying vats** and **weaving tools**, suggest that royal wardrobes were not just symbols of wealth but also a reflection of artistic expression and cultural identity.

Additionally, **jewelry** was an integral part of royal life, with **gold**, **silver**, and **precious stones** being used to create intricate designs that reflected the craftsmanship of the period. Excavations have revealed **jewelry-making workshops** and **smithy tools**, indicating the importance of adornments in the court. **Portraits and miniatures** of the period, preserved in palace archives, also provide a visual record of the types of **crowns**, **necklaces**, **armbands**, and **earrings** worn by the Rajput nobility.

10.2.5 Entertainment and Artistic Patronage

The royal families of Rajasthan were great patrons of the **arts**, and this is evident in the extensive archaeological evidence of **paintings**, **sculptures**, and **music**. **Court paintings**, depicting scenes of hunting, religious ceremonies, and royal life, were a significant aspect of courtly culture. **Archaeological studies** have uncovered fragments of these paintings in palaces like **Udaipur's City Palace** and **Bundi Palace**. These **miniature paintings** provide a glimpse into the entertainment and leisure activities of the royal courts, which included **theatrical performances**, **musical recitals**, and **dance dramas**.

Moreover, the discovery of **musical instruments** during excavations, including **stringed instruments**, **drums**, and **flutes**, reveals the importance of music in royal entertainment. Royal patronage extended to musicians, poets, and dancers, who performed during festivals and ceremonies. **Artistic patronage** was also extended to the **sculptors** and **architects** who adorned palaces with carvings and intricate designs.

10.2.6 Religious and Ceremonial Life

Religious life played a central role in the court, with rituals and ceremonies being conducted to honor deities and celebrate royal victories. Archaeological studies of **temples** and **shrines** within palace complexes have provided insights into the spiritual life of the royal family. Artifacts such as **ritual objects**, **sacred manuscripts**, and **iconography** of deities have been found, highlighting the religious devotion of the Rajput rulers. Palaces often included **private chapels** or **temples**, where daily rituals were conducted by court priests.

10.3 Art and Culture Depicted in Murals and Frescoes

The palaces, forts, and havelis of Rajasthan are adorned with some of the most exquisite **murals** and **frescoes** in India. These vibrant works of art, dating back several centuries, provide a fascinating glimpse into the art, culture, and societal norms of the region's royal past. The murals and frescoes, which often cover entire walls or ceilings, are a visual storytelling medium that immortalizes not only the aesthetics of the time but also the deep cultural and religious values held by the Rajput rulers and their subjects. These artworks are a testament to Rajasthan's enduring legacy of **artistic excellence** and **cultural richness**.

10.3.1 Techniques and Styles of Murals and Frescoes

Murals and frescoes in Rajasthan are primarily created using two methods: **dry fresco** (also known as *fresco-secco*) and **wet fresco** (or *buon fresco*). The *buon fresco* technique involves painting on freshly applied wet lime plaster, where pigments are absorbed by the plaster as it dries, making the artwork highly durable. The *fresco-secco* method, on the other hand, involves painting on a dry surface using pigments mixed with a binding medium, which allows for greater detailing but is less durable over time. Both techniques are seen across various palaces, forts, and temples, each reflecting the **regional variation** and **artistic preferences** of the era.

Rajasthani murals are known for their **vivid colors**, made from **natural pigments** such as crushed minerals, stones, plant dyes, and even gold and silver dust. The themes range from **courtly scenes** and **battle depictions** to **mythological stories** and **religious motifs**. The style of painting is deeply rooted in the **Rajput tradition**, but over time, influences from **Mughal**, **Persian**, and even **European art** began to blend into these works, creating a unique fusion.

10.3.2 Royal Court Life and Historical Events

One of the central themes of murals and frescoes in Rajasthan is the **depiction of royal life**. Palaces like **Udaipur's City Palace**, **Bundi Palace**, and **Amer Fort** house murals that vividly capture the **lavish lifestyles** of the Rajput kings and their courts. These paintings depict scenes of **royal processions**, **hunting expeditions**, **court ceremonies**, and **military exploits**. For example, the frescoes in the **Zenana Mahal** (Women's Palace) at Udaipur's City Palace depict detailed scenes of royal women engaged in daily activities, such as weaving, playing music, or enjoying leisure time in gardens.

The murals also document significant **historical events**, such as battles and alliances. The **battle scenes** often emphasize the valor and bravery of Rajput warriors, who are depicted riding horses or elephants into combat, their swords raised in victory. The **Amer Fort** is particularly known for its murals of **Rajput-Mughal interactions**, which highlight the alliances and conflicts between these two powerful groups. These paintings not only serve as historical records but also reflect the **Rajput ideals of honor, bravery, and loyalty**.

10.3.3 Religious and Mythological Themes

A large portion of the murals and frescoes in Rajasthan depict **religious and mythological themes**, which were central to the cultural life of the Rajput rulers. The walls of temples, as well as palace interiors, are covered with images of **Hindu deities**, including **Krishna**, **Rama**, **Shiva**, and **Durga**. The **Nathdwara Temple** near Udaipur, a major center of Krishna worship, is famous for its murals that depict episodes from the life of **Lord Krishna**, particularly the **Ras Leela**, where Krishna dances with the gopis. These frescoes, painted in vibrant colors, show the playful and divine aspects of Krishna's character.

Similarly, **Bundi Palace** is renowned for its murals depicting scenes from the **Ramayana** and **Mahabharata**, the two great epics of Indian mythology. These scenes are filled with expressive figures, rich detailing, and symbolic elements that bring the stories to life. The **religious devotion** of the Rajput rulers is clearly reflected in these works, as temples were often commissioned alongside royal palaces, with the murals serving as both decoration and spiritual expression.

10.3.4 Folk Traditions and Daily Life

Beyond the grandeur of royal and religious themes, the murals and frescoes of Rajasthan also depict **folk traditions** and aspects of **everyday life**. These artworks often portray **festivals**, **farming practices**, and **local customs** that were part of the cultural fabric of Rajasthan. The paintings frequently showcase scenes from local festivals like **Holi**, **Diwali**, and **Teej**, where the vibrant colors of the murals mirror the celebratory atmosphere of these occasions.

At **Shekhawati**, a region often referred to as the **open-air art gallery of Rajasthan**, the **havelis** (mansions) are adorned with murals that depict **local culture**, **marriages**, **trading activities**, and **festive celebrations**. These frescoes also highlight the **interactions between common people** and the elite, portraying **traders**, **farmers**, and **artisans** alongside nobles and royalty, thereby creating a comprehensive picture of Rajasthani society.

10.3.5 Mughal and Persian Influence on Rajput Murals

During the **Mughal era**, the cultural exchange between the Mughals and Rajputs had a profound impact on the art of Rajasthan. **Mughal influence** is particularly visible in the **floral patterns**, **geometric designs**, and **miniature painting style** that were incorporated into the murals. The use of **subtle shading**, **naturalism**, and **perspective**, techniques that were hallmarks of Mughal art, can be seen in many Rajput palaces, especially those with direct Mughal interactions, like **Amber Fort** and **Jaipur's City Palace**.

For instance, the frescoes in **Amber Fort's Sheesh Mahal** (Mirror Palace) show the fine blending of **Persian floral motifs** with the traditional **Rajput court scenes**. These works reflect the mutual admiration and exchange of artistic techniques between the two cultures, leading to a rich fusion of styles that enhanced the visual appeal of Rajput murals. The **perspective of nature** in these murals is also a notable Mughal influence, where **trees**, **birds**, and

gardens are painted with greater realism than the traditional stylized depictions of the past.

10.3.6 Decorative Art and Symbolism

The murals and frescoes of Rajasthan are also laden with **symbolic meanings** and decorative elements that go beyond their aesthetic appeal. The use of **lotuses**, **peacocks**, **elephants**, and **horses** in the murals often has symbolic significance, representing purity, grace, strength, and royalty, respectively. These symbols were frequently used to reinforce the power and divine right of the Rajput rulers.

The **intricate geometric patterns** and **floral designs** found in the frescoes also serve a decorative function, while simultaneously symbolizing **order**, **beauty**, and the **cosmic connection** between humans and the divine. The use of **gold leaf** in many of the frescoes adds a sense of grandeur and divine light, often used in religious depictions to highlight the sacred nature of the scene.

10.3.7 Preservation and Restoration Efforts

Over time, many of these murals and frescoes have suffered from **environmental damage**, **neglect**, and **human intervention**. However, there have been increasing efforts to **preserve** and **restore** these artworks. Institutions like the **Archaeological Survey of India (ASI)**, in collaboration with private heritage conservation groups, have initiated projects to restore the faded colors and damaged sections of the frescoes, ensuring that they remain intact for future generations to appreciate.

For example, **Shekhawati's havelis**, which had fallen into disrepair, are now being restored with careful attention to maintaining the original techniques and styles. Similarly, **Amer Fort's murals** have undergone restoration, particularly the **Sheesh Mahal**, where the intricate mirror work and frescoes are being meticulously repaired.

CHAPTER ELEVEN

Water Management Systems: Stepwells and Reservoirs

11.1 Role of Water Management in Rajasthan's Arid Climate

Rajasthan, the largest state in India, is predominantly characterized by its **arid and semi-arid climate**, especially in the **Thar Desert** region. With sparse rainfall and extreme temperatures, water has always been a precious resource in this state. Despite these harsh conditions, Rajasthan has a rich tradition of innovative **water management practices** developed over centuries. The people of Rajasthan adapted to their environment through ingenious engineering and conservation methods, which allowed them to sustain agriculture, settlements, and daily life in the face of persistent water scarcity. This chapter explores the historical and cultural significance of water management in Rajasthan and how these systems have evolved to meet the needs of a growing population while protecting natural resources.

11.1.1 Traditional Water Harvesting Systems

Rajasthan has a long history of traditional **water harvesting systems**, many of which were developed and perfected by local communities. These systems were built in response to the erratic rainfall and dry conditions, ensuring that every drop of water was stored and used efficiently. Among the most important traditional water management systems are **baoris**, **kunds**, **johads**, and **talabs**.

- **Baoris** (or **stepwells)** are deep wells that were dug into the earth and surrounded by stepped structures to access the water. These stepwells not only served as vital water storage systems but also as cool resting places during the hot summer months. Examples of famous baoris include the **Chand Baori** in **Abhaneri** and **Rani-ki-Vav** in **Patan**.

- **Kunds** are underground tanks constructed to capture rainwater, especially in the desert areas. These structures have dome-shaped roofs to prevent evaporation and are often built near temples, serving as community water storage systems for both drinking and ritual purposes.

- **Johads** are small earthen check dams or embankments that capture and store rainwater. These structures slow down water runoff and allow for groundwater recharge, benefiting agriculture and livestock. Johads were especially common in the **Aravalli Hills**, where rainfall is slightly more abundant than in the desert.

- **Talabs** (lakes) and **bandhis** (reservoirs) were also built in Rajasthan to store large amounts of water. **Man-made lakes** like the **Jaisamand Lake** and **Fateh Sagar Lake** in **Udaipur** are examples of such structures, which were often constructed by kings to support agriculture and the population.

11.1.2 Role of Stepwells in Water Conservation

Stepwells, also known as **baolis** or **vavs**, are a unique architectural form found in Rajasthan that played a vital role in water conservation. These structures are not only engineering marvels but also symbols of the community-driven approach to managing water resources. Built as deep underground wells with tiered steps, stepwells allowed people to access water even during the driest months of the year. The deeper the well, the more water it could store, making these structures indispensable for Rajasthan's survival.

The construction of stepwells began around the **6th century** and reached its peak during the **medieval period** under the patronage of Rajput kings. Stepwells such as the **Panna Meena ka Kund** in **Jaipur** and **Toorji ka Jhalra** in

Jodhpur not only provided water but also became social hubs for the community, where people gathered for various activities. Women, in particular, played a central role in maintaining and using these wells, as they were responsible for fetching water for their families.

11.1.3 Agricultural Practices and Irrigation Techniques

Agriculture in Rajasthan has always been a challenge due to the state's extreme climate, but traditional irrigation techniques have enabled the people to cultivate crops even in the harshest conditions. **Canal systems** and **kundis** (small earthen dams) were used to divert and channel water into fields, where crops such as **millets**, **pulses**, and **oilseeds** were grown. In regions near rivers, such as the **Chambal** and **Mahi**, **lift irrigation** systems were implemented to draw water into agricultural fields. The use of **ghul** (small irrigation channels) helped ensure that water was distributed evenly across the fields, maximizing its utility.

Another innovative technique is the **khadin system**, which involves building a long embankment at the lower end of a sloping farmland to collect rainwater runoff. This collected water saturates the soil, allowing crops to be grown on the moisture-retentive soil for several months after the rains have ceased. The **khadin system** is especially popular in the **Jaisalmer** region and is considered one of the oldest methods of **rainwater harvesting** and water conservation.

11.1.4 Sacredness of Water in Rajasthani Culture

Water in Rajasthan is not just a physical necessity but holds deep **religious** and **cultural significance**. Due to its scarcity, water is considered sacred, and its sources are often treated with reverence. Many of the traditional water harvesting systems, such as **stepwells** and **lakes**, were built near temples or within palace grounds, reflecting the spiritual importance of water. Rituals and festivals are often centered around water bodies, and offering water to travelers or animals is considered a form of **punya** (religious merit).

The practice of **jhalra**, or dedicating water structures to deities, was common in Rajasthan. These structures were built with the belief that they would not only serve the people but also please the gods, ensuring continued rainfall and prosperity for the region. In **Pushkar**, the famous **Pushkar Lake** is believed to have been created by the tears of Lord Brahma, making it one of the holiest pilgrimage sites in India. Pilgrims bathe in the lake as part of purification rituals, and the water is considered to have healing properties.

11.1.5 Modern Water Management Efforts

With the growing pressures of population, urbanization, and climate change, Rajasthan faces significant challenges in sustaining its traditional water management practices. However, efforts are being made to integrate these age-old methods with modern technology. Government initiatives such as the **Rajasthan Water Sector Restructuring Project (RWSRP)** and the **Integrated Watershed Management Programme (IWMP)** aim to rehabilitate traditional water structures while promoting **sustainable water use**.

Additionally, **rainwater harvesting** has become a critical aspect of modern water management strategies. Many **urban households** in cities like Jaipur and Jodhpur are incorporating **rainwater collection systems** into their homes to supplement their water supply. Programs to **recharge groundwater** and promote **drip irrigation** are also being implemented to make agriculture more water-efficient.

Non-governmental organizations (NGOs) and **local communities** continue to play an essential role in reviving ancient water harvesting systems and educating people about water conservation. For example, the work of the **Tarun Bharat Sangh** in reviving **johads** and **kunds** in the **Alwar district** has garnered national and international recognition, showcasing the importance of community involvement in sustainable water management.

11.2 Architectural Significance of Stepwells: Chand Baori, Toorji Ka Jhalra

Rajasthan's stepwells, known locally as **baoris** or **vavs**, represent a unique aspect of India's **water management architecture** and cultural heritage. These structures, built to provide water in the arid regions of Rajasthan, are a testament to the **architectural ingenuity** and **artistic creativity** of the past. Among the numerous stepwells in Rajasthan, **Chand Baori** and **Toorji Ka Jhalra** stand out as monumental examples of this unique form of architecture, both reflecting the region's historical relationship with water conservation, as well as its rich **aesthetic traditions**.

11.2.1 Chand Baori: A Marvel of Geometric Precision

Located in the village of **Abhaneri**, near Jaipur, **Chand Baori** is one of the deepest and largest stepwells in India. Constructed around the **9th century** during the reign of **King Chanda of the Nikumbha Dynasty**, this architectural wonder is over **13 stories deep**, with **3,500 narrow steps** that descend in perfect symmetry to a depth of about **100 feet**.

The **geometric design** of Chand Baori is nothing short of extraordinary. The meticulously aligned steps form a visual masterpiece, creating a pattern of light and shadow that shifts with the movement of the sun. This design is not merely decorative but also functional. The steps were designed to allow access to the well even when water levels dropped significantly during the hot and dry months. The steep descent into the earth helped keep the water cool, making the stepwell a natural air-conditioning system for the villagers who used it.

Architecturally, Chand Baori is an excellent example of **early medieval Hindu craftsmanship**, combining utility with aesthetics. The lower levels of the stepwell are adorned with **intricate carvings** and sculptures, including images of **Hindu deities** such as **Durga** and **Ganesha**, along with decorative panels depicting **mythological scenes**. The integration of **religious motifs** within a functional structure highlights the spiritual significance of water in Indian culture.

11.2.2 Toorji Ka Jhalra: A Regal Water Reservoir

Toorji Ka Jhalra, located in the heart of **Jodhpur**, is another stunning example of stepwell architecture. Built in the **18th century** by a queen consort, it served as a water reservoir for the local population, particularly during times of drought. While smaller in scale compared to Chand Baori, Toorji Ka Jhalra stands out for its **refined design** and **aesthetic beauty**.

Constructed from **red sandstone**, the stepwell features **ornate carvings** and sculptures typical of **Rajput architecture**. The steps are arranged in a zigzag pattern that leads to the water, creating a **visual harmony** with the surrounding landscape. Unlike Chand Baori, which primarily served a utilitarian purpose, Toorji Ka Jhalra was designed to be a **social hub**, where people gathered not only to draw water but also to interact and participate in religious rituals.

The **restoration** of Toorji Ka Jhalra in recent years has brought attention to the stepwell's architectural and cultural significance. During the restoration process, **centuries-old carvings** were uncovered, depicting **celestial nymphs**, **dancing figures**, and **mythological creatures**. These carvings reflect the artistic skills of the local artisans who built the stepwell, as well as the **cultural fusion** between **Rajput art** and **Mughal influences** that were prevalent during that time.

11.2.3 Water Conservation and Engineering

Both Chand Baori and Toorji Ka Jhalra showcase the **engineering brilliance** of Rajasthan's past, particularly in water-scarce regions. Stepwells were built to manage the **seasonal fluctuations** in water availability, capturing rainwater during the monsoon and storing it for the dry months. The design of these wells was often highly **sophisticated**, incorporating **rainwater harvesting** and **groundwater recharge** mechanisms, making them effective tools for **water conservation**.

The placement of stepwells was often strategic, located near **trade routes** or **temples**, where they could serve both practical and symbolic purposes. In the case of **Chand Baori**, its proximity to the **Harshat Mata Temple** suggests that the stepwell also had a **ritualistic function**, providing water for religious ceremonies and pilgrimages. Similarly, Toorji Ka Jhalra, being located in a royal city, was likely intended to symbolize the benevolence of the queen who commissioned it, reinforcing the **social and political power** of the ruling elite through the provision of water.

11.2.4 Social and Cultural Significance

Stepwells like Chand Baori and Toorji Ka Jhalra were not just utilitarian structures; they were integral to the **social fabric** of their communities. These stepwells were often the center of social life, where people gathered for daily chores, such as fetching water, washing clothes, and bathing. For women, in particular, stepwells were a **social space**, where they could meet and interact with others in the community.

In addition to their social function, stepwells also held a **spiritual significance**. Water has always been revered in Indian culture, symbolizing **purity**, **life**, and **fertility**. The **ritualistic aspects** of water usage were often incorporated into the design of the stepwells. Chand Baori's proximity to the **Harshat Mata Temple** suggests that it may have played a role in **religious ceremonies** or **offerings** to the goddess. Similarly, the carvings and sculptures found in these stepwells often depict **deities** and **mythological scenes**, reinforcing the connection between water and the **divine**.

11.2.5 Decline and Restoration Efforts

With the advent of **modern water management systems**, the use of stepwells gradually declined, and many of them fell into disrepair. However, in recent years, there has been a growing recognition of the **architectural and cultural significance** of these structures. **Restoration projects**, particularly in tourist regions like **Jodhpur** and **Jaipur**, have brought new life to these ancient wells.

Toorji Ka Jhalra, for example, has been meticulously restored and is now a popular spot for tourists and locals alike. The restoration has not only preserved the **architectural beauty** of the stepwell but also revived its use as a **community gathering place**. Similarly, efforts have been made to preserve **Chand Baori**, which remains one of the most visited historical sites in Rajasthan. These restoration projects are crucial in ensuring that the **cultural heritage** and **engineering marvels** of Rajasthan's stepwells are preserved for future generations.

11.3 Reservoirs, Lakes, and Canal Systems

Rajasthan, being a largely arid and desert region, has historically faced significant challenges in water management. However, the state's ancient and medieval civilizations developed innovative methods to ensure a stable water supply, resulting in the creation of impressive **reservoirs**, **lakes**, and **canal systems**. These structures were not only engineering marvels but also played a crucial role in the **socio-economic development** of the region, supporting agriculture, human settlements, and religious practices. The **archaeological explorations** of Rajasthan have revealed a wealth of information about these water management systems, showcasing the **ingenuity** and **foresight** of its early inhabitants.

11.3.1 Early Reservoirs and Water Harvesting Structures

One of the earliest known methods of water management in Rajasthan was the construction of **reservoirs** or **water harvesting structures**. These were designed to collect and store **rainwater**, which could then be used throughout the year for drinking, irrigation, and other purposes. Archaeological findings from **Kalibangan** and **Ahar** suggest that early civilizations in the region had sophisticated knowledge of water conservation techniques.

Reservoirs like the **Jaisalmer's Gadsisar Lake**, built in the 14th century, are prime examples of how artificial lakes were constructed to cater to the water needs of the local population. Gadsisar Lake, surrounded by **temples** and **shrines**, not only provided water but also became a significant religious site, indicating the dual importance of these water bodies in both practical and spiritual life.

11.3.2 Lakes of Rajasthan: A Lifeline for Desert Dwellers

Several **man-made lakes** were constructed across Rajasthan, turning the state's dry landscape into an area where **urban centers** and **agriculture** could flourish. Some of the most famous lakes in Rajasthan include **Pichola Lake** in Udaipur, **Fateh Sagar Lake**, and **Sambhar Salt Lake**, each of which holds historical significance and is linked to the broader **water conservation traditions** of the state.

- **Pichola Lake**: One of the oldest and most iconic lakes, **Lake Pichola** was constructed in the 14th century by a local banjara (tribal) leader. Its expansion under Maharana Udai Singh II, who founded the city of Udaipur, turned it into a key water source. Pichola Lake, with its **islands**, **palaces**, and **temples**, became not just a water reservoir but a center of **political power** and **cultural activities**.

- **Fateh Sagar Lake**: An extension of Pichola Lake, **Fateh Sagar Lake** was built in the late 17th century and is surrounded by hills, creating a **picturesque** setting. It played a vital role in the irrigation systems of Udaipur, ensuring water supply during the dry seasons.

- **Sambhar Salt Lake**: Unlike other lakes, the **Sambhar Salt Lake** is renowned for being **India's largest inland salt lake**. Though its primary function was salt production, it also helped in **groundwater recharge** and acted as a significant water source for nearby areas.

These lakes were not just important for their water-harvesting capacities but also became central to the **urban planning** and **architectural heritage** of cities. Temples, palaces, and havelis were often constructed around these lakes, transforming them into cultural and religious hubs.

11.3.3 Canal Systems: Engineering Marvels of Rajasthan

In addition to reservoirs and lakes, Rajasthan's historical water management also relied on an intricate network of **canal systems**. The state's **medieval rulers** recognized the importance of canal construction to divert water from rivers into reservoirs and fields, particularly in the **semi-arid and arid regions** where rainfall was scarce.

One of the most significant ancient canal systems is the **Gang Canal**, constructed during the 1920s in the northwestern part of Rajasthan, utilizing water from the **Sutlej River**. Though it is a more recent construction, it represents the culmination of a long history of canal engineering in the region. The **Indira Gandhi Canal**, one of the longest canals in India, continues this tradition of

large-scale water transportation, making the deserts of western Rajasthan more suitable for human habitation and agriculture.

In earlier times, smaller canals were developed to carry water from **rainwater-fed tanks** to agricultural fields. These were constructed with the **local topography** in mind, ensuring minimal water wastage. **Stepwells**, such as those found in **Abhaneri** and **Jodhpur**, also played a critical role in both storing water and facilitating its easy access.

11.3.4 Stepwells: Ingenious Water Storage Systems

Rajasthan's unique contribution to India's water management heritage is its **stepwells** (*baoris* or *baolis*), which serve as another form of reservoir. These **underground structures** are designed with a series of steps descending down to the water level, allowing easy access to the water stored within, even as the water level fluctuated with the seasons.

- **Chand Baori**: Located in the village of Abhaneri, **Chand Baori** is one of the most famous stepwells in Rajasthan and one of the largest and deepest in India. Built during the 9th century by King Chanda of the **Chauhan dynasty**, it showcases a **complex engineering** and **architectural design**, with thousands of steps arranged in a geometric pattern. Chand Baori not only served as a water reservoir but also as a **community gathering space** during the hot summer months.

- **Toorji Ka Jhalra**: Another notable example is **Toorji Ka Jhalra** in Jodhpur, a 250-year-old stepwell. This structure is intricately carved from sandstone and reflects the **practicality** and **artistry** involved in water storage methods in Rajasthan.

These stepwells were often elaborately decorated with **carvings** and **sculptures**, reflecting the **religious** and **cultural significance** of water. They served both practical and **ritualistic purposes**, providing water for daily needs while also being associated with various **rituals** and **festivals**.

11.3.5 Religious and Cultural Significance of Water Bodies

In Rajasthan, water has always been more than just a resource—it holds deep **religious** and **cultural significance**. Lakes and reservoirs were often dedicated to deities, with temples built along their shores. For example, **Pushkar Lake** is considered one of the holiest sites in Hinduism, believed to have been created by the god Brahma. Pilgrims come from all over the country to bathe in its waters, seeking spiritual cleansing and blessings.

Similarly, many of the reservoirs and lakes were constructed with an eye toward **religious duty**. Kings and nobles saw the construction of water bodies as an act of **dharma**, ensuring that they left a lasting legacy for their people. **Ghat structures**, where people could descend to the water for bathing or prayer, are commonly found along these lakes, further emphasizing their role in religious life.

11.3.6 Legacy and Continuing Relevance

Today, many of Rajasthan's ancient and medieval reservoirs, lakes, and canal systems are still in use, providing vital resources in an otherwise dry landscape. Archaeological explorations and restoration efforts are ongoing, ensuring that these historical water management systems are preserved for future generations. They stand as a testament to the **sustainable water management practices** developed by the region's early inhabitants and continue to inspire modern water conservation efforts.

CHAPTER TWELVE

Cultural Artifacts: Pottery, Textiles, and Jewelry

12.1 Craftsmanship Through the Ages

Rajasthan's history of craftsmanship is a reflection of its rich cultural heritage, spanning centuries of artistic innovation and excellence. The craftsmanship of Rajasthan has evolved significantly through the ages, influenced by the region's rulers, religious practices, and geographic features. Rajasthan's crafts not only catered to local demands but also became highly sought after in distant lands, leading to a thriving tradition of trade and cultural exchange. This chapter will explore the history of Rajasthani craftsmanship, focusing on various forms of art, from intricate textiles to metalwork, pottery, and jewelry, while considering the influence of different periods and dynasties on these crafts.

12.1.1 Early Craftsmanship: Prehistoric and Early Civilizations

Craftsmanship in Rajasthan can be traced back to prehistoric times when the region's early inhabitants developed basic tools and decorative items from stone and clay. Archaeological evidence from sites like **Kalibangan** and **Ahar** suggests that early settlements in Rajasthan were involved in creating pottery, stone tools, and simple adornments made from bones and shells. The **Harappan** influence, particularly in the **Kalibangan** region, brought with it the knowledge of terracotta figurines, pottery, and bead-making, which were essential aspects of early craftsmanship.

With the advent of the **Iron Age**, artisans in Rajasthan began to work with metals like iron and copper, marking the beginning of a metallurgical tradition that would later thrive under various dynasties.

12.1.2 Craftsmanship Under the Rajputs

The rise of the **Rajput** kingdoms during the **medieval period** had a profound impact on Rajasthani craftsmanship. The Rajputs, known for their patronage of the arts, created a flourishing environment for artisans, who were tasked with adorning palaces, forts, and temples with intricate carvings, sculptures, and paintings. This period saw the development of various crafts, such as:

- **Textile Weaving and Dyeing**: Rajasthan became famous for its vibrant textiles, including **bandhani** (tie-dye), **leheriya** (wave-patterned fabrics), and **block printing**. These techniques were developed using natural dyes and were often used to create garments for the royal families and the nobility. The city of **Sanganer** became known for its block-printing artisans, while **Ajrakh** printing flourished in the desert regions.

- **Metalwork**: Rajput rulers commissioned metalworkers to create weapons, armor, and ceremonial objects. The **jaali** (latticework) and **toranas** (archways) of forts like **Chittorgarh** and **Mehrangarh** were adorned with intricate metal designs, showcasing the skill of Rajasthani artisans.

- **Jewelry Making**: The art of jewelry making reached new heights during this period. Artisans in Rajasthan crafted exquisite **kundan** (gold jewelry set with gemstones) and **meenakari** (enamel work) jewelry, which became synonymous with the region. The **royal courts** often employed dedicated jewelers to create elaborate pieces for royal weddings, religious ceremonies, and festivals.

12.1.3 Mughal Influence on Rajasthani Craftsmanship

The **Mughal Empire** had a significant impact on the craftsmanship of Rajasthan. Although the Mughals and the Rajputs were often at odds politically, they also shared a deep mutual respect for art and culture. The **Mughal-Rajput alliance**, cemented through marriage and diplomacy, led to a cultural exchange that enriched Rajasthani craftsmanship.

- **Miniature Paintings**: Mughal influence is evident in the development of **Rajasthani miniature paintings**, which became a hallmark of the region's artistic tradition. The schools of **Mewar**, **Marwar**, **Kota**, and **Bundi** each developed their unique styles, blending Mughal techniques with local themes, such as depictions of Rajput kings, religious figures, and scenes from the **Ramayana** and **Mahabharata**.

- **Architecture and Decorative Arts**: Mughal influence also extended to architecture, where craftsmen incorporated intricate **floral patterns**, **geometric designs**, and **inlay work** into the palaces and forts of Rajasthan. The **Amber Fort** and the **City Palace of Jaipur** are prime examples of Mughal-inspired craftsmanship, with their ornate facades, mirrored halls, and intricately carved pillars.

12.1.4 Craftsmanship in the Colonial Period

The **British colonial era** brought both challenges and new opportunities for Rajasthan's craftsmen. While the traditional patronage system of the Rajput courts was in decline, new markets opened up, both within India and abroad, for handcrafted goods. The British had a particular interest in Rajasthani **textiles**, **carpets**, and **jewelry**, and many local artisans began to cater to these markets.

- **Textiles for Export**: Textile production, particularly in the regions of **Jaipur** and **Jodhpur**, expanded to meet international demand. **Block printing** on cotton became highly sought after in Europe, and Rajasthan's **silk weavers** began producing elaborate saris and fabrics for both Indian and European markets.

- **Blue Pottery**: One of the most significant innovations of the colonial period was the development of **Jaipur Blue Pottery**. Introduced to Rajasthan by **Turkic and Persian** artisans, blue pottery flourished under British patronage. This unique craft, characterized by its vibrant blue color and intricate designs, became a symbol of Rajasthani craftsmanship and continues to be a popular art form today.

12.1.5 Contemporary Craftsmanship and Global Influence

In modern times, Rajasthani craftsmanship has continued to thrive, blending traditional techniques with contemporary innovations. The state's artisans have adapted to the changing demands of a globalized world, producing goods that appeal to both local and international markets.

- **Handicrafts for the Modern World**: Rajasthani crafts, such as **textiles**, **pottery**, **metalwork**, and **jewelry**, have found new life in modern design. Many artisans are now incorporating contemporary aesthetics into their traditional crafts, resulting in unique products that appeal to a global audience. The city of **Jodhpur** has emerged as a hub for **furniture design**, where traditional woodworking techniques are used to create modern pieces for export.

- **Sustainable Craftsmanship**: In recent years, there has been a growing emphasis on **sustainability** in craftsmanship. Artisans are using eco-friendly materials and processes to create handcrafted goods that reflect Rajasthan's commitment to preserving its natural resources. **Recycled textiles**, **organic dyes**, and **handwoven fabrics** are becoming more popular, especially among younger generations of artisans.

- **Revival of Dying Arts**: Efforts have been made to preserve dying crafts such as **phad painting**, **lacquer work**, and **pichwai painting**. These traditional art forms, which were once on the verge of extinction, have been revived through government initiatives, NGO support, and the efforts of local artisans committed to passing down their knowledge to future generations.

12.2 Archaeological Evidence of Traditional Crafts

Rajasthan, known for its **rich cultural and artistic heritage**, has been a hub of various traditional crafts for centuries. The region's unique geographical position, combined with its historical interactions with **different civilizations**—including the **Indus Valley**, **Rajput dynasties**, and later, the **Mughals**—has contributed to a **vibrant craft tradition**. Archaeological excavations across Rajasthan have uncovered significant evidence of **traditional crafts**, ranging from **pottery** and **textile production** to **metalwork** and **stone carving**. These findings offer insight into the **artisanal expertise** of ancient societies in Rajasthan, highlighting how these crafts not only served practical purposes but also reflected the **aesthetic preferences** and **cultural values** of the time.

12.2.1 Pottery: Craftsmanship in Clay

One of the most notable craft traditions in Rajasthan, as revealed by archaeological studies, is **pottery**. Excavations at sites like **Kalibangan** and **Ahar** have uncovered a variety of **earthenware** items, including storage jars, cooking pots, and water vessels. The pottery styles vary across regions and time periods, but many examples share certain **distinctive features**, such as **black-and-red ware** with intricate **geometric patterns**.

The discovery of **wheel-made pottery** indicates the use of advanced techniques even in **prehistoric times**. Pottery from these ancient sites also reflects **technological innovations**, such as the application of specific **glazing**

techniques and the firing of clay at high temperatures to produce more durable and finely crafted items. The inclusion of **decorative motifs**—floral patterns, animal figures, and religious symbols—on these pots suggests that they were not merely utilitarian objects but also had significant **aesthetic and symbolic roles** in the society.

12.2.2 Textile Production: Weaving and Dyeing

Rajasthan has long been associated with **textile production**, particularly the art of **weaving** and **dyeing**. Archaeological evidence of **looms**, **spindles**, and **dyed fabrics** has been discovered at various sites, indicating the region's long-standing tradition of **textile craftsmanship**. Textiles from Rajasthan, renowned for their **bright colors** and **intricate designs**, are closely linked to the natural environment. For instance, the region's arid climate encouraged the development of **light, breathable fabrics** made from **cotton** and **silk**.

Ancient techniques such as **tie-dyeing** or **bandhani**, still practiced today, have their roots in **pre-modern Rajasthan**. Archaeological findings from **Jodhpur** and **Jaipur** suggest that traditional dyeing techniques, such as the use of **vegetable-based dyes**, were well-established by the **medieval period**. These findings underscore the importance of textiles not only as a **commodity** in trade but also as a medium through which **cultural identity** and **social status** were expressed.

12.2.3 Metalwork: The Craft of Iron, Copper, and Bronze

The evidence of **metalworking** in Rajasthan can be traced back to the **Bronze Age**, with early findings of **copper tools** and **bronze sculptures** discovered at sites such as **Balathal**. These findings reveal the mastery of **metal alloying techniques** and the production of **ornamental items** alongside more practical tools. **Copper hoards**, particularly from the **Ahar-Banas culture**, suggest that the people of ancient Rajasthan possessed advanced knowledge of **metal extraction and smelting**.

By the **Iron Age**, archaeological studies point to the transition to **ironworking**, a development that greatly impacted **agricultural tools**, **weapons**, and **construction materials**. The production of **iron swords**, **daggers**, and **axes**, as well as **bronze figurines**, exemplifies the importance of metalwork in both **military** and **cultural spheres**.

In addition to weapons and tools, **jewelry** production became a significant craft in Rajasthan. Excavations have unearthed **ornamental artifacts** made from **precious metals** like **gold** and **silver**, often adorned with **semi-precious stones** such as **lapis lazuli**, **agate**, and **carnelian**. These luxurious items reflect not only the **craftsmanship of artisans** but also the **trade connections** Rajasthan had with other regions, as the stones were often imported from distant places.

12.2.4 Stone Carving: From Utility to Art

Stone carving, another ancient craft in Rajasthan, has left behind an extensive archaeological record. Sites like **Chittorgarh** and **Jaisalmer** are home to numerous examples of **intricately carved stone** in the form of **temples**, **forts**, and **palaces**. However, even beyond the monumental structures, smaller **artifacts** such as **stone utensils**, **tools**, and **decorative items** have been found, showcasing the daily use of **stonework** in Rajasthan.

The variety of **stone types** available in Rajasthan—such as **sandstone**, **marble**, and **granite**—allowed for the development of a wide range of **artistic expressions**. The **precision** with which stones were cut and shaped into elaborate sculptures and relief work is evident from the remains of temples and fortifications across the region. **Jain temples** at **Ranakpur** and **Dilwara** are prime examples of the **sculptural finesse** achieved by Rajasthan's stone carvers, reflecting a craft that combined religious devotion with artistic excellence.

12.2.5 Crafting Techniques and Tools

Archaeological evidence also sheds light on the **tools** and **techniques** used by artisans in ancient Rajasthan. **Metal chisels**, **hammers**, **files**, and other tools found at various excavation sites demonstrate the **precision** and **skill** with which craftsmen worked. The use of **rudimentary hand tools**, however, did not limit the artisans' creativity; rather, it showcases their ability to produce **complex designs** using **basic yet effective technologies**.

Techniques such as **lost-wax casting** were employed for producing **metal sculptures**, particularly during the **medieval period**, as evidenced by findings from **Nagaur** and **Ajmer**. This method, along with the use of **stone polishing** techniques, allowed for the creation of **finely detailed artifacts**. The tools and techniques uncovered in these archaeological studies point to a **deep understanding** of material properties and a **long tradition** of craft specialization that evolved over the centuries.

12.2.6 Trade and Craftsmanship in Ancient Rajasthan

The archaeological evidence of traditional crafts in Rajasthan also highlights the region's role in **interregional trade**. As a key part of the **medieval trade routes**, Rajasthan became a center for the exchange of goods such as **textiles, jewelry**, and **metalware**. The city of **Jaisalmer**, strategically located along the **Silk Road**, was particularly important in this trade network, serving as a conduit for goods moving between **India, Central Asia**, and the **Middle East**.

The production of luxury items for both **domestic use** and **export** indicates that Rajasthan's artisans were highly valued not only within the region but across broader trade networks. **Textiles dyed with indigo**, **embellished garments**, and **ornamental jewelry** were highly sought after by merchants, contributing to the **economic prosperity** of the region. The demand for these items also spurred innovation, leading to the refinement of existing techniques and the development of new ones.

12.3 Preservation of Cultural Heritage through Artifacts

The preservation of cultural heritage through **artifacts** plays a crucial role in safeguarding the rich history and traditions of Rajasthan. As a land with an ancient and vibrant civilization, Rajasthan's **artifacts**—ranging from **sculptures**, **pottery**, **coins**, **jewelry**, and **manuscripts**—offer invaluable insights into the lifestyles, artistic sensibilities, and historical events that have shaped the region. These artifacts, unearthed through systematic **archaeological explorations**, are vital not only in reconstructing the past but also in ensuring that future generations remain connected to the state's rich cultural legacy.

12.3.1 Artifacts as Historical Narratives

Artifacts serve as **tangible links** to the past, allowing historians, archaeologists, and the general public to engage with historical events in a direct and meaningful way. In Rajasthan, artifacts dating back to the **Indus Valley Civilization**, the **Rajput kingdoms**, and the **Mughal era** have been discovered at various archaeological sites. These objects often bear unique **symbols**, **inscriptions**, and **craftsmanship** that convey stories about **trade**, **religion**, and **social practices**.

For example, the **terracotta figurines** and **pottery** found at sites like **Kalibangan** and **Ahar** provide insights into the daily lives and religious practices of the region's ancient inhabitants. Similarly, **Rajput swords**, **armor**, and **royal insignia** reveal the martial culture and the valor of Rajasthan's ruling clans. These artifacts allow researchers to piece together the cultural mosaic of Rajasthan's various historical periods.

12.3.2 Museums: Custodians of Rajasthan's Cultural Artifacts

Museums in Rajasthan play a critical role in the **preservation and display** of artifacts, acting as **repositories** of the state's cultural heritage. Institutions such as the **Albert Hall Museum** in Jaipur, the **Mehrangarh Fort Museum** in Jodhpur, and the **City Palace Museum** in Udaipur house vast collections of artifacts ranging from **ancient coins** to **paintings** and **textiles**.

- **Albert Hall Museum**: One of the oldest museums in Rajasthan, it holds a vast collection of **metal objects**, **carpets**, and **ivory sculptures** that reflect the rich artistic traditions of the region. The museum's archaeological collection includes important pieces from **Indus Valley** sites as well as from **Buddhist** and **Jain** centers in Rajasthan.

- **Mehrangarh Fort Museum**: This museum showcases **Rajput-era artifacts**, including **palanquins**, **elephant**

howdahs, and **miniature paintings**, highlighting the royal heritage of Rajasthan. The **armor** and **weaponry** collection is particularly significant, offering insights into the military traditions of the region.

- **City Palace Museum**: In Udaipur, this museum houses a significant collection of **Rajasthani miniatures**, **silver objects**, and **historic manuscripts**, providing a glimpse into the lavish lifestyles and **artistic patronage** of the Mewar rulers.

These museums not only preserve these objects but also **curate exhibits** that educate the public about their historical importance. They play a pivotal role in safeguarding the **physical heritage** of Rajasthan, ensuring that the artifacts are protected from deterioration and remain accessible to scholars and visitors alike.

12.3.3 Archaeological Excavations and Artifact Discovery

Archaeological excavations in Rajasthan have uncovered a wealth of artifacts that have deepened our understanding of the state's historical development. Sites such as **Kalibangan**, **Ahar**, and **Balathal** have yielded important relics from the **Harappan civilization**, including **pottery**, **beads**, and **tools**, which point to a sophisticated and interconnected society.

- **Kalibangan**: Excavations here have revealed **Harappan pottery**, **brick structures**, and **fire altars**, indicating the region's participation in the broader **Indus Valley culture**. The artifacts found at Kalibangan illustrate both the urban planning of the time and the religious practices that were central to Harappan life.

- **Ahar**: Known for its **chalcolithic** (copper age) culture, Ahar has produced numerous **copper tools**, **stone beads**, and **ceramic remains**. These artifacts are key to understanding the **early agricultural** and **metallurgical** practices in Rajasthan.

- **Balathal**: This site has provided evidence of **pre-Harappan settlements**, with the discovery of **microlithic tools** and **chalcolithic pottery**. The artifacts from Balathal shed light on the **evolution of human settlement** and technology in the region.

The careful excavation, cataloging, and study of these artifacts ensure that they are properly preserved and that their historical context is understood. **Conservation efforts**, both at the excavation site and in museums, play a vital role in preventing these artifacts from degrading, allowing them to be passed down to future generations.

12.3.4 Conservation Challenges and Efforts

Preserving Rajasthan's artifacts presents numerous challenges, especially considering the region's **harsh climate** and the **age** of many of the objects. The extreme temperatures and **aridity** can cause rapid deterioration of **organic materials** like wood, textiles, and manuscripts. Furthermore, **urbanization** and **development projects** pose a threat to undiscovered archaeological sites, making it essential to balance modern growth with the preservation of cultural heritage.

To address these challenges, there have been concerted efforts by both the **state government** and **heritage conservation organizations** to implement measures for the **protection and conservation** of artifacts. Modern conservation techniques, such as **climate-controlled storage**, **chemical treatments**, and **digital archiving**, have been adopted to ensure the long-term preservation of fragile objects.

- **Digital Preservation**: Many artifacts are now being digitized, with high-resolution **3D scanning** allowing for the creation of digital records that can be studied and shared without risking damage to the original objects. This is particularly important for **manuscripts** and **paintings**, which are susceptible to fading and wear over time.

- **Public Awareness**: Initiatives to promote **public awareness** of the importance of cultural heritage have also been undertaken. Educational programs, exhibitions, and **heritage walks** are organized to engage the public, fostering a sense of ownership and responsibility for the preservation of these artifacts.

12.3.5 Artifacts and the Revival of Cultural Identity

The preservation of artifacts is not just about **academic study**; it is also about the **revival** and **reinforcement** of Rajasthan's cultural identity. These objects serve as a source of pride for local communities, helping them stay connected to their **ancestral traditions**. Festivals, **craft revivals**, and **cultural performances** are often centered around the historical narratives uncovered through artifacts, ensuring that the **living traditions** of Rajasthan continue alongside its preserved heritage.

For example, the **craftsmanship** seen in ancient jewelry, textiles, and pottery has inspired **modern artisans** in Rajasthan, leading to a **renaissance** in traditional crafts. Workshops and **artisan programs** often reference **historical designs**, ensuring that the cultural techniques and aesthetics represented by the artifacts continue to influence **contemporary art** and **craft**.

CHAPTER THIRTEEN

Inscriptional Evidence and Written Records

13.1 Study of Stone and Metal Inscriptions in Rajasthan

Inscriptions, both on stone and metal, form one of the most crucial sources of historical knowledge, especially in the context of ancient and medieval Indian history. Rajasthan, with its rich legacy of powerful kingdoms, intricate trade routes, and architectural grandeur, boasts a vast number of inscriptions that provide valuable insights into the region's past. These inscriptions, etched on temple walls, pillars, copper plates, and other monuments, not only reveal important aspects of political history but also shed light on social, religious, and economic life.

13.1.1 Significance of Inscriptions as Historical Sources

Inscriptions serve as primary historical documents that provide first-hand information about different time periods. Unlike manuscripts, which can be prone to later interpolations and damage over time, inscriptions are usually contemporaneous with the events they describe. In Rajasthan, inscriptions give us direct access to the reigns of various rulers, their military conquests, the establishment of temples, religious donations, and the social and economic conditions prevalent during their reigns.

Stone inscriptions, commonly found on temple walls, stepwells, and forts, often contain details about donations made by kings, queens, and local nobility for religious or civic purposes. These inscriptions provide important information about the patronage extended to temples and other institutions, and the relationships between rulers and religious establishments. Similarly, **metal inscriptions**, particularly copper plate grants, were often issued as official records of land grants or tax exemptions. These copper plates are invaluable in reconstructing local governance and administrative systems.

13.1.2 Key Locations of Inscriptions in Rajasthan

Rajasthan is home to many significant sites that house a wide variety of inscriptions, ranging from early periods to late medieval times. The inscriptions are primarily in languages such as **Sanskrit**, **Prakrit**, and **Rajasthani**, and often in scripts like **Brahmi**, **Nagari**, and **Persian-Arabic** in later periods.

- **Chittorgarh**: The **Chittorgarh Fort**, one of the most prominent forts in Rajasthan, houses several stone inscriptions dating back to the **Mewar dynasty**. These inscriptions describe the valiant battles fought by Rajput kings, the construction of temples, and donations to various religious institutions.

- **Ranakpur**: The **Ranakpur Jain Temple**, renowned for its stunning architecture, is also home to numerous inscriptions, which provide insight into the **Jain patronage** in Rajasthan. The inscriptions describe the temple's construction during the reign of **Rana Kumbha**, one of the most powerful Rajput rulers, and his generous contributions to Jainism.

- **Dilwara Temples**: The **Dilwara Temples** in **Mount Abu** are another important site for inscriptions. The meticulous records etched into the stone walls of these temples provide details about the construction phases, financial contributions by merchants and nobility, and the influence of Jain leaders on Rajasthani society during the medieval period.

- **Jodhpur and Bikaner**: The cities of **Jodhpur** and **Bikaner** have yielded a wealth of metal inscriptions, particularly in the form of **copper plate grants**. These grants often contain records of land given to religious figures, farmers, or officials as rewards for service. They also give details about the tax exemptions granted to various landowners, shedding light on the economic policies of different rulers.

13.1.3 Early Stone Inscriptions: Gupta and Post-Gupta Period

The earliest inscriptions in Rajasthan date back to the **Gupta period** (4th to 6th centuries CE), which marked the beginning of classical Indian civilization. The **Gupta empire** stretched across much of northern India, including parts of Rajasthan. Stone inscriptions from this era are typically in Sanskrit and are found primarily in religious contexts, such as temple dedications and records of land grants to Brahmins and religious institutions.

A significant post-Gupta inscription is the **Banskhera Inscription** of **Harsha**, dating back to the **7th century** CE. This copper plate inscription provides insight into Harsha's reign and his efforts to maintain a strong administrative structure. The inscription is a key document for understanding the political landscape of Rajasthan during this time and offers clues about the relationship between the central and local authorities.

13.1.4 Medieval Rajput Inscriptions

The **medieval period**, dominated by the Rajput clans, saw a significant increase in the number of inscriptions. These inscriptions primarily reflect the political and religious patronage of the **Rajput kings**, their military conquests, and their efforts to legitimize their rule by supporting temples and religious orders.

For instance, the **Kumbhalgarh inscriptions** found at the **Kumbhalgarh Fort** celebrate the military victories of **Rana Kumbha** and his architectural contributions to the region. Other Rajput inscriptions, like those at the **Eklingji Temple**, emphasize the devotion of Rajput rulers to **Shiva** and their claim to divine right through religious support.

In **Jainism**, many Jain temples, such as those in **Ranakpur** and **Osian**, have inscriptions that highlight the role of wealthy Jain merchants in supporting temple construction and religious activities. These inscriptions show how religious patronage was not limited to kings but also involved a broader spectrum of society.

13.1.5 Metal Inscriptions: Copper Plates and Grants

While stone inscriptions were primarily used for public displays, metal inscriptions, particularly **copper plates**, were used to record official grants and donations. These plates were portable and served as legal documents that could be referred to in case of disputes.

One of the earliest examples of a copper plate inscription in Rajasthan is the **Ghatiyala inscription**, dating to the **9th century CE**. This inscription, written in **Nagari script**, records a land grant made by a local ruler. The inscription is notable for its detail, providing information about the boundaries of the land, the conditions of the grant, and the religious significance attached to it.

These grants often provided insights into the economic conditions of the time, as they described the land's productivity, taxes levied, and exemptions provided. Many of these copper plates were issued by **Rajput kings** to Brahmins or religious institutions as a means of legitimizing their rule through religious merit.

13.1.6 Persian Inscriptions and Mughal Influence

The **Mughal period** brought a new wave of inscriptions in **Persian**, reflecting the influence of Islamic rule in Rajasthan. The Mughals, especially under **Akbar** and his successors, engaged with the Rajput rulers of Rajasthan, leading to a fusion of **Rajput-Mughal** architecture and culture. Persian inscriptions are found in places like the **Amber Fort** and **Jaipur**, where Mughal influence was strong.

These inscriptions often praised the Mughal emperors, recorded military campaigns, or commemorated the construction of mosques and other Islamic structures. They also marked significant alliances between the Mughals and Rajput rulers, reflecting the blend of cultures during this period.

13.1.7 Preservation and Study of Inscriptions

The study of inscriptions in Rajasthan has been an ongoing process, with several scholars dedicating their efforts to deciphering these ancient records. **Epigraphists** and **archaeologists** play a crucial role in identifying, translating, and interpreting these inscriptions to reconstruct the historical narrative of Rajasthan.

Efforts are also being made to preserve these inscriptions, many of which have suffered damage due to environmental factors, neglect, or vandalism. Institutions like the **Archaeological Survey of India (ASI)** have taken steps to document and conserve these invaluable records. Modern techniques, such as **3D scanning** and **digital archiving**, are also being employed to create lasting records of inscriptions for future generations.

13.2 Interpretation of Ancient Languages and Scripts

The study of **ancient languages and scripts** in Rajasthan plays a vital role in understanding the region's **historical narratives**, **cultural evolution**, and **social dynamics**. Decoding these scripts not only unveils the political and administrative systems of ancient times but also provides insights into the **religious practices**, **economic conditions**, and **artistic expressions** of the past. Rajasthan, being a land rich in **historical significance**, has been home to various dynasties, each of which left behind an array of **epigraphic records** and **inscriptions** in multiple scripts, including **Brahmi**, **Sanskrit**, **Prakrit**, and **Nagari**. The archaeological findings of **inscriptions**, **seals**, and **coins** across the region have been critical in piecing together the linguistic history of Rajasthan.

13.2.1 The Brahmi Script: Rajasthan's Earliest Writing System

One of the earliest scripts found in Rajasthan is the **Brahmi script**, which dates back to the **3rd century BCE** and was used during the **Mauryan Empire**. The Brahmi script is considered the **precursor** to many Indian scripts, including **Devanagari**, and its presence in Rajasthan indicates the region's interaction with the larger **pan-Indian cultural and political systems**.

Inscriptions in Brahmi have been discovered in regions such as **Bairat** (modern **Viratnagar**) and **Udaipur**. These inscriptions primarily include **edicts** and **royal decrees**, particularly those issued by Emperor **Ashoka**, who sought to spread his message of **Dhamma** (righteousness) throughout his empire. The Bairat Edict, found near Jaipur, is one of the most significant examples, detailing Ashoka's **Buddhist beliefs** and his commitment to **moral governance**.

The interpretation of Brahmi script has been crucial in understanding the **spread of Buddhism** in Rajasthan and its interactions with local cultures. The **decipherment** of Brahmi, pioneered by **James Prinsep** in the 19th century, opened the door to understanding the earliest phases of written communication in Rajasthan, shedding light on the **political history** of the Mauryan and post-Mauryan periods.

13.2.2 Sanskrit and the Gupta Script: The Golden Age of Literature

With the advent of the **Gupta Empire** (4th–6th centuries CE), **Sanskrit** emerged as the **dominant language** for inscriptions and official communication. The **Gupta script**, a later development of Brahmi, was used extensively in Rajasthan during this period. Inscriptions in Sanskrit, found in **temples**, **pillars**, and **copper plates**, reveal the flourishing of **literature**, **science**, and **religion** under Gupta patronage.

The **Ahar inscriptions** near **Udaipur** provide valuable evidence of the **Gupta era's administrative system**, religious practices, and donations to **temples** and **monasteries**. These inscriptions, written in elegant Sanskrit, also highlight the influence of **Hinduism** and the patronage of **Brahminical institutions** during this time. The use of Sanskrit in these epigraphs reflects the **sophistication** of the Gupta courts and their role in standardizing Sanskrit as the **lingua franca** for intellectual and administrative activities.

Sanskrit inscriptions have also helped in identifying key **dynastic lineages**, such as the **Gurjara-Pratiharas**, who ruled parts of Rajasthan and played a crucial role in resisting early **Arab invasions**. Their inscriptions, often found in **temple complexes**, provide details on the **military conquests**, **land grants**, and **religious endowments** of the ruling elite.

13.2.3 Prakrit and Early Vernacular Languages

While Sanskrit was the language of the elite, **Prakrit**, a more **colloquial form** of language, was widely used by the common people. Prakrit inscriptions have been found in various **Jain temples** and **monastic complexes**, particularly in areas like **Ranakpur** and **Mount Abu**. Prakrit was commonly used for **religious texts**, especially those associated with the **Jain** and **Buddhist traditions**.

The **Shila Lekha** (rock inscriptions) in Prakrit found in **Rajasthan's cave temples** provide valuable insights into the **rituals** and **daily lives** of the common people, as well as the **religious donations** made by merchants and artisans to monastic communities. The presence of Prakrit in Rajasthan's inscriptions highlights the **multi-lingual environment** of the region, where various dialects coexisted with classical Sanskrit.

13.2.4 Nagari Script and Medieval Rajasthan

By the **medieval period**, the **Nagari script**, an offshoot of Brahmi, became widely used in Rajasthan for writing **Sanskrit** and **regional dialects**. This script, particularly its **Devanagari variant**, was employed extensively in **temple inscriptions**, **land grant records**, and **royal decrees**. The inscriptions from this period provide a rich source of information about **Rajput kingdoms**, their **military exploits**, and their **religious patronage**.

The **Rajput dynasties**, such as the **Sisodias of Mewar** and the **Rathores of Marwar**, left behind numerous inscriptions in Nagari, many of which can be found in the **fortresses** and **temple complexes** of **Chittorgarh**, **Kumbhalgarh**, and **Mehrangarh**. These inscriptions detail the **genealogies** of the ruling houses, the construction of **fortifications** and **palaces**, and the **religious donations** made by the kings to **Hindu temples** and **Jain shrines**.

The Nagari script also facilitated the recording of **Rajput military history**, with numerous inscriptions glorifying the **valor** and **martial achievements** of Rajput warriors. These inscriptions, often poetic in nature, extolled the virtues of **honor**, **bravery**, and **sacrifice**—values central to the Rajput ethos.

13.2.5 Jain Inscriptions and the Role of Script in Religious Traditions

Rajasthan has been an important center for **Jainism**, and the **Jain inscriptions** found across the region offer a window into the religious life of ancient and medieval Rajasthan. Written primarily in **Prakrit**, **Sanskrit**, and later in **Nagari**, these inscriptions are often associated with **temples**, **stupas**, and **monastic complexes**.

The **Dilwara Temples** on **Mount Abu** and the **Ranakpur Temple** near Udaipur house some of the most significant Jain inscriptions. These texts, etched into the **walls**, **pillars**, and **ceilings** of the temples, describe the **construction process**, the names of the **patrons** (often wealthy Jain merchants), and the **religious ceremonies** conducted in these sacred spaces. The inscriptions also provide details on the **iconography** and **ritual practices** associated with the temples, helping scholars understand the **doctrinal evolution** of Jainism in Rajasthan.

13.2.6 Seals and Coins: Economic and Political Records

Apart from stone inscriptions, **seals** and **coins** bearing ancient scripts have been critical in interpreting the **economic** and **political history** of Rajasthan. **Seals** with inscriptions in **Brahmi** and **Kharosthi** have been found at **Kalibangan**, a significant **Harappan site** in Rajasthan, indicating that the region was part of a broader **trade network** during the **Indus Valley Civilization**.

The **coins** issued by various rulers in Rajasthan, particularly during the medieval period, often carried inscriptions in **Nagari** or **Arabic**, reflecting the **cosmopolitan nature** of the region's economy and its connections with both **Hindu** and **Islamic rulers**. The interpretation of these coin inscriptions provides valuable information on the **economic policies**, **trade routes**, and **foreign relations** of the region.

13.2.7 Challenges in Interpretation

While Rajasthan's inscriptions offer a wealth of information, interpreting ancient languages and scripts presents several challenges. Many inscriptions have been **damaged** over time due to **weathering** or **human interference**, making them difficult to decipher. Additionally, the **regional variations** in language use, particularly in the case of **vernacular dialects**, complicate efforts to fully understand the content of the inscriptions.

The study of these ancient languages requires **specialized knowledge** of **paleography** (the study of ancient writing) and **epigraphy** (the study of inscriptions), and ongoing research continues to reveal new interpretations of Rajasthan's historical records.

13.3 Impact of Written Records on Understanding Historical Timelines

Written records play a pivotal role in the understanding of historical timelines, particularly in regions as historically rich and culturally diverse as Rajasthan. These records—ranging from **ancient inscriptions**, **royal decrees**, **manuscripts**, and **travelogues**—offer vital insights into the **political**, **social**, and **economic** developments that shaped the region over millennia. Archaeological excavations combined with these **documentary sources** enable historians and archaeologists to construct a more **comprehensive** and **accurate** timeline of events, highlighting the influence of various **dynasties**, **religious movements**, and **trade networks** on Rajasthan's evolution.

13.3.1 Inscriptions as Historical Milestones

Inscriptions found on **temples**, **forts**, **monuments**, and **copper plates** serve as primary written records that document key events in Rajasthan's history. These inscriptions often commemorate the reigns of rulers, significant battles, land grants, and religious endowments, providing chronological markers that are invaluable for constructing historical timelines.

- **Chittorgarh and Ranthambore Inscriptions**: Inscriptions found at forts like **Chittorgarh** and **Ranthambore** offer details about the **Rajput dynasties** that ruled these areas. They record the **ascension of**

kings, their victories, and their contributions to religious institutions. For example, the inscriptions at Chittorgarh detail the reign of the **Sisodia dynasty**, highlighting the fort's role as a bastion of Rajput resistance against **Mughal expansion**. These inscriptions also help historians understand the sequence of rulers, providing clear markers of succession and political shifts.

- **Copper Plate Grants**: Copper plates discovered in Rajasthan offer important insights into **land grants** and **tax exemptions** given by rulers to religious institutions or individuals. These records help track the **economic policies** of different kingdoms, revealing the land distribution systems and the role of religion in governance. The **Ahar Copper Plates**, for instance, shed light on the socio-political framework of the **Guhila dynasty** of Mewar, outlining territorial grants that contributed to the growth of local religious and social structures.

By correlating these inscriptions with **archaeological findings**, historians can pinpoint the dates of construction for **fortifications**, **temples**, and other monumental structures. This allows for the accurate mapping of **dynastic periods** and the architectural styles that flourished during them, creating a more nuanced understanding of the **chronological evolution** of Rajasthan's cultural landscape.

13.3.2 Manuscripts and Chronicles: Documenting Dynasties and Events

Manuscripts, particularly those created during the **medieval period**, provide rich documentation of Rajasthan's **dynastic history** and the political changes that shaped the region. These texts, often written in **Sanskrit**, **Rajasthani**, **Persian**, or **Arabic**, include **royal chronicles**, **genealogies**, and **poetic epics** that highlight the exploits of rulers, their interactions with neighboring kingdoms, and significant military campaigns.

- **Prithviraj Raso**: One of the most famous literary works in Rajasthan's history, the **Prithviraj Raso**, written by **Chand Bardai**, chronicles the life and heroic exploits of **Prithviraj Chauhan**. While it is a semi-legendary account, it offers valuable insights into the **Rajput era** and helps establish a timeline for the **Chauhan dynasty's** rise and conflicts with **Muslim invaders**, including the **Ghurids**. While some details are exaggerated or romanticized, the text serves as an important cultural artifact, offering a window into the values, battles, and alliances of the time.

- **Khyat Literature**: This genre of **historical ballads** and **biographies** written by **Charans** (traditional bards) offers insight into the lives of **Rajput rulers** and their deeds. **Charan poets** like **Mohanlal Charan** and **Nathji Charan** documented significant events, including battles, diplomatic treaties, and royal ceremonies. These written records allow historians to trace the political and military alliances that shaped Rajasthan during the

medieval period, offering a perspective on **Mughal-Rajput relations** and the influence of the **Maratha invasions**.

- **Persian Histories**: During the Mughal period, **Persian chroniclers** documented significant events related to Rajasthan, particularly the interactions between **Mughal emperors** and the Rajput kingdoms. Works such as the **Ain-i-Akbari** and **Akbarnama**, written by **Abu'l Fazl**, provide crucial information about the **political alliances** between the Mughals and Rajput rulers like **Raja Man Singh** and **Raja Jai Singh**. These records help establish the timeline of **Rajput integration** into the Mughal administrative framework and their military contributions to the empire.

By comparing these written records with **archaeological data**, such as the **construction dates of forts** and **battlefield remains**, historians are able to create a detailed chronology of political events and **cultural exchanges** during the Mughal-Rajput period.

13.3.3 Travelogues and Foreign Accounts: A Broader Perspective

In addition to local sources, foreign accounts from travelers who visited Rajasthan during different historical periods offer a broader perspective on the region's development. These travelogues, written by **Arab**, **Persian**, **Chinese**, and **European** visitors, provide unique insights into the **socio-political conditions**, **trade networks**, and

architectural achievements of the region.

- **Ibn Battuta**: The famous Moroccan traveler **Ibn Battuta** passed through Rajasthan during his journeys across the **Indian subcontinent**. His writings offer a glimpse into the **Delhi Sultanate's control** over parts of Rajasthan and the state of the **Rajput kingdoms** during the 14th century. He documented the **fortifications**, **trade routes**, and **cultural practices** he observed, contributing valuable information to our understanding of medieval Rajasthan's role in regional politics.

- **Tavernier and Bernier**: European travelers like **Jean-Baptiste Tavernier** and **François Bernier**, who visited Rajasthan during the Mughal period, recorded their observations about the **economy**, **architecture**, and **military strength** of the Rajput states. Their accounts highlight the grandeur of **Rajput courts**, the architectural splendor of cities like **Amber** and **Jaipur**, and the role of Rajputs in Mughal military campaigns. These records are essential for establishing timelines of **Mughal-Rajput interactions** and for understanding the influence of **European trade networks** on Rajasthan.

These foreign accounts, while sometimes biased or incomplete, offer a valuable external perspective that complements local written records. By comparing these accounts with indigenous manuscripts and inscriptions, historians can establish more **accurate timelines** of Rajasthan's political and economic history.

13.3.4 Challenges in Interpreting Written Records

While written records are invaluable for constructing historical timelines, they are not without challenges. Many written sources, particularly **chronicles** and **epic poems**, contain **embellishments** or are influenced by the **political motives** of their authors. As a result, historians must carefully **cross-reference** written records with **archaeological evidence** and other contemporary documents to arrive at a balanced and accurate timeline.

Additionally, the **deciphering** of ancient scripts, particularly those in **Prakrit**, **Brahmi**, or **Sanskrit**, presents another challenge. Some inscriptions or manuscripts are **damaged** or **incomplete**, leading to gaps in the historical record. Nevertheless, advancements in **epigraphy** and **manuscript preservation** continue to improve our understanding of these records, ensuring that they remain a key source for historical reconstruction.

13.3.5 Bridging the Past and Present Through Written Records

In sum, written records, whether in the form of inscriptions, manuscripts, or foreign accounts, serve as essential tools for understanding Rajasthan's historical timelines. These records help bridge the **past and present**, offering modern scholars a way to reconstruct the **chronological progression** of **dynasties**, **cultural**

movements, and **architectural developments**. By combining these written sources with **material artifacts** unearthed through archaeological excavations, historians are able to paint a more comprehensive picture of Rajasthan's long and varied history. This integrated approach ensures that the **rich heritage** of Rajasthan continues to inform and inspire both academic research and public interest in the region's past.

CHAPTER FOURTEEN

Rajasthan's Archaeological Excavations: Techniques and Discoveries

14.1 Major Archaeological Excavations and Key Findings

Rajasthan, with its rich historical and cultural legacy, has been the site of numerous archaeological excavations over the years. These excavations have yielded crucial evidence about ancient civilizations, trade routes, religious practices, and socio-political dynamics in the region. The discoveries from these excavations have added depth to our understanding of Rajasthan's past, stretching back to the **Stone Age** and moving through the **Harappan**, **Vedic**, **Buddhist**, **Rajput**, and **Mughal periods**. This chapter will focus on major archaeological excavations conducted across Rajasthan and their key findings, which have brought to light the historical significance of the region.

14.1.1 Kalibangan: The Harappan Settlement in Rajasthan

One of the most significant archaeological excavations in Rajasthan is at **Kalibangan**, located on the banks of the **Ghaggar River** in the **Hanumangarh district**. Kalibangan is one of the prominent sites of the **Indus Valley Civilization**, or Harappan culture, known for its urban planning, advanced drainage systems, and use of baked bricks.

Excavations at Kalibangan, conducted by the **Archaeological Survey of India (ASI)**, have revealed evidence of both a **Pre-Harappan** and a **Harappan settlement**. The pre-Harappan phase, dating back to around **3500 BCE**, is characterized by mudbrick structures, while the mature Harappan phase shows the use of baked bricks and advanced urban planning.

- **Key Findings:**
    - **Fire Altars:** One of the most remarkable discoveries at Kalibangan is the series of fire altars, indicating the religious and ritualistic practices of the people. These fire altars suggest that **Vedic** rituals were possibly performed in the region.
    - **Ploughed Field:** Kalibangan also holds the distinction of having the earliest evidence of a **ploughed agricultural field** in India, showing that

the region had a well-established agricultural economy.

- **Pottery**: The excavation unearthed a large number of painted and unpainted pots, which are important for understanding the artistic and cultural practices of the Harappans.

14.1.2 Ahar and Balathal: Chalcolithic Culture

The sites of **Ahar** and **Balathal**, located in **Udaipur district**, represent some of the most important **Chalcolithic** (Copper Age) settlements in Rajasthan, dating from **3000 BCE to 1500 BCE**. These sites provide evidence of early human settlements that practiced agriculture, metallurgy, and pottery production.

- **Key Findings at Ahar**:
    - **Copper Artifacts**: Ahar is often referred to as the **Copper Age Culture** because of the large number of copper artifacts discovered at the site. Tools, weapons, and ornaments made from copper suggest the inhabitants had advanced metallurgical skills.
    - **Red-Black Pottery**: The Ahar culture is also known for its distinctive **Red-Black Ware** pottery, characterized by red slip with black designs, which has been found in abundance at the site.

- **Granaries**: The discovery of large **granaries** suggests that the Ahar people were engaged in large-scale grain storage and trade, which indicates a settled agricultural lifestyle.

- **Key Findings at Balathal**:
  - **Stone Structures**: Balathal has yielded evidence of well-planned stone houses, indicative of a settled, organized society.
  - **Burial Sites**: The excavation of **burial sites** provides insight into the burial practices of the Chalcolithic people, who buried their dead with grave goods like pottery and copper ornaments.
  - **Agricultural Tools**: Various stone tools used for agriculture have been discovered, suggesting that the people of Balathal were engaged in farming and domestication of animals.

14.1.3 Bairat: A Buddhist Site

Bairat, located in the **Jaipur district**, is an important **Buddhist archaeological site** dating back to the **Mauryan period**. The site has yielded significant evidence of early Buddhism, including remnants of **stupas** and **monastic complexes**.

- **Key Findings**:
  - **Ashokan Edicts**: One of the most notable finds at Bairat is the **rock edict of Emperor Ashoka**, dating to the **3rd century BCE**. This edict contains one of Ashoka's famous inscriptions promoting Buddhist teachings and ethical governance.
  - **Stupa Remains**: Excavations have revealed the remains of a **Buddhist stupa**, which was likely an important religious center for Buddhist monks in ancient times.
  - **Monastic Complex**: Remnants of a **monastery** were also found, indicating that Bairat was a thriving center of Buddhist learning and culture during the Mauryan and post-Mauryan periods.

14.1.4 Bagor: A Mesolithic Site

The **Bagor** site, located on the banks of the **Kothari River** in the **Bhilwara district**, is one of the largest **Mesolithic** (Middle Stone Age) settlements in India. Excavations at Bagor have revealed evidence of early human occupation, dating back to around **5000 BCE**.

- **Key Findings**:
  - **Microliths**: The most significant discovery at Bagor is the large number of **microliths**, small stone tools

that were used for hunting and other daily activities. These tools are made of **chert**, **chalcedony**, and **quartz**.

- **Animal Bones**: The presence of animal bones, particularly from domesticated animals like **cattle**, **sheep**, and **goats**, suggests that the people of Bagor practiced **animal husbandry** alongside hunting and gathering.

- **Circular Huts**: Excavations also revealed the remains of circular **hut-like structures**, which indicate the early development of settled communities in the region.

14.1.5 Osian: Temple Architecture and Sculptures

The town of **Osian**, located in the **Jodhpur district**, is famous for its **temples** and sculptures dating from the **8th to the 12th centuries** CE. Osian was a significant center of Brahmanical and Jain religious activities during the early medieval period, and its temples reflect a high level of architectural and artistic achievement.

- Key Findings:

  - **Hindu and Jain Temples**: The site has yielded several important temples, including the **Sun Temple**, **Harihara Temples**, and **Mahavira Temple**. These temples are remarkable for their intricate carvings and unique architectural styles.

- **Sculptures**: The temples of Osian are adorned with exquisitely carved **sculptures**, including figures of gods, goddesses, and mythical creatures. These sculptures provide insights into the religious and cultural symbolism of the time.

- **Architectural Elements**: The temples display advanced techniques of **shikharas** (spires), **mandapas** (pillared halls), and **toranas** (ornate gateways), which influenced later temple architecture in Rajasthan.

14.1.6 Excavations at Jaisalmer: Desert Civilization

The city of **Jaisalmer**, known for its **desert landscape** and historic fort, has also been the site of significant archaeological exploration. Excavations in and around Jaisalmer have revealed evidence of human settlement in the **Thar Desert** dating back to ancient times.

- **Key Findings**:
  - **Pottery and Tools**: Discoveries of **pottery** and **stone tools** suggest that early human communities adapted to the harsh desert environment by developing unique survival strategies.

- **Fortifications**: The **Jaisalmer Fort** itself, which dates back to the **12th century**, has been studied extensively. Archaeologists have uncovered evidence of the fort's construction techniques, water management systems, and defense strategies, which were crucial for survival in the desert.

- **Water Conservation**: The excavation of ancient **stepwells** and **reservoirs** near Jaisalmer highlights the sophisticated water conservation techniques used by the inhabitants of the region to manage scarce resources in the arid desert climate.

14.2 Methods Used in Discovering and Preserving Ancient Sites

The preservation and discovery of ancient sites in Rajasthan necessitate a multifaceted approach that combines advanced technology, meticulous archaeological techniques, and collaborative efforts among various stakeholders. Given the rich historical tapestry of Rajasthan, which includes structures, artifacts, and inscriptions dating back to ancient civilizations, the methods employed in discovering and preserving these sites are crucial for ensuring their integrity and accessibility for future generations.

14.2.1 Archaeological Surveys and Excavations

Archaeological surveys form the cornerstone of discovering ancient sites. These surveys involve systematic investigations of specific geographic areas to identify potential archaeological sites. In Rajasthan, archaeologists employ both **field surveys** and **remote sensing** techniques to locate ancient structures and artifacts. Field surveys often include walking across landscapes, documenting the location of surface artifacts, and assessing the potential for excavation.

Excavations are subsequently conducted to uncover buried materials. These excavations can be **test pits** or larger trench excavations designed to reveal stratified layers of occupation. Each layer is meticulously documented, and artifacts are carefully cataloged to establish a chronology of human activity at the site. For instance, the excavation of sites like **Kalibangan** has revealed the urban planning and architecture of the **Indus Valley Civilization**, offering invaluable insights into ancient life.

14.2.2 Remote Sensing and Geospatial Technologies

In recent years, the advent of **remote sensing** and **geospatial technologies** has revolutionized the methods used in archaeological discovery. Techniques such as **LiDAR** (Light Detection and Ranging) allow archaeologists to survey vast areas without the need for extensive ground excavation. LiDAR can penetrate forest canopies, revealing previously hidden structures such as temples, roads, and settlements.

Geographical Information Systems (GIS) also play a critical role in analyzing spatial data related to archaeological sites. By layering different types of data—such as topography, hydrology, and settlement patterns—archaeologists can make informed decisions about where to excavate and how to interpret the findings. GIS has been particularly useful in Rajasthan, where the rugged terrain and arid climate can obscure archaeological features.

14.2.3 Scientific Analysis and Dating Techniques

To gain a deeper understanding of the age and context of artifacts, scientists employ various dating techniques, including **radiocarbon dating**, **thermoluminescence dating**, and **optically stimulated luminescence (OSL)**.

- **Radiocarbon dating** is used to date organic materials, providing a timeframe for human activity at a site. This technique has been instrumental in dating archaeological remains from the **Neolithic** to the **Medieval period** in Rajasthan.

- **Thermoluminescence** and **OSL** are used for dating ceramics and sediments, respectively. These techniques measure the last time the materials were exposed to heat or light, providing further context for the artifacts' chronological placement within a site's stratigraphy.

The results from these scientific analyses contribute to a more nuanced understanding of Rajasthan's historical timeline and the interactions between various cultures.

14.2.4 Conservation Techniques and Practices

Once ancient sites are discovered, the focus shifts to their preservation. Effective conservation methods are vital for protecting these sites from deterioration due to environmental factors, tourism, and human activity.

- **Site management plans** are often developed to outline specific strategies for conservation, including stabilization of structures, restoration of damaged areas, and visitor management practices. For instance, in places like **Chittorgarh Fort**, ongoing efforts have been made to preserve its ramparts and palaces while accommodating tourism.

- **Materials conservation** is another critical aspect. Conservators analyze the materials used in ancient structures, developing techniques to repair or replace damaged sections while maintaining historical authenticity. This includes using compatible materials and traditional building techniques to ensure that restorations blend seamlessly with the original structure.

- **Climate monitoring** is also essential. Changes in temperature and humidity can significantly affect the integrity of archaeological sites. By implementing climate control measures and utilizing technology to monitor environmental conditions, archaeologists can take proactive steps to mitigate potential damage.

14.2.5 Community Involvement and Education

Engaging local communities in the discovery and preservation of archaeological sites has proven to be a successful strategy. Local populations often possess invaluable knowledge about their region's history and geography. By involving them in the preservation process, archaeologists foster a sense of ownership and pride in the cultural heritage of their area.

- **Public education** programs play a crucial role in raising awareness about the importance of preserving archaeological sites. Workshops, guided tours, and informational materials can educate both locals and tourists about the significance of these sites, encouraging responsible visitation and stewardship.

- Collaborations between archaeologists and local governments can also lead to more effective preservation strategies. Initiatives that promote sustainable tourism can benefit both the economy and the preservation of archaeological sites.

14.2.6 Legal Framework and Policies

The preservation of ancient sites in Rajasthan is supported by legal frameworks and policies established by the **Indian government** and various heritage organizations. Laws such as the **Ancient Monuments and Archaeological Sites and Remains Act** of 1958 provide guidelines for the protection and management of archaeological sites.

- The establishment of **protected sites** ensures that significant archaeological locations are safeguarded from development and degradation. Regular monitoring and enforcement of conservation measures are critical components of these legal frameworks.
- International organizations like **UNESCO** also contribute to preservation efforts. Sites recognized as **World Heritage Sites**, such as the **Hampi** and **Khajuraho** temples, benefit from international funding and expertise for conservation initiatives.

14.2.7 Challenges in Preservation

Despite the robust methods employed in discovering and preserving ancient sites, challenges remain. Urban development and infrastructure projects often threaten archaeological sites, leading to irreversible damage. Balancing modernization with heritage preservation is a continual struggle for archaeologists and heritage advocates.

Additionally, limited funding and resources can hinder conservation efforts. Collaborating with international organizations and securing grants can provide the necessary support for preservation projects.

14.3 Collaborations with National and International Archaeologists

The field of archaeology in Rajasthan has greatly benefited from collaborations between **national** and **international** archaeologists. These partnerships have fostered a rich exchange of knowledge, techniques, and resources, leading to significant advancements in the understanding of the region's archaeological heritage. By bringing together diverse perspectives and expertise, these collaborations enhance research quality and promote a holistic approach to preserving and interpreting Rajasthan's archaeological sites.

14.3.1 Significance of Collaborations in Archaeological Research

Collaborations in archaeology play a critical role in addressing complex research questions and enhancing the overall impact of archaeological projects. National and international archaeologists bring distinct methodologies, cultural backgrounds, and academic experiences that enrich the research landscape. Such partnerships can facilitate the following:

- **Resource Sharing**: Collaborative efforts often lead to the pooling of resources, including funding, equipment, and personnel. This shared approach enables more extensive fieldwork, advanced technology usage, and access to specialized knowledge that might be lacking in a single institution or region.

- **Knowledge Exchange**: Collaborations promote the sharing of expertise in various fields, such as **geophysics**, **remote sensing**, **conservation techniques**, and **historical research methods**. This exchange of knowledge contributes to refining research methodologies and expanding the scope of archaeological inquiries.

- **Enhanced Publication Opportunities**: Working with international archaeologists can improve the visibility of research findings. Collaborative publications often reach broader audiences, raising awareness of Rajasthan's archaeological significance and attracting more attention from scholars and enthusiasts worldwide.

14.3.2 Case Studies of Successful Collaborations

Numerous successful collaborations have emerged in Rajasthan, demonstrating the efficacy of partnerships in archaeological research.

- **The Rajasthan Archaeological Project**: This initiative involves collaborations between Indian archaeologists and international experts from institutions like the **University of Pennsylvania** and the **University of California**. The project focuses on understanding the early urbanization of Rajasthan and its connections with the broader Indian subcontinent. Through systematic excavations, these collaborative efforts have revealed significant urban planning features in sites like **Kalibangan** and **Ahar**, enhancing our understanding of the **Indus Valley Civilization**'s influence on the region.

- **Buddhist Sites Excavation**: The excavation of important Buddhist sites in Rajasthan, such as **Sanchi** and **Ajmer**, has attracted collaborative efforts from both national and international archaeologists. Teams comprising members from **Indian universities** and international institutions like **Harvard University** have conducted extensive research on the architectural styles and artistic expressions present at these sites. The collaboration has resulted in the publication of comprehensive studies and reports that detail the evolution of Buddhist architecture in Rajasthan, shedding light on its cultural significance.

- **Desert Archaeology Project**: This project, which focuses on the archaeological exploration of the **Thar Desert**, involves collaborations between Indian archaeologists and international teams from universities in the **United States**, **Germany**, and **France**. The project aims to investigate ancient trade routes, settlement patterns, and the interaction between nomadic and settled communities in the desert. By combining archaeological excavations, **geospatial analysis**, and **ethnographic studies**, this collaborative effort has generated a wealth of data that enhances our understanding of Rajasthan's past.

14.3.3 Challenges in Collaborative Archaeological Efforts

Despite the numerous benefits, collaborative archaeological projects can also face challenges:

- **Cultural Differences**: Different cultural perspectives and academic practices may lead to misunderstandings or conflicts among collaborators. It is crucial to establish clear communication channels and shared goals from the outset to mitigate these issues.

- **Funding and Resource Allocation**: Collaborations often require substantial funding and resource allocation, which can be a complex process. Securing funding from multiple sources can complicate project management, necessitating transparency and effective planning.

- **Intellectual Property Rights**: The question of intellectual property rights can arise in collaborative projects, particularly when it comes to the ownership of research findings and published materials. Establishing clear agreements regarding authorship and data sharing is essential to avoid potential disputes.

14.3.4 Future Directions for Collaborative Archaeology

As archaeological research continues to evolve, there are several potential directions for enhancing collaborations between national and international archaeologists in Rajasthan:

1. **Leveraging Technology**: The integration of modern technology, such as **3D modeling**, **remote sensing**, and **geographic information systems (GIS)**, can facilitate joint research initiatives. Collaborative projects can benefit from using cutting-edge tools to analyze archaeological sites and improve data collection and analysis.

2. **Public Engagement**: Collaborative efforts can extend beyond academic circles to include local communities. Engaging with local stakeholders and fostering public interest in archaeology can lead to greater support for preservation initiatives and increased awareness of Rajasthan's cultural heritage.

3. **Sustainable Practices**: Promoting sustainable archaeological practices through collaboration is

essential for preserving Rajasthan's archaeological sites. International collaborations can help implement best practices for site management, conservation, and heritage preservation.

4. **Capacity Building**: Establishing training programs for local archaeologists and students can empower communities and promote sustainable archaeological practices. International collaborators can contribute expertise and resources to enhance the skills of the local workforce, fostering a new generation of archaeologists in Rajasthan.

CHAPTER FIFTEEN

Challenges in Preserving Rajasthan's Archaeological Heritage

15.1 Issues of Conservation and Restoration

The archaeological heritage of Rajasthan, characterized by its ancient temples, forts, palaces, and various historical sites, represents an invaluable asset to both Indian culture and the global historical narrative. However, these sites face numerous challenges related to conservation and restoration. This chapter will delve into the key issues confronting the conservation and restoration efforts in Rajasthan, emphasizing the importance of preserving this rich cultural heritage for future generations.

15.1.1 The Impact of Natural Elements

Rajasthan's climate is primarily characterized by extreme temperatures, arid conditions, and seasonal monsoons. These environmental factors pose significant challenges to the preservation of archaeological sites.

- **Erosion**: The strong winds and occasional rain can lead to erosion, causing damage to ancient structures. Over time, this can result in the degradation of walls, sculptures, and intricate carvings.

- **Salt Crystallization**: In regions with high salinity in the soil, salt crystallization occurs when moisture evaporates, leading to the deterioration of stone materials. This phenomenon affects many historical buildings, particularly those constructed from sandstone and limestone, which are prevalent in Rajasthan.

- **Vegetation Growth**: The growth of vegetation, particularly roots of trees and shrubs, can cause structural instability. These roots can penetrate cracks in the stone, further exacerbating the deterioration process.

15.1.2 Human Activities and Urbanization

Rapid urbanization and development in Rajasthan have led to significant threats to archaeological sites. As cities expand, many historical sites find themselves in precarious situations.

- **Encroachment**: With increasing population density, there is often encroachment on archaeological sites. Buildings, roads, and other infrastructure can impede access to these sites and cause direct damage to the structures.

- **Pollution**: Urban pollution, including air and water pollution, poses a significant threat to the integrity of archaeological sites. Pollutants can lead to the chemical deterioration of stone materials, affecting the structural and aesthetic aspects of these historical sites.

- **Tourism Pressure**: While tourism is vital for the local economy, it can also lead to the degradation of archaeological sites. Increased foot traffic can wear down stone surfaces, and inadequate visitor management can result in vandalism or unintended damage to delicate structures.

15.1.3 Inadequate Funding and Resources

Conservation and restoration projects require substantial funding and resources. Unfortunately, many archaeological sites in Rajasthan face financial constraints that limit effective conservation efforts.

- **Lack of Government Support**: Despite the rich cultural heritage of Rajasthan, there often is inadequate government support and funding allocated for the preservation of archaeological sites. This lack of financial resources can hinder necessary restoration work, leaving sites vulnerable to further deterioration.

- **Insufficient Training and Expertise**: Effective conservation requires skilled professionals with knowledge in archaeology, architecture, and materials science. However, there is often a shortage of trained conservationists, making it difficult to undertake comprehensive restoration projects.

- **Prioritization of Projects**: Limited resources also mean that conservation efforts may not prioritize the most vulnerable sites. As a result, many important sites may remain neglected while others receive attention, leading to uneven conservation efforts across the state.

15.1.4 Ethical Considerations in Restoration

Restoration efforts often raise ethical questions about authenticity and the role of intervention in preserving archaeological heritage.

- **Authenticity vs. Restoration**: There is an ongoing debate among conservationists regarding the extent to which restoration should be undertaken. While some argue for minimal intervention to maintain the authenticity of a site, others advocate for more extensive restoration to prevent further decay. This debate is especially significant in a region like Rajasthan, where many structures are deeply intertwined with local cultural identity.

- **Cultural Sensitivity**: Restoration efforts should also be sensitive to the cultural and spiritual significance of a site. Many archaeological sites in Rajasthan are not merely historical relics but are still active places of worship or cultural practices. Conservationists must consider the beliefs and practices of local communities when planning restoration projects.

- **Public Involvement**: Engaging local communities in conservation efforts can enhance the effectiveness of restoration projects. However, balancing expert opinions with local knowledge and concerns can be challenging. Fostering a sense of ownership and pride among local residents is crucial for the long-term success of conservation efforts.

15.1.5 Case Studies of Conservation Efforts

Several notable conservation projects in Rajasthan serve as examples of both the challenges and successes in archaeological preservation.

- **Restoration of Chittorgarh Fort**: This UNESCO World Heritage Site has undergone significant restoration efforts in recent years. The challenges faced during this project included addressing structural instability and preserving the fort's historical authenticity. The restoration process involved careful planning, extensive research, and collaboration with local experts to ensure that the fort retains its historical significance.

- **Conservation of Dilwara Temples**: The Dilwara Temples in **Mount Abu**, known for their intricate marble carvings, have faced threats from pollution and tourism. Restoration efforts have focused on cleaning the carvings and controlling visitor access to prevent further wear. The project emphasizes the importance of public awareness and education regarding the significance of preserving such sites.

- **Revival of Jaisalmer Fort**: The Jaisalmer Fort, a living fort with residents and businesses, has faced challenges related to urbanization and tourism. Efforts to balance the needs of the local population while preserving the fort's historical integrity are ongoing. Restoration projects have aimed to address structural issues while maintaining the fort's unique character.

15.2 Impact of Urbanization and Tourism on Archaeological Sites

Urbanization and tourism significantly impact archaeological sites in Rajasthan, a region celebrated for its rich history and cultural heritage. As cities expand and tourism flourishes, the pressures on these ancient sites intensify, posing challenges to their preservation and integrity. Understanding these impacts is crucial for implementing effective management strategies that balance development, tourism, and the safeguarding of archaeological heritage.

15.2.1 Urbanization and Its Effects

Urbanization in Rajasthan has been accelerated by population growth, economic development, and migration. Cities like Jaipur, Udaipur, and Jodhpur have witnessed rapid expansion, often encroaching upon archaeological sites and historical landmarks.

- **Land Use Changes**: As urban areas expand, the demand for land increases, leading to the conversion of open spaces, including archaeological sites, into residential, commercial, and industrial zones. This encroachment can result in the destruction of historical structures and artifacts, diminishing the cultural landscape.

- **Infrastructure Development**: Urbanization typically involves significant infrastructure projects, such as roads, bridges, and public utilities. Such development can disturb archaeological layers and lead to irreversible damage. For instance, construction activities in areas adjacent to sites like **Chittorgarh Fort** have raised concerns about the potential destruction of ancient remains buried beneath the surface.

- **Pollution and Environmental Degradation**: The rapid growth of urban centers brings about increased pollution, including air, water, and noise pollution. These factors can negatively affect the preservation of ancient structures, which may be susceptible to deterioration from environmental stressors. The historic sandstone used in many Rajput forts and palaces can erode due to pollutants, leading to costly repairs and restoration efforts.

15.2.2 Tourism and Its Dual Nature

Tourism is a double-edged sword for archaeological sites in Rajasthan. On one hand, it provides economic benefits and promotes cultural awareness; on the other, it poses significant risks to the preservation of these sites.

- **Economic Benefits**: Tourism generates revenue for local economies and creates jobs in various sectors, including hospitality, transportation, and crafts. Historical sites such as the **Hawa Mahal**, **Amber Fort**, and **Mehrangarh Fort** attract millions of visitors annually, contributing significantly to Rajasthan's economy. This financial influx can be reinvested into site maintenance, conservation, and community development.

- **Visitor Impact**: The influx of tourists can lead to physical wear and tear on archaeological sites. High foot traffic can damage fragile structures, erode pathways, and displace artifacts. For example, the delicate frescoes in the **City Palace** in Jaipur face deterioration due to exposure to sunlight and humidity, exacerbated by the large number of visitors.

- **Commercialization**: The commodification of heritage sites can dilute their cultural significance. To cater to tourists, some sites may undergo alterations, such as the addition of modern amenities or entertainment facilities, which can undermine their historical authenticity. The **Pushkar Camel Fair**, while a vibrant cultural event, exemplifies how commercialization can overshadow the intrinsic value of local traditions and heritage.

15.2.3 Challenges in Management and Conservation

The challenges posed by urbanization and tourism require effective management strategies to protect archaeological sites in Rajasthan.

- **Balancing Development and Preservation**: Policymakers and heritage organizations must find ways to accommodate urban growth while safeguarding archaeological sites. This may involve establishing **buffer zones** around sensitive areas, restricting development activities, and promoting sustainable land-use practices that consider the historical context of the region.

- **Implementing Sustainable Tourism Practices**: Encouraging sustainable tourism can help mitigate the negative impacts on archaeological sites. Initiatives such as **visitor management** plans, education programs, and eco-friendly tourism practices can ensure that tourism contributes positively to site preservation. For example, limiting the number of visitors at certain times or implementing guided tours can help reduce wear on fragile areas.

- **Community Involvement**: Engaging local communities in the management and preservation of archaeological sites can lead to more effective conservation efforts. By fostering a sense of ownership and pride in their heritage, communities are more likely to support preservation initiatives. Training local guides and artisans can also enhance the cultural experience for tourists while promoting traditional crafts.

15.2.4 Case Studies of Impact

Several notable case studies illustrate the impacts of urbanization and tourism on archaeological sites in Rajasthan:

- **Amber Fort**: The Amber Fort, a UNESCO World Heritage Site, attracts thousands of tourists daily. While tourism has spurred local economic development, the sheer volume of visitors has led to concerns about the degradation of the fort's structures and artifacts. Efforts are underway to implement visitor management systems and conservation programs to address these challenges.

- **Hawa Mahal**: The Hawa Mahal, known for its intricate latticework and architectural beauty, faces challenges related to tourism. Measures to control foot traffic and enhance site maintenance are crucial to preserving its unique features.

- **Ranakpur Temples**: The Ranakpur Temples, renowned for their stunning marble architecture, have implemented strict guidelines to control visitor access and ensure the conservation of their intricate carvings. This approach serves as a model for managing tourism while preserving the site's integrity.

15.2.5 Future Directions and Recommendations

To ensure the preservation of Rajasthan's archaeological heritage in the face of urbanization and tourism, several recommendations can be made:

- **Integrated Planning**: Urban planning should incorporate archaeological considerations, with input from archaeologists, conservationists, and local communities. This collaborative approach can help mitigate the negative effects of urban expansion.

- **Investment in Conservation**: Increased funding and resources for archaeological research and site management are essential for effective preservation efforts. Partnerships with international organizations and NGOs can provide additional support for conservation initiatives.

- **Public Awareness Campaigns**: Raising awareness about the significance of archaeological sites among tourists and locals can foster a culture of respect and responsibility towards heritage preservation. Educational programs can emphasize the importance of protecting these sites for future generations.

15.3 Efforts by Government and Non-Governmental Organizations

The archaeological landscape of Rajasthan is enriched by the concerted efforts of both governmental and non-governmental organizations (NGOs). These entities work collaboratively to preserve, protect, and promote the region's archaeological heritage, ensuring that it is not only studied and understood but also appreciated by future generations. This section will discuss the various initiatives undertaken by government bodies and NGOs, highlighting their roles in archaeological research, conservation, education, and community engagement.

15.3.1 Government Initiatives in Archaeology

The government of Rajasthan plays a pivotal role in promoting archaeological studies and heritage conservation. Several departments and agencies are involved in these efforts:

- **Archaeological Survey of India (ASI)**: The ASI is the primary national body responsible for archaeological research and the protection of cultural heritage in India. In Rajasthan, the ASI has been instrumental in conducting excavations, documenting historical sites, and implementing conservation projects. Notable initiatives include the restoration of key monuments, such as the **Hawa Mahal** and the **Amber Fort**, which attract thousands of tourists each year.

- **Rajasthan State Archaeology Department**: This department focuses on the archaeological research specific to the state. It undertakes surveys, excavations, and conservation efforts at various sites across Rajasthan, including **Kalibangan**, **Ahar**, and **Bikaner**. The department also organizes seminars and workshops to promote research and raise awareness about the importance of preserving Rajasthan's archaeological heritage.

- **Tourism Development Initiatives**: The Rajasthan government recognizes the economic potential of its archaeological sites in attracting tourists. Through various tourism development schemes, the government promotes heritage tourism, which directly benefits local communities and enhances funding for archaeological projects. The establishment of **Heritage Walks** and **Cultural Festivals** in cities like **Jaipur** and **Udaipur** draws attention to the state's rich cultural heritage and encourages visitors to explore archaeological sites.

- **Legislative Measures**: The government has enacted laws and policies to protect archaeological sites and monuments. The **Ancient Monuments and Archaeological Sites and Remains Act** is a significant legal framework that governs the preservation of historical structures and sites. This legislation empowers authorities to take action against encroachments and unauthorized construction near archaeological sites, ensuring their integrity is maintained.

15.3.2 Non-Governmental Organizations and Their Contributions

Non-governmental organizations play a crucial role in complementing government efforts in archaeological preservation and education. These organizations often focus on community engagement, advocacy, and capacity-building initiatives.

- **INTACH (Indian National Trust for Art and Cultural Heritage)**: INTACH is one of the leading NGOs dedicated to heritage conservation in India. In Rajasthan, INTACH works on various projects aimed at raising awareness about the importance of preserving cultural heritage. The organization conducts workshops, training sessions, and heritage walks, engaging local communities in the conservation process and fostering a sense of ownership over their cultural resources.

- **Rajasthan Patrika Foundation**: This NGO focuses on promoting awareness about Rajasthan's cultural heritage through educational programs and public campaigns. The foundation organizes exhibitions, lectures, and workshops to educate the public about the significance of archaeological sites and the need for their preservation. Their efforts help inspire community involvement in conservation activities and foster a deeper appreciation for Rajasthan's rich history.

- **Heritage Trusts and Local NGOs**: Various local NGOs and heritage trusts in Rajasthan work tirelessly to preserve and promote specific sites or communities. For instance, the **Bikaner Heritage Trust** focuses on preserving the architectural heritage of Bikaner and promoting sustainable tourism practices. These organizations often collaborate with local artisans, encouraging traditional crafts and skills that contribute to the preservation of cultural heritage.

15.3.3 Community Engagement and Education

Both government and NGOs recognize the importance of community involvement in archaeological preservation. Engaging local communities ensures that they understand the value of their heritage and actively participate in its conservation.

- **Awareness Programs**: Educational programs aimed at schools and local communities emphasize the importance of Rajasthan's archaeological heritage. Workshops and seminars organized by government bodies and NGOs help disseminate knowledge about local history, encouraging younger generations to take an active interest in preserving their cultural heritage.

- **Volunteer Programs**: Some NGOs offer volunteer programs that allow local residents to participate in archaeological excavations and conservation projects. These programs foster a sense of pride in local heritage and empower communities to take ownership of their archaeological sites.

- **Heritage Festivals**: Events such as heritage festivals and cultural fairs celebrate Rajasthan's rich history and traditions. These events often feature exhibitions, performances, and workshops that highlight local arts and crafts, promoting cultural tourism and raising awareness about the importance of heritage conservation.

15.3.4 Challenges and Future Directions

Despite the significant efforts made by government and non-government organizations, several challenges remain in the preservation of Rajasthan's archaeological heritage:

- **Funding Constraints**: Limited financial resources can hinder the implementation of conservation projects and research initiatives. Securing sustained funding from both government and private sources is essential for the long-term success of preservation efforts.

- **Balancing Development and Conservation**: Rapid urbanization and infrastructure development pose significant threats to archaeological sites. Finding a balance between development needs and the preservation of cultural heritage is a complex challenge that requires collaborative planning and innovative solutions.

- **Awareness and Advocacy**: While efforts have been made to raise awareness about the importance of archaeological preservation, there is still a need for more extensive advocacy campaigns to engage broader audiences. Collaborations between government bodies, NGOs, and local communities can enhance awareness and promote the significance of Rajasthan's archaeological heritage.

CHAPTER SIXTEEN

The Mysteries of Rajasthan's Lost Cities

16.1 Exploring Lesser-Known Cities: Nagari, Barmer, Osian

Rajasthan, known for its majestic forts, palaces, and vibrant culture, is home to several lesser-known cities that hold immense historical and archaeological significance. Among these cities are **Nagari**, **Barmer**, and **Osian**, each of which offers unique insights into the rich tapestry of Rajasthan's past. While Jaipur, Jodhpur, and Udaipur often steal the spotlight, these lesser-known locations invite exploration and appreciation for their distinct cultural heritage and archaeological findings.

16.1.1 Nagari: The Forgotten Capital

Nestled in the **Chittorgarh district**, **Nagari** was once the capital of the **Mewar kingdom** during the 6th century CE. This ancient city is often overlooked in favor of its more famous neighbors, yet it boasts a wealth of historical significance.

- **Historical Context**: The history of Nagari is intertwined with the rise and fall of the **Mewar dynasty**. Established by **Maharana Kumbha**, the city served as a significant center of trade and commerce during its heyday. However, by the 14th century, Nagari's prominence waned as the capital moved to **Chittorgarh**, leading to its gradual decline.

- **Archaeological Significance**: Archaeological excavations at Nagari have unveiled various remnants of its past, including ruins of palaces, temples, and ancient water reservoirs. Notably, the site features a collection of temples dedicated to **Shiva**, **Vishnu**, and **Goddess Durga**, which exhibit intricate carvings and inscriptions. The most famous temple is the **Siva temple**, known for its remarkable sculptures that depict various deities and mythological scenes.

- **Cultural Heritage**: Nagari's cultural heritage is also reflected in its traditional crafts. The region is known for its skilled artisans who create exquisite pottery, textiles, and jewelry. The local economy is supported by agriculture, particularly the cultivation of crops such as **millets**, **wheat**, and **barley**. This agrarian lifestyle, coupled with traditional craftsmanship, contributes to the unique character of Nagari.

- **Tourism Potential**: Despite its historical importance, Nagari remains relatively unexplored by tourists. This presents an opportunity for heritage tourism, where visitors can immerse themselves in the city's rich history while supporting local artisans and preserving traditional crafts. Efforts to promote Nagari as a tourist destination could include organizing guided tours, cultural festivals, and workshops to showcase local craftsmanship.

16.1.2 Barmer: The Gateway to the Thar Desert

Barmer, located in the western part of Rajasthan, is often associated with the vast **Thar Desert** and its arid landscapes. The city has a rich history and cultural heritage that reflects the resilience and creativity of its inhabitants.

- **Historical Context**: Barmer was founded in the 13th century by **Rao Bar Singh**, and it served as a crucial center for trade and commerce along the ancient trade routes connecting Rajasthan to Gujarat and beyond. The region's strategic location made it a melting pot of cultures, facilitating the exchange of goods and ideas.

- **Archaeological Significance**: Barmer is home to several archaeological sites, including the **Someshwar Temple**, which dates back to the 12th century. This temple showcases intricate carvings and architectural styles influenced by both **Hindu** and **Jain** traditions. The ruins of ancient fortifications, stepwells, and havelis are also scattered throughout the region, providing a glimpse into Barmer's glorious past.

- **Cultural Heritage**: The culture of Barmer is vibrant and diverse, characterized by folk music, dance, and colorful handicrafts. The city is renowned for its **block printing** and **tie-dye textiles**, which are produced using traditional methods passed down through generations. The **Barmer Camel Festival**, held annually, showcases the region's rich cultural heritage, featuring camel races, folk performances, and handicraft exhibitions.

- **Tourism Potential**: Barmer's unique desert landscape and cultural richness offer significant tourism potential. Adventure tourism activities such as camel safaris, desert camping, and cultural tours can attract visitors seeking authentic experiences. Additionally, promoting local handicrafts and supporting artisans can contribute to sustainable economic development in the region.

16.1.3 Osian: The Ancient Oasis

Osian, located near **Jodhpur**, is often referred to as the "Khajuraho of Rajasthan" due to its exquisite temples adorned with intricate carvings. This ancient town, once a flourishing trade center, holds a wealth of historical and architectural significance.

- **Historical Context**: Osian's history dates back to the **6th century CE**, when it served as a prominent center for **Brahmanical** and **Jain** religions. The town thrived during the **Pratihara dynasty**, and its strategic location along trade routes contributed to its prosperity.

- **Archaeological Significance**: Osian is renowned for its ancient temples, particularly the **Suriya Mandir** and **Mahavira Temple**. These temples are notable for their stunning sculptures depicting various deities, celestial beings, and intricate floral motifs. The craftsmanship exhibited in these temples reflects the artistic excellence of the era.

- **Cultural Heritage**: The town's culture is deeply intertwined with its religious significance. Osian is still a site of pilgrimage for many devotees, and the festivals celebrated here attract visitors from far and wide. The local cuisine, influenced by Rajasthani traditions, adds another layer to Osian's cultural heritage. Dishes such as **dal bati churma** and **gatte ki sabzi** are popular among locals and tourists alike.

- **Tourism Potential**: Osian's rich cultural and architectural heritage presents opportunities for heritage tourism. Efforts to promote Osian as a tourist destination could include guided heritage walks, cultural festivals, and culinary experiences that highlight the town's unique traditions. By focusing on sustainable tourism practices, Osian can retain its cultural authenticity while benefiting economically from increased visitor interest.

16.1.4 Challenges and Opportunities

While these lesser-known cities possess immense historical and cultural significance, they face several challenges that need to be addressed to unlock their full potential.

- **Awareness and Promotion**: One of the primary challenges is raising awareness about these cities among tourists and travelers. Unlike popular destinations like Jaipur and Udaipur, Nagari, Barmer, and Osian often remain off the radar for many visitors. Targeted marketing campaigns that highlight their unique attractions, historical importance, and cultural heritage can help draw attention to these cities.

- **Infrastructure Development**: To support tourism, it is essential to invest in infrastructure development. Improving transportation, accommodations, and amenities can enhance the visitor experience and encourage longer stays. Collaboration with local communities and stakeholders is vital to ensure that development aligns with preserving the cultural heritage.

- **Community Involvement**: Engaging local communities in tourism initiatives can foster a sense of ownership and pride in their heritage. By involving local artisans, guides, and residents in tourism activities, these cities can create authentic experiences that benefit both visitors and the local economy.

- **Sustainable Practices**: As tourism grows, it is crucial to adopt sustainable practices that minimize the impact on the environment and cultural heritage. Implementing responsible tourism initiatives, such as promoting eco-friendly accommodations, minimizing waste, and supporting local businesses, can contribute to the long-term sustainability of these destinations.

16.2 Forgotten Histories Unearthed through Archaeological Findings

The state of Rajasthan is not just a tapestry of vibrant cultures and majestic landscapes; it is also a treasure trove of archaeological findings that have the potential to rewrite our understanding of Indian history. Over the years, various excavations and studies in Rajasthan have unearthed artifacts, structures, and inscriptions that reveal insights into the lives, beliefs, and practices of its ancient inhabitants. This chapter explores the forgotten histories of Rajasthan, shedding light on the archaeological discoveries that have unveiled the region's rich past.

16.2.1 The Significance of Archaeological Research

Archaeology serves as a crucial tool in reconstructing histories that have been lost to time. The findings from

Rajasthan illustrate how systematic excavations and studies can reveal stories about early civilizations, social structures, and cultural practices. Understanding these archaeological discoveries is vital for several reasons:

- **Historical Context**: The artifacts and structures discovered in Rajasthan provide essential context for understanding the broader narrative of Indian history. They help fill gaps in our knowledge, revealing how ancient societies developed, interacted, and transformed over time.

- **Cultural Heritage**: Each finding contributes to the rich cultural heritage of Rajasthan, enriching the state's identity and allowing for a deeper appreciation of its diverse traditions. This cultural heritage is an integral part of the identity of both local communities and the nation as a whole.

- **Preservation of Knowledge**: By documenting and preserving archaeological findings, researchers ensure that this knowledge is passed down to future generations. This preservation effort contributes to a sense of pride in local history and fosters a collective identity.

16.2.2 Major Archaeological Discoveries in Rajasthan

Various archaeological sites across Rajasthan have yielded significant findings that have reshaped our understanding of the region's history. Some of the most notable discoveries include:

- **Kalibangan**: An important site of the **Indus Valley Civilization**, Kalibangan, located in the **Hanumangarh district**, has revealed extensive urban planning and agricultural practices. Excavations have unearthed well-planned streets, drainage systems, and evidence of advanced farming techniques, indicating a highly organized society. The discovery of ceramic seals and other artifacts suggests that Kalibangan was a vital center for trade and commerce.

- **Ahar**: Close to **Udaipur**, Ahar is another significant archaeological site linked to the **Chandela dynasty**. Excavations at Ahar have uncovered a complex of burial sites, including **copper and bronze tools**, pottery, and jewelry. The site reflects a rich funerary tradition, highlighting the social stratification and artistic craftsmanship of the time. The findings from Ahar offer insights into the spiritual beliefs and practices of its inhabitants.

- **Brahmapuri**: This site, near **Ajmer**, has gained attention for its unique pottery styles and terracotta figurines. The discoveries at Brahmapuri suggest a flourishing settlement with a vibrant cultural life. The artifacts found here provide evidence of trade connections with other regions, indicating that Rajasthan was part of a larger economic network.

- **Chandravati**: This site, located in **Sirohi district**, is noteworthy for its ancient temples and inscriptions. The discoveries include sculptural representations of deities, indicating the religious practices of the time. Inscriptions in the **Nagari script** provide invaluable information about the historical context and patronage of temple architecture in the region.

16.2.3 Unveiling Social Structures and Daily Life

The archaeological findings in Rajasthan have also shed light on the social structures and daily lives of its ancient inhabitants. Various artifacts have revealed insights into their economic activities, domestic life, and cultural practices.

- **Economic Activities**: The presence of tools and implements indicates a diverse range of economic activities. Evidence of agriculture, pottery, metallurgy, and trade suggests that ancient communities in Rajasthan were economically vibrant. The discovery of weights and measures points to a sophisticated trading system, reflecting the region's role in ancient commerce.

- **Domestic Life**: Excavations have revealed the remnants of dwellings, including mud-brick houses and cooking utensils. These findings provide a glimpse into the daily lives of ancient residents, their dietary habits, and their domestic routines. The presence of storage jars and cooking pots indicates the importance of agriculture and food preparation in their daily lives.

- **Cultural Practices**: Artifacts such as figurines, pottery, and jewelry reflect the artistic expressions and cultural practices of the time. These items not only showcase the craftsmanship of ancient artisans but also provide insights into the spiritual beliefs and rituals practiced by these communities. For instance, terracotta figurines discovered at various sites often depict fertility symbols, indicating the importance of agricultural fertility in their beliefs.

16.2.4 The Role of Inscriptions in Understanding History

Inscriptions play a crucial role in understanding the historical context of Rajasthan. They provide direct evidence of political, social, and cultural developments in the region.

- **Political History**: Inscriptions from various dynasties, such as the **Mauryas**, **Guptas**, and **Rajputs**, shed light on the political landscape of Rajasthan. They often commemorate victories, royal decrees, and patronage of temples, offering insights into the power dynamics of the time.

- **Cultural Continuity**: Inscriptions also highlight the continuity of cultural practices over centuries. Many inscriptions reference local deities and rituals, demonstrating how ancient beliefs have persisted through time. This continuity of culture is essential for understanding the identity of contemporary Rajasthan.

- **Language and Script**: The variety of scripts found in inscriptions, including **Brahmi**, **Kharosthi**, and **Nagari**, reflects the linguistic diversity of the region. Studying these inscriptions not only enhances our understanding of historical languages but also provides insights into the evolution of written communication in Rajasthan.

16.2.5 The Future of Archaeological Research in Rajasthan

Despite the significant findings, there is still much to uncover in Rajasthan. Continued archaeological research is essential to further understanding the region's rich history.

- **Multidisciplinary Approaches**: Future archaeological endeavors should adopt multidisciplinary approaches that integrate archaeology with history, anthropology, and environmental studies. This holistic perspective can provide a more comprehensive understanding of the region's past.

- **Community Involvement**: Engaging local communities in archaeological research can foster a sense of ownership and pride in their heritage. Community participation in excavations, documentation, and preservation efforts can enhance the sustainability of archaeological projects.

- **Technological Advancements**: The incorporation of modern technologies, such as remote sensing, GIS mapping, and 3D modeling, can significantly enhance archaeological research. These technologies can facilitate the documentation of sites and provide insights into ancient landscapes, allowing researchers to visualize historical settlements and trade routes.

- **Awareness and Education**: Raising awareness about the importance of archaeological findings is crucial for garnering public interest and support. Educational programs, workshops, and exhibitions can help bridge the gap between academia and the general public, fostering a greater appreciation for the region's heritage.

16.3 Theories Around the Decline of These Cities

The decline of ancient cities is a recurring theme in the study of history, and Rajasthan is no exception. As a region marked by the rise and fall of various civilizations, the archaeological record reflects significant shifts in population, economy, and culture. This chapter explores the various theories surrounding the decline of lesser-known cities in Rajasthan, such as Nagari, Barmer, and Osian, examining factors that contributed to their diminished prominence over time.

16.3.1 Environmental Factors

One of the primary theories surrounding the decline of ancient cities in Rajasthan is the impact of environmental changes. The region's arid climate and vulnerability to fluctuations in weather patterns have historically influenced agricultural productivity and resource availability.

- **Climate Change**: Research suggests that climatic shifts, including prolonged droughts or sudden shifts to wetter conditions, could have severely impacted the agricultural viability of these cities. As agriculture formed the backbone of the economy, any decline in crop yields would have led to food shortages, population displacement, and ultimately, urban decline. For instance, Nagari's decline is believed to have coincided with a period of decreased rainfall, making it increasingly difficult to sustain its population.

- **Resource Depletion**: Overexploitation of local resources, such as water and timber, could have contributed to the decline of these cities. As populations grew, the demand for resources intensified, leading to unsustainable practices. In areas like Barmer, where water scarcity is a persistent issue, the inability to maintain adequate water supply systems could have severely hampered agricultural and economic activities.

16.3.2 Socio-Political Factors

The socio-political dynamics of the region played a crucial role in shaping the fortunes of its cities. Various internal and external pressures often led to the decline of urban centers.

- **Dynastic Changes**: The rise and fall of ruling dynasties significantly influenced the political landscape of Rajasthan. For example, as the **Rajput clans** fought for control, many smaller cities lost their autonomy and significance. In Nagari, shifting power dynamics led to a loss of political importance as the capital moved to **Chittorgarh**, resulting in decreased investment in local infrastructure and security.

- **Invasions and Conflicts**: Invasions by external forces, such as the **Mughals**, **Afghans**, and later the British, had profound effects on the stability of local governments. Osian, which thrived during the **Pratihara dynasty**, faced considerable disruption as power shifted to larger, more fortified cities. These conflicts not only led to destruction but also caused populations to flee, further accelerating urban decline.

- **Social Unrest**: Internal conflicts, including disputes among local clans and societal divisions, could have led to instability. As rival factions vied for control, cities like Barmer experienced internal strife, weakening their administrative structures and reducing their ability to govern effectively.

16.3.3 Economic Decline

The economic foundations of ancient cities were critical to their sustainability. As trade routes shifted and economic practices evolved, many cities faced challenges that contributed to their decline.

- **Trade Route Changes**: The strategic locations of cities like Nagari and Barmer once made them significant trading hubs. However, changes in trade routes, especially during periods of political turmoil, could lead to economic isolation. As trade shifted toward larger cities, the economies of smaller towns dwindled, making them less viable.

- **Decline of Traditional Industries**: Many ancient cities thrived on specific industries, such as agriculture, pottery, and textile production. As demand for these goods changed or competition increased, the economic base of these cities weakened. The decline of local crafts and traditional industries could lead to a loss of livelihoods, prompting migration to more prosperous areas.

16.3.4 Cultural and Religious Shifts

Cultural and religious changes also played a role in the decline of cities in Rajasthan, particularly as new beliefs and practices emerged.

- **Shifts in Religious Practices**: The rise of new religious movements or the spread of different belief systems can lead to the decline of established cultural practices. In cities like Osian, the prominence of **Brahmanical** traditions may have waned with the growth of **Jainism** and later **Islam**, affecting local patronage of temples and shrines.

- **Cultural Assimilation**: As cities were absorbed into larger empires or experienced demographic changes, their cultural identities often transformed. The fusion of different cultures may have led to the dilution of local traditions, contributing to a sense of loss and decline among residents.

16.3.5 Archaeological Evidence and Case Studies

Archaeological findings provide crucial evidence to support these theories of decline. Excavations and studies in Nagari, Barmer, and Osian reveal patterns that align with the aforementioned factors.

- **Nagari**: Archaeological excavations in Nagari indicate a decline in urban infrastructure and agricultural practices. The remnants of abandoned structures and a decrease in artifact diversity suggest that the city's population dwindled significantly as agricultural challenges mounted.

- **Barmer**: In Barmer, archaeological studies have uncovered evidence of resource depletion, particularly concerning water management systems. The remnants of ancient stepwells indicate attempts to adapt to water scarcity, but their eventual abandonment points to the challenges faced by the city in sustaining its population.

- **Osian**: The temples in Osian, once thriving centers of worship, show signs of neglect over time. Inscriptions indicate a decline in patronage, aligning with the broader cultural shifts as the region transitioned into new religious paradigms.

CHAPTER SEVENTEEN

Rajasthan's Desert Civilizations: Life Amidst the Dunes

17.1 How Ancient Civilizations Adapted to the Thar Desert

The Thar Desert, also known as the Great Indian Desert, stretches across the northwestern part of India and eastern Pakistan. This expansive desert, characterized by its arid climate, sandy terrain, and extreme temperature variations, presents unique challenges to human habitation. Despite these harsh conditions, ancient civilizations flourished in the Thar Desert, demonstrating remarkable adaptability and resilience. This chapter explores the various ways in which these civilizations adapted to their environment, focusing on their strategies for water management, agriculture, trade, and social organization.

17.1.1 Water Management Strategies

Water is the lifeblood of any civilization, and in the arid expanse of the Thar Desert, effective water management was crucial for survival. Ancient communities developed innovative techniques to harness and conserve water resources, allowing them to thrive in an otherwise inhospitable environment.

- **Stepwells and Tanks**: One of the most notable engineering achievements in the Thar Desert was the construction of stepwells and tanks. These structures served as reservoirs for storing rainwater, providing a reliable water source during the dry months. Stepwells were often adorned with intricate carvings and served not only practical purposes but also as sites for social and religious gatherings. The famous **Baoris** of Rajasthan, such as the **Rani Padmini Baori** in Chittorgarh, exemplify the sophisticated water management techniques employed by ancient civilizations.

- **Canals and Irrigation**: Ancient inhabitants also constructed canals and irrigation systems to divert water from rivers and streams to their agricultural fields. The **Ghaggar-Hakra River**, which once flowed through the region, was utilized for irrigation, enabling the cultivation of crops in an otherwise barren landscape. These irrigation practices not only sustained local agriculture but also supported larger populations, contributing to the development of settlements.

- **Rainwater Harvesting**: Recognizing the sporadic nature of rainfall in the Thar Desert, ancient communities developed methods for rainwater harvesting. They constructed ponds and small embankments to capture and store runoff during the monsoon season. These techniques not only provided water for drinking and irrigation but also helped recharge groundwater supplies, ensuring long-term sustainability.

17.1.2 Agricultural Adaptations

Agriculture in the Thar Desert required innovative approaches to cope with limited water availability and extreme temperatures. Ancient civilizations developed a range of agricultural practices tailored to the unique conditions of the desert environment.

- **Crop Selection**: The choice of crops was critical for success in the Thar Desert. Ancient farmers opted for drought-resistant varieties, such as **millets**, **barley**, and **gram**, which could thrive in sandy soils with minimal water. These hardy crops were well-suited to the desert's climatic conditions and provided essential nutrition for local populations.

- **Mixed Farming**: Many ancient communities practiced mixed farming, combining crop cultivation with animal husbandry. This approach provided a diversified source of food and income. Livestock, such as camels, goats, and sheep, not only supplied meat and milk but also served as vital transportation for goods across the vast desert landscape. The symbiotic relationship between crops and livestock enhanced the resilience of these communities.

- **Transhumance**: Some groups engaged in transhumance, a practice of seasonal movement with livestock to access grazing lands. As vegetation varied throughout the year, herders would migrate between higher altitudes in the summer and the desert plains in the winter. This adaptive strategy allowed communities to optimize their resource use and maintain livestock health, ensuring food security.

17.1.3 Trade and Economic Networks

The Thar Desert's arid landscape did not isolate ancient civilizations; rather, it became a conduit for trade and cultural exchange. The strategic location of settlements within the desert facilitated connections between different regions, allowing for the exchange of goods, ideas, and technologies.

- **Trade Routes**: The Thar Desert served as a crucial link between the Indian subcontinent and Central Asia. Ancient trade routes traversed the desert, enabling the movement of valuable commodities such as spices, textiles, and precious metals. Towns like **Osian** and **Bikaner** emerged as key trading hubs, attracting merchants and travelers from distant lands.

- **Cultural Exchange**: The interaction between different cultures along trade routes led to a rich exchange of ideas and traditions. The fusion of artistic styles, religious beliefs, and technological innovations enriched the cultural tapestry of the region. For instance, the introduction of new agricultural techniques and crafts contributed to the evolution of local practices, enhancing the resilience of communities.

- **Market Centers**: Ancient civilizations established market centers within the Thar Desert, facilitating the exchange of goods and services. These markets served as social hubs where traders and consumers could interact, fostering economic growth. The organization of fairs and festivals further promoted trade, drawing visitors from surrounding areas and enhancing cultural connections.

17.1.4 Social Organization and Community Resilience

The ability of ancient civilizations to adapt to the Thar Desert also stemmed from their social organization and community resilience. The harsh environment necessitated cooperation and collaboration among individuals, leading to the development of strong social structures.

- **Clan Systems**: Many communities in the Thar Desert organized themselves into clans or tribes, fostering a sense of identity and solidarity. These social structures facilitated resource sharing and mutual support, enabling communities to withstand the challenges posed by the environment. Clan-based systems also played a crucial role in conflict resolution and decision-making, ensuring a cohesive response to external threats.

- **Cultural Practices and Rituals**: The challenges of desert life often spurred the development of unique cultural practices and rituals. Festivals celebrating the arrival of rain or the harvest season reinforced community bonds and provided opportunities for social cohesion. These cultural expressions not only served as a means of coping with adversity but also fostered a sense of belonging among community members.

- **Leadership and Governance**: Effective leadership was vital for navigating the challenges of desert life. Ancient civilizations often appointed leaders or chieftains who were responsible for managing resources, resolving conflicts, and coordinating communal efforts. This governance structure allowed for efficient decision-making and resource allocation, enhancing the community's resilience to environmental fluctuations.

17.1.5 Spiritual Beliefs and Adaptation

The harshness of the Thar Desert also influenced the spiritual beliefs and practices of its inhabitants. Many communities developed a rich tapestry of religious and spiritual traditions that reflected their connection to the environment.

- **Nature Worship**: The unpredictable nature of the desert environment often led communities to develop a profound respect for natural forces. Many ancient civilizations practiced nature worship, venerating deities associated with rain, fertility, and agricultural abundance. These beliefs served as a means of seeking favor from higher powers and mitigating the risks associated with living in an arid landscape.

- **Sacred Sites**: The Thar Desert is dotted with sacred sites and shrines that reflect the spiritual significance of the landscape. Temples dedicated to local deities were often constructed near water sources, symbolizing the interconnectedness of life and the environment. Pilgrimages to these sacred sites fostered a sense of community and collective identity, reinforcing the cultural heritage of desert inhabitants.

- **Rituals and Festivals**: Festivals celebrating seasonal changes or agricultural cycles were integral to the social fabric of ancient communities. These rituals provided opportunities for communal gatherings and reaffirmed cultural identity. Celebrations associated with the arrival of rain were particularly significant, as they marked the renewal of life in the arid landscape.

17.2 Survival Strategies: Water Sourcing, Agriculture, and Settlements

The Thar Desert, with its arid climate and limited water resources, posed significant challenges for ancient civilizations striving to survive and thrive in this unforgiving environment. However, these communities developed a range of innovative survival strategies, particularly in the areas of water sourcing, agriculture, and settlement patterns. Their ingenuity and adaptability allowed them to make the most of the available resources, leading to sustainable living practices that have endured through generations.

17.2.1 Water Sourcing Strategies

Water scarcity in the Thar Desert necessitated the development of sophisticated water sourcing strategies. Ancient inhabitants recognized the vital importance of water for survival and employed various techniques to harness and conserve this precious resource.

- **Stepwells and Reservoirs**: The construction of stepwells, known as **baoris**, and reservoirs was a significant achievement of ancient civilizations in Rajasthan. These structures allowed communities to store rainwater during the monsoon season, providing a reliable water supply throughout the year. Stepwells often featured intricate architectural designs, with steps leading down to the water level. These communal gathering spaces served not only practical purposes but also played a central role in the social and cultural life of the community.

- **Water Harvesting Techniques**: The arid landscape prompted the implementation of innovative water harvesting techniques. Ancient communities created small ponds and embankments to capture runoff from seasonal rains, allowing them to store water for later use. These techniques helped recharge groundwater supplies and facilitated irrigation, ensuring that crops could be cultivated even during dry spells.

- **Canal Systems**: In some areas, ancient civilizations developed canal systems to divert water from rivers and streams to their agricultural fields. For example, the **Ghaggar-Hakra River**, which once flowed through the region, was utilized for irrigation purposes. By directing water flow to arable land, communities could cultivate crops, ensuring food security in an otherwise challenging environment.

17.2.2 Agricultural Innovations

Agriculture in the Thar Desert required creative adaptations to cope with limited rainfall and extreme temperatures. Ancient farmers developed various strategies to maximize agricultural productivity while minimizing reliance on water.

- **Drought-Resistant Crops**: The cultivation of drought-resistant crops was essential for agricultural success in the Thar Desert. Ancient farmers opted for hardy varieties such as **millets**, **barley**, and **gram**, which were well-suited to the arid climate. These crops not only required less water but also thrived in sandy soils, making them ideal for cultivation in the desert landscape.

- **Crop Rotation and Mixed Farming**: To enhance soil fertility and optimize resource use, ancient communities practiced crop rotation and mixed farming. By alternating crops and planting legumes alongside cereals, they improved soil quality and reduced pest infestations. Additionally, integrating livestock into farming practices allowed for the recycling of nutrients through manure, contributing to healthier crops.

- **Transhumance and Pastoralism**: Some groups engaged in transhumance, a seasonal movement of livestock between grazing grounds. This practice allowed communities to access fresh pastures during different times of the year, promoting sustainable use of available resources. By migrating with their herds, pastoralists could adapt to changing environmental conditions while ensuring the health and productivity of their livestock.

17.2.3 Settlement Patterns

The settlement patterns of ancient civilizations in the Thar Desert were influenced by water availability, agricultural practices, and social organization. Communities strategically chose locations for their settlements, taking into account the challenges posed by the arid environment.

- **Proximity to Water Sources**: Settlements were often established near water sources, such as stepwells, rivers, or seasonal ponds. This proximity allowed communities to easily access water for drinking, irrigation, and livestock care. Towns like **Bikaner** and **Nagari** were strategically located near these vital resources, facilitating agricultural activities and trade.

- **Fortified Settlements**: In response to external threats and the harsh desert environment, many ancient civilizations constructed fortified settlements. These structures provided protection against invasions and served as centers for trade and social interaction. The fortifications also played a crucial role in resource management, allowing communities to defend their water sources and agricultural lands.

- **Adaptation to Mobility**: Some communities adopted a more mobile lifestyle, moving between seasonal camps to optimize resource use. This adaptive strategy allowed groups to take advantage of temporary water sources and grazing lands, ensuring their survival in an unpredictable environment. The use of portable shelters and the ability to migrate as needed were essential survival strategies for these nomadic groups.

17.2.4 Social and Cultural Adaptations

The survival strategies of ancient civilizations in the Thar Desert were not solely focused on physical sustenance; they also encompassed social and cultural adaptations that fostered resilience and cohesion within communities.

- **Community Cooperation**: The challenges of desert life encouraged strong communal ties and cooperation among residents. The sharing of resources, such as water and grazing land, was essential for survival. Communities often organized collective efforts to maintain and manage water sources, ensuring equitable access for all members.

- **Cultural Practices and Beliefs**: The harsh environment influenced cultural practices and belief systems within ancient communities. Rituals related to water conservation, agriculture, and seasonal changes played a significant role in fostering a sense of identity and belonging. Festivals celebrating the arrival of rain or the harvest season reinforced social bonds and provided opportunities for communal gatherings.

- **Knowledge Transfer and Innovation**: The transfer of knowledge and innovations across generations was crucial for the survival of ancient civilizations. Techniques related to water management, agricultural practices, and resource conservation were passed down through oral traditions, ensuring that communities could adapt to changing conditions. This sharing of knowledge allowed for continuous improvement and resilience in the face of adversity.

17.3 Interaction Between Desert Tribes and Urban Centers

The interaction between desert tribes and urban centers in Rajasthan is a fascinating aspect of the region's history, showcasing the dynamic relationships between nomadic groups and settled communities. These interactions were shaped by a variety of factors, including trade, cultural exchange, political alliances, and social networks. As a result, they played a significant role in shaping the economic, cultural, and social landscape of Rajasthan. This chapter delves into the various dimensions of these interactions, highlighting their implications for both desert tribes and urban centers.

17.3.1 Historical Context of Desert Tribes

Desert tribes in Rajasthan, such as the **Rajputs**, **Bishnois**, **Ramsnehi**, and **Bakarwals**, have traditionally adapted to the challenging conditions of the Thar Desert. These groups developed unique survival strategies that revolved around pastoralism, agriculture, and trade. Their deep-rooted knowledge of the desert environment allowed them to thrive despite its harshness.

- **Pastoralism and Mobility**: Many desert tribes relied heavily on livestock for their livelihoods. They practiced pastoralism, moving between seasonal pastures to access grazing land and water sources. This mobility was a key adaptation to the desert's arid climate, allowing them to optimize resource use and maintain healthy herds.

- **Cultural Identity**: The desert tribes cultivated distinct cultural identities shaped by their environment. Their traditions, customs, and social structures reflected a deep connection to the land and its resources. Oral histories, music, and art played vital roles in preserving their heritage and fostering a sense of community.

17.3.2 Urban Centers as Economic Hubs

Urban centers in Rajasthan, such as **Jaipur**, **Bikaner**, and **Jaisalmer**, emerged as significant economic hubs due to their strategic locations along trade routes. These cities facilitated the exchange of goods and ideas, attracting traders, artisans, and scholars from diverse backgrounds.

- **Trade and Commerce**: The interaction between desert tribes and urban centers was primarily driven by trade. Desert tribes served as vital suppliers of livestock, wool, and other raw materials, which were in high demand in urban markets. In exchange, urban centers provided manufactured goods, textiles, and agricultural produce. This reciprocal relationship fostered economic interdependence and enriched the local economies of both desert tribes and urban centers.

- **Market Dynamics**: Urban markets became vital venues for desert tribes to sell their products and acquire goods from urban artisans. Traditional markets, fairs, and festivals often facilitated these exchanges, creating a vibrant atmosphere for trade and cultural interaction. For instance, the **Camel Festival in Bikaner** attracted tribes from surrounding areas, providing a platform for commerce and social engagement.

17.3.3 Cultural Exchange and Influence

The interaction between desert tribes and urban centers extended beyond economic transactions; it also facilitated significant cultural exchange. This exchange enriched the cultural tapestry of Rajasthan, resulting in a blending of traditions, art forms, and social practices.

- **Art and Craftsmanship**: The craftsmanship of desert tribes, particularly in textiles and handicrafts, found its way into urban markets. The intricate designs and techniques developed by these tribes influenced urban artisans, leading to the emergence of hybrid styles that incorporated elements from both rural and urban aesthetics. The fusion of styles resulted in unique artistic expressions, such as vibrant Rajasthani quilts and embroidered textiles.

- **Cultural Practices**: Cultural practices, such as music, dance, and folklore, also experienced cross-pollination between desert tribes and urban centers. Urban centers became venues for cultural performances, where traditional desert music and dance forms were showcased. Festivals and celebrations in urban areas often featured the participation of desert tribes, promoting cultural exchange and mutual appreciation.

- **Language and Literature**: The interaction between desert tribes and urban centers influenced language and literature in Rajasthan. The oral traditions of desert tribes enriched local dialects, while urban centers became centers for literary expression. Poets and storytellers often traveled between these spaces, sharing tales and narratives that reflected the shared experiences of both groups.

17.3.4 Political Alliances and Conflicts

The relationship between desert tribes and urban centers was not solely characterized by cooperation; it also involved political alliances and conflicts. The shifting dynamics of power in the region influenced these interactions and shaped the course of Rajasthan's history.

- **Alliances for Defense**: Desert tribes often formed alliances with urban centers for mutual protection against external threats. These alliances allowed for coordinated defense strategies, enabling both parties to safeguard their territories. The Rajput clans, for example, forged alliances with urban centers to counter invasions and maintain their autonomy.

- **Territorial Disputes**: However, territorial disputes occasionally arose between desert tribes and urban centers, leading to conflicts over land and resources. As urban centers expanded, they encroached upon traditional grazing lands used by desert tribes. This conflict over land use often resulted in tensions and confrontations, prompting negotiations or skirmishes to resolve disputes.

- **Integration into Political Systems**: Over time, some desert tribes integrated into the political systems of urban centers, becoming part of the ruling elite. This integration allowed desert tribes to exert influence in governance and decision-making processes, shaping the political landscape of Rajasthan. Leaders from desert tribes often held important positions in urban administration, reflecting the interconnectedness of these two groups.

17.3.5 Social Networks and Community Building

The interaction between desert tribes and urban centers facilitated the development of social networks that transcended geographic boundaries. These networks played a crucial role in fostering a sense of community and solidarity among diverse groups.

- **Intermarriage and Kinship**: Intermarriage between desert tribes and urban residents contributed to social cohesion and cultural blending. These marriages fostered ties between different communities, creating networks of kinship that transcended tribal and urban identities. The resulting familial connections strengthened social bonds and facilitated collaboration in various domains.

- **Community Events and Gatherings**: Events such as fairs, festivals, and religious celebrations provided opportunities for social interaction between desert tribes and urban residents. These gatherings allowed individuals to forge friendships, share experiences, and celebrate their cultural heritage together. The communal nature of these events reinforced the sense of belonging and interconnectedness among diverse groups.

CHAPTER EIGHTEEN

Legends and Folklore: Decoding Archaeology through Oral Traditions

18.1 How Folklore Has Guided Archaeological Explorations

Folklore, a vital element of cultural heritage, encompasses the myths, legends, tales, and traditions that characterize a community's identity. In Rajasthan, a region rich in history and culture, folklore has played an instrumental role in guiding archaeological explorations. These narratives not only preserve the memories of past civilizations but also provide essential clues about historical sites, helping archaeologists identify significant locations and understand their cultural context. This chapter examines the influence of folklore on archaeological research in Rajasthan, illustrating how legends have shaped exploration and interpretation of the region's rich archaeological landscape.

18.1.1 The Interplay Between Folklore and Archaeology

Folklore serves as a bridge between past and present, connecting communities to their histories. In Rajasthan, stories of kings, queens, and mythical beings permeate the cultural fabric, providing insights into social structures, religious beliefs, and historical events. These narratives often contain kernels of truth that can guide archaeologists in their search for artifacts and sites.

For instance, local legends about lost cities or sacred places often lead archaeologists to conduct investigations in specific areas. When communities share stories of ancient temples, battlefields, or royal residences, archaeologists can use these accounts as a starting point for their research. The blend of oral traditions with scientific inquiry facilitates a holistic understanding of the region's past, allowing researchers to frame their explorations within the cultural narratives that have persisted over centuries.

18.1.2 Myths as Catalysts for Discovery

Many archaeological discoveries in Rajasthan have been inspired by local folklore. A notable example is the story of the lost city of **Sambhar**, known for its salt lake. Legends suggest that Sambhar was once a flourishing city that met a tragic fate, submerged under water or destroyed by a calamity. This narrative has driven archaeological efforts to uncover evidence of ancient habitation and trade in the region.

In excavations at Sambhar, researchers have unearthed pottery shards, tools, and remnants of structures that suggest the presence of a thriving settlement. The correlation between folklore and material culture not only confirms the existence of an ancient city but also highlights the significance of Sambhar as a trade center, further enriching the understanding of Rajasthan's historical landscape.

18.1.3 Folklore as a Source of Cultural Identity

Folklore is integral to the cultural identity of communities, providing a sense of belonging and continuity. In Rajasthan, stories about legendary figures like **Maharana Pratap** and **Rani Padmini** not only celebrate valor and honor but also serve as reminders of the region's historical struggles against invasions and oppression. These narratives influence local perceptions of historical sites and enhance the significance of archaeological findings.

For example, the **Chittorgarh Fort**, associated with Rani Padmini, draws significant attention due to its legendary connections. Folklore surrounding Rani Padmini has prompted numerous studies and archaeological explorations at the site, leading to discoveries that illuminate the fort's strategic importance and architectural features. This synergy between folklore and archaeology fosters a deeper appreciation of the fort's historical significance, highlighting its role as a symbol of Rajput pride.

18.1.4 Documenting and Preserving Folklore

As archaeological explorations continue, the documentation and preservation of folklore become crucial. Collaborating with local communities allows researchers to gather stories that might otherwise be lost to time. By recording these narratives, archaeologists can create a comprehensive framework for understanding the historical significance of various sites.

Moreover, integrating folklore into archaeological practices enriches the interpretation of findings. When artifacts are discovered, researchers can contextualize them within the stories and legends associated with those locations. This approach enhances the narrative surrounding archaeological discoveries, making them more relatable and engaging for both scholars and the public.

18.1.5 Challenges in Integrating Folklore and Archaeology

While the interplay between folklore and archaeology offers valuable insights, it is not without challenges. The fluid nature of folklore can complicate the verification of historical accuracy. Myths often undergo transformations as they are passed down through generations, leading to variations in narratives that may obscure historical facts. Archaeologists must approach these stories with a critical lens, balancing the cultural significance of folklore with the rigor of scientific inquiry.

Additionally, there can be discrepancies between local beliefs and academic interpretations. Scholars must navigate these differences sensitively, respecting the cultural context of folklore while ensuring that their research is grounded in archaeological evidence. Collaborative efforts between archaeologists and local communities can help bridge these gaps, fostering mutual understanding and respect.

18.2 Legends of Kings, Queens, and Warriors Linked to Archaeological Sites

The historical tapestry of Rajasthan is intricately woven with the legends of its kings, queens, and warriors, whose tales of valor, romance, and tragedy resonate throughout the region. These legends, often passed down through generations, have become a crucial component of Rajasthan's cultural identity and significantly influence the archaeological exploration of various sites across the state. The intertwining of folklore and history provides a unique lens through which to understand the socio-political dynamics of ancient Rajasthan and the enduring legacy of its rulers. This chapter delves into the captivating legends associated with prominent figures and sites, illustrating how these narratives have shaped archaeological endeavors.

18.2.1 The Legend of Rani Padmini and Chittorgarh Fort

One of the most famous legends in Rajasthan is that of **Rani Padmini**, a beautiful queen of Chittorgarh, who is celebrated for her courage and honor. The story unfolds against the backdrop of **Chittorgarh Fort**, a UNESCO World Heritage Site, which stands as a testament to the valor of the Rajput clans. According to legend, Rani Padmini's beauty attracted the attention of **Alauddin Khilji**, the Sultan of Delhi. Determined to possess her, Khilji laid siege to the fort. Rani Padmini, embodying the ideals of Rajput honor and dignity, chose to commit **jauhar**—a mass self-immolation—alongside other women rather than be captured.

This legendary narrative has fueled both literary and artistic expressions, inspiring poets, playwrights, and filmmakers. Archaeologically, the fort's remnants, including the **Rani Padmini Palace** and various temples, have been subjects of extensive study, revealing insights into the fortification techniques, architecture, and lifestyle of the era. The legend continues to attract scholars and tourists alike, making Chittorgarh Fort a focal point for both historical and cultural exploration.

18.2.2 Maharana Pratap and the Battle of Haldighati

Another iconic figure in Rajasthani history is **Maharana Pratap**, the valiant king of **Mewar**, known for his fierce resistance against Mughal expansion. The **Battle of Haldighati**, fought in 1576 between Maharana Pratap and the Mughal army led by **Raja Man Singh**, is steeped in legend and heroism. According to folklore, Maharana Pratap rode his loyal horse, **Chetak**, during the battle. The tale goes that Chetak, despite sustaining injuries, leaped over a ravine to ensure Maharana's escape, showcasing an extraordinary bond between the king and his steed.

Archaeological explorations at **Haldighati** have revealed remnants of battlefields, weaponry, and fortifications that provide context to this legendary confrontation. The site, along with the nearby **Chetak Samadhi**, commemorates both the king's valor and the cultural importance of equestrianism in Rajasthani folklore. These discoveries not only validate historical narratives but also deepen our understanding of the military strategies employed by Rajput warriors during this tumultuous period.

18.2.3 The Tragic Love Story of Dhola-Maru

The legend of **Dhola-Maru**, a classic romantic tale, reflects the themes of love, honor, and sacrifice prevalent in Rajasthani folklore. Set against the backdrop of the **Mewar** region, this story tells of the love between Dhola, a prince, and Maru, a beautiful princess. The narrative unfolds with themes of betrayal, longing, and the ultimate reunion of the lovers against all odds.

The archaeological site of **Nathdwara**, known for its rich cultural heritage, is often associated with the Dhola-

Maru legend. The tales surrounding these characters have inspired numerous artistic expressions, including paintings and folk dances. Archaeological studies in this region often uncover artifacts and murals that depict scenes from the story, providing a tangible connection to the past and enriching the cultural landscape of Rajasthan.

18.2.4 The Legacy of Raja Man Singh and Amer Fort

Raja Man Singh, a prominent Rajput general in the Mughal court, is another legendary figure linked to archaeological sites in Rajasthan. His contributions to architecture and military strategy are significant, with the **Amer Fort** in Jaipur standing as a testament to his legacy. The fort's construction reflects a blend of Mughal and Rajput architectural styles, symbolizing the cultural amalgamation of the time.

According to legend, Raja Man Singh was not only a skilled warrior but also a patron of arts and culture. His connection to Amer Fort has led to extensive archaeological investigations, revealing intricate frescoes, elaborate gateways, and intricate water management systems. The fort continues to be a popular tourist destination, drawing visitors eager to explore the historical narratives intertwined with its architecture.

18.2.5 The Influence of Folklore on Archaeological Interpretations

The legends of kings, queens, and warriors provide rich narratives that inform archaeological interpretations. While folklore may embellish certain aspects of historical events, it often captures the cultural values, social dynamics, and regional identities of the time. Archaeologists often approach their findings with an awareness of these legends, using them to contextualize their discoveries and engage with local communities.

For instance, the stories of valor associated with Rajput warriors foster a sense of pride and identity among local populations. Archaeological sites linked to these legends often become sites of cultural memory, where communities gather to celebrate their heritage. This interplay between folklore and archaeology not only enriches the understanding of the past but also fosters a sense of belonging and continuity within contemporary society.

18.2.6 Challenges in Interpreting Folklore and History

While the legends surrounding kings, queens, and warriors provide valuable insights, they also pose challenges for archaeologists. The line between myth and reality can be blurred, making it essential for researchers to critically evaluate the narratives they encounter. Archaeologists must balance the allure of folklore with the need for rigorous scientific methodology, ensuring that their interpretations are grounded in tangible evidence.

Additionally, cultural sensitivity is crucial when engaging with local communities and their legends. Researchers must approach these narratives with respect, acknowledging their significance while avoiding any misrepresentation or oversimplification. Building trust with local populations can enhance the quality of archaeological investigations and foster collaborative efforts in preserving both the cultural heritage and the stories that define it.

18.3 Cross-Referencing Myths with Historical Artifacts

The exploration of Rajasthan's archaeological sites reveals a complex tapestry of myths, legends, and historical artifacts that collectively shape our understanding of the region's past. Cross-referencing these myths with archaeological findings allows researchers to glean insights into the social, cultural, and political dynamics of ancient Rajasthan. This chapter delves into the methodology of cross-referencing myths with historical artifacts, providing examples that illustrate the profound connections between folklore and material culture.

18.3.1 The Importance of Myths in Historical Context

Myths serve as foundational narratives that encapsulate the values, beliefs, and histories of cultures. In Rajasthan, myths often reflect themes of heroism, morality, and the interplay between divine and mortal realms. These stories, while sometimes embellished, can offer historical clues regarding societal structures, conflicts, and daily life. Archaeologists can leverage these narratives to formulate hypotheses about ancient civilizations, focusing their efforts on specific sites or artifacts that resonate with these tales.

For example, the legend of **Rani Padmini**, associated with **Chittorgarh Fort**, illustrates the ideals of honor and sacrifice among the Rajputs. The tales of her beauty and bravery highlight the significance of women's roles in societal narratives. When excavating the fort, archaeologists have discovered various artifacts, including jewelry and weapons, which offer insights into the daily lives and cultural practices of the Rajput elite. Cross-referencing these findings with the myth of Rani Padmini allows researchers to create a more nuanced understanding of the fort's historical significance and the societal values it embodied.

18.3.2 Methodological Approaches to Cross-Referencing

Cross-referencing myths with historical artifacts requires a multi-disciplinary approach that combines archaeological research, historical analysis, and folklore studies. Archaeologists often begin by identifying relevant myths and legends associated with specific sites. Once these narratives are established, they can guide archaeological investigations, focusing on artifacts that align with the themes or characters within the myths.

For instance, at the site of **Bhangarh Fort**, known for its haunting legends, researchers have uncovered various remnants of structures, pottery, and tools. The folklore surrounding the fort—primarily involving tragic love stories and supernatural occurrences—provides a contextual framework for interpreting the archaeological findings. By examining the types of artifacts discovered and their alignment with the narratives, archaeologists can begin to construct a story about the inhabitants' lifestyle, rituals, and social organization.

Additionally, archaeologists often collaborate with local historians, folklore experts, and cultural anthropologists to enrich their understanding of the myths and legends tied to specific sites. This collaboration fosters a holistic view that integrates local knowledge and cultural significance into the archaeological process.

18.3.3 Case Studies of Successful Cross-Referencing

One prominent example of successful cross-referencing is found at the **Amer Fort** in Jaipur. The legends surrounding Raja Man Singh, a key figure in the fort's history, provide insight into the architectural features and military strategies employed by the Rajputs. According to folklore, the fort was built to symbolize the strength and unity of the Rajput clans.

Archaeological studies at Amer Fort have revealed a complex system of fortifications, water management, and architectural grandeur that aligns with the narratives of strength and resilience. By analyzing the layout and materials used in construction, researchers have drawn parallels between the fort's physical attributes and the ideals encapsulated in the legends. This synergy between myth and artifact enhances our understanding of the socio-political dynamics of the time and underscores the fort's significance as a symbol of Rajput identity.

Another compelling case study can be found at the site of **Kalibangan**, an important Harappan site in Rajasthan. The myths surrounding the Saraswati River, often regarded as a sacred river in Hindu tradition, have led archaeologists to explore its ancient course and tributaries. Legends suggest that the river was once a lifeline for early civilizations, influencing their agricultural practices and settlement patterns.

Archaeological findings at Kalibangan, including advanced irrigation systems and agricultural tools, provide evidence of sophisticated agricultural practices that align with the mythological narratives. By cross-referencing the legends with material evidence, researchers can better understand how ancient societies adapted to their environments and leveraged natural resources for survival.

18.3.4 Challenges in Cross-Referencing Myths and Artifacts

While the integration of myths and historical artifacts can enhance our understanding of Rajasthan's past, it also presents challenges. Myths are often fluid, subject to reinterpretation and adaptation over time. As a result, the accuracy and authenticity of these narratives can vary, complicating efforts to correlate them with archaeological findings.

Furthermore, there is a risk of oversimplifying or misinterpreting the myths when attempting to align them with material culture. Researchers must approach the process of cross-referencing with caution, ensuring that they do not conflate folklore with factual history. Critical evaluation and triangulation of sources are essential to maintain the integrity of the archaeological interpretations.

Local communities also play a significant role in shaping the narratives surrounding myths and archaeological sites. Their perspectives can differ from scholarly interpretations, leading to potential conflicts in understanding the significance of certain artifacts. Engaging with local populations and respecting their interpretations of myths can enhance archaeological research and ensure that it aligns with the cultural heritage of the community.

CHAPTER NINETEEN

UNSOLVED ARCHAEOLOGICAL MYSTERIES OF RAJASTHAN

19.1 Incomplete Excavations and Unexplained Artifacts

The archaeological landscape of Rajasthan is marked by a rich tapestry of history, culture, and art that dates back millennia. However, despite significant advancements in archaeological techniques and methodologies, many sites in this region remain partially excavated or have yielded artifacts that lack proper contextualization. This chapter delves into the complexities surrounding incomplete excavations and the presence of unexplained artifacts, highlighting the implications for understanding Rajasthan's historical narrative.

19.1.1 The Nature of Incomplete Excavations

Incomplete excavations are a common challenge in archaeology, particularly in a region as expansive and diverse as Rajasthan. Factors contributing to this issue include limited funding, political instability, and the sheer scale of the sites. In many instances, excavations are initiated with great enthusiasm but may stall due to budgetary constraints or logistical challenges. Consequently, only portions of significant archaeological sites are explored, leaving many questions unanswered.

For example, **Kalibangan**, a prominent site of the Indus Valley Civilization, has been only partially excavated. Initial excavations conducted in the 1960s uncovered streets, drainage systems, and pottery, but much of the site remains unexplored. The absence of comprehensive excavation hampers a holistic understanding of the settlement's layout, population, and socio-economic structures. Researchers can only hypothesize about the unexcavated areas, limiting insights into how the site functioned within the broader context of the Indus Valley Civilization.

19.1.2 The Role of Unexplained Artifacts

In addition to incomplete excavations, the presence of unexplained artifacts poses another significant challenge in reconstructing the past. Artifacts discovered during excavations often lack clear context, making it difficult to ascertain their purpose, usage, and cultural significance. The identification of such artifacts is vital for piecing together the lifestyle and traditions of ancient communities.

For instance, at the **Ahar site**, archaeologists have discovered numerous terracotta figurines that remain enigmatic. While some researchers speculate that these figures may represent deities or symbols of fertility, others argue they could be toys or ritualistic items. Without sufficient contextual data—such as the location of discovery or associated artifacts—conclusive interpretations remain elusive. This ambiguity can lead to varying theories and interpretations, complicating the narrative surrounding the culture that produced these artifacts.

19.1.3 Challenges in Interpretation

The interpretation of incomplete excavations and unexplained artifacts is fraught with challenges. Archaeologists often rely on comparative analysis, drawing parallels between artifacts from Rajasthan and those found in other regions. However, such comparisons can be problematic, as cultural practices and meanings may differ significantly across communities. Additionally, artifacts can be misinterpreted due to preconceived notions or biases, leading to flawed conclusions about their function and cultural significance.

In some cases, the interpretation of unexplained artifacts is influenced by contemporary beliefs and practices. For example, the use of specific motifs in artifacts may be interpreted through the lens of modern cultural significance rather than historical context. This can lead to misrepresentations of ancient practices, hindering a clear understanding of the cultural dynamics of the time.

19.1.4 The Impact of Political and Cultural Factors

Political and cultural factors significantly influence the progress of archaeological explorations and the interpretation of artifacts. In Rajasthan, the cultural pride associated with historical sites can lead to pressure on archaeologists to produce findings that align with popular narratives. This may result in a reluctance to confront ambiguity or question established interpretations, perpetuating misconceptions and incomplete understandings.

Moreover, political instability can disrupt ongoing excavations and hinder collaborations between researchers. For example, local conflicts or changes in governance can lead to the suspension of archaeological projects, leaving significant sites unexamined. This lack of continuity can result in the loss of vital information and artifacts, further complicating efforts to piece together the historical puzzle.

19.1.5 Case Studies of Incomplete Excavations and Unexplained Artifacts

A notable case study of incomplete excavation is found at **Bhinmal**, a site believed to have been an important center for trade and commerce during ancient times.

Excavations have revealed several layers of habitation, but much of the site remains unexplored. The limited scope of excavations raises questions about the socio-economic structure of the inhabitants and their interactions with neighboring regions.

Unexplained artifacts from Bhinmal, such as intricate seals and ornaments, lack clear parallels in other archaeological contexts. This absence of comparative data makes it challenging to determine their purpose and significance within the local culture. Researchers continue to debate the origins and functions of these artifacts, underscoring the complexity of understanding Rajasthan's historical narrative.

Another compelling example is the archaeological site of **Jaisalmer**, known for its sandstone architecture and strategic location along ancient trade routes. While significant structures have been excavated, many areas of the city remain untouched. Artifacts unearthed in Jaisalmer, such as coins and pottery, have not been fully analyzed, leading to gaps in understanding the economic systems and trade networks of the time. The lack of comprehensive excavation limits the ability to construct a complete picture of the city's historical role and significance.

19.1.6 Future Directions and Solutions

To address the challenges posed by incomplete excavations and unexplained artifacts, archaeologists in Rajasthan must adopt innovative strategies. Collaborative approaches that involve local communities can enhance archaeological research by incorporating local knowledge and cultural perspectives. Community involvement can also foster greater interest in preserving and protecting archaeological sites.

Additionally, employing advanced technologies, such as ground-penetrating radar and 3D modeling, can facilitate more effective exploration of sites, allowing researchers to identify areas of interest without extensive excavation. These tools can provide valuable insights into subsurface features, guiding future excavations and prioritizing areas for study.

Furthermore, interdisciplinary research that combines archaeology with anthropology, history, and art history can provide a richer understanding of the cultural context of artifacts. By engaging with experts from various fields, archaeologists can develop more comprehensive interpretations of artifacts and their significance within ancient socictics.

19.2 Theories About Ancient Technologies or Knowledge

The study of ancient technologies and knowledge systems is crucial for understanding the advancements and capabilities of early civilizations. In Rajasthan, archaeological findings reveal a rich tapestry of technologies, from sophisticated agricultural practices to advanced metallurgy, showcasing the ingenuity of ancient societies. This chapter explores various theories surrounding the technologies and knowledge possessed by these civilizations, drawing connections between archaeological evidence and the broader historical context of the region.

19.2.1 Agricultural Innovations

One of the most significant areas of ancient technology in Rajasthan is agriculture. Given the arid climate and the challenges posed by the Thar Desert, early inhabitants developed innovative techniques to sustain their livelihoods. Archaeological sites, such as **Kalibangan**, provide evidence of advanced agricultural practices, including irrigation systems and crop rotation.

Theories suggest that the inhabitants of Kalibangan employed a combination of floodplain agriculture and irrigation from the Ghaggar-Hakra River system. The remnants of canals and fields indicate a systematic approach to water management, which would have been vital for cultivating crops like wheat, barley, and pulses. This knowledge of irrigation not only highlights the ingenuity of ancient agricultural practices but also suggests a sophisticated understanding of hydrology and soil management.

Additionally, theories posit that early inhabitants were aware of the importance of crop diversity. Archaeobotanical studies have revealed the presence of various plant remains, indicating that these communities practiced mixed farming. This adaptability would have allowed them to maximize yields and ensure food security, demonstrating a deep understanding of local ecosystems and agricultural cycles.

19.2.2 Metallurgy and Material Sciences

Rajasthan is renowned for its rich deposits of metals, particularly copper, lead, and iron. The evolution of metallurgy in the region reflects significant technological advancements. Archaeological evidence from sites like **Bhirrana** and **Ganeshwar** shows that ancient communities engaged in complex metallurgical processes, such as smelting and alloying.

Theories regarding ancient metallurgy suggest that early metallurgists in Rajasthan possessed advanced knowledge of chemical properties and reactions. The discovery of crucibles and slag at these sites indicates that artisans experimented with different metal ores to produce superior alloys. For example, the production of bronze—a copper-tin alloy—would have required precise knowledge of melting points and proportions, showcasing the technological prowess of these ancient societies.

Moreover, evidence of ironworking in Rajasthan suggests a significant transition in material culture. Theories propose that the introduction of iron technology revolutionized agriculture and warfare, leading to increased agricultural productivity and the development of more effective weapons. The strategic importance of iron tools and weapons could have influenced social hierarchies and trade networks, underscoring the interconnectedness of technology, economy, and society.

19.2.3 Architectural Techniques

The architectural heritage of Rajasthan reflects advanced building technologies and knowledge of materials. The region is home to numerous forts, palaces, and temples, many of which exhibit intricate designs and engineering marvels. Theories about ancient architectural techniques suggest that builders employed a combination of local materials, innovative construction methods, and advanced knowledge of geometry.

For instance, the construction of **Jaisalmer Fort**, with its distinctive yellow sandstone, showcases the use of locally sourced materials that blend harmoniously with the desert landscape. Theories indicate that builders utilized an understanding of thermal dynamics to create structures that remain cool during the scorching days and warm during chilly nights. The design of thick walls and strategically placed windows reflects an awareness of climate and environmental conditions.

Additionally, the intricate carvings and frescoes found in temples such as **Dilwara** and **Ranakpur** demonstrate a high level of craftsmanship and artistic knowledge. Theories suggest that artisans possessed advanced techniques in stone carving and decorative arts, with influences from various cultural exchanges along trade routes. This artistry not only highlights the technical skills of ancient craftsmen but also reflects the cultural and religious values of the societies that commissioned these structures.

19.2.4 Water Management Systems

In a region characterized by aridity, ancient societies in Rajasthan developed sophisticated water management systems that showcased their ingenuity and adaptability. Theories surrounding these systems suggest that early inhabitants employed a combination of techniques to harness and store water, essential for agriculture and daily life.

Archaeological findings indicate the presence of **stepwells**, tanks, and reservoirs, which facilitated water storage and distribution. For example, the **Baoris** (stepwells) found throughout Rajasthan exemplify the advanced engineering skills of ancient communities. Theories propose that these structures were not only practical solutions to water scarcity but also reflected social and communal values, serving as gathering places and centers of social interaction.

The design of these water management systems suggests an intricate understanding of hydrology and geomorphology. Theories posit that ancient engineers carefully considered the topography and geology of the land to maximize water retention and minimize evaporation. This knowledge would have been crucial for sustaining agricultural practices and supporting growing populations in an arid environment.

19.2.5 Knowledge Transmission and Cultural Exchange

The advancements in ancient technologies in Rajasthan can be attributed to the transmission of knowledge across generations and cultures. Theories suggest that trade routes connecting Rajasthan with other regions facilitated the exchange of ideas, materials, and techniques. This cultural exchange played a pivotal role in the evolution of technologies and knowledge systems.

Archaeological evidence from sites like **Hampi** and **Mandalay** indicates that traders and artisans traveled across vast distances, sharing innovations in metallurgy, agriculture, and architecture. The presence of similar artifacts and architectural styles in distant regions suggests a network of knowledge transfer that transcended geographic boundaries.

Moreover, local traditions and oral histories have preserved ancient knowledge systems, allowing communities to adapt and innovate over time. Theories propose that this continuity of knowledge is reflected in the resilience and adaptability of Rajasthan's inhabitants, who have managed to thrive in challenging environmental conditions.

19.3 Open-Ended Questions for Future Discoveries

The exploration of ancient technologies and knowledge systems in Rajasthan has unveiled a wealth of information about its past civilizations. However, numerous open-ended questions remain that can guide future archaeological discoveries and deepen our understanding of the region's history. This chapter outlines critical questions that researchers, archaeologists, and historians can explore as they continue to investigate Rajasthan's archaeological landscape.

19.3.1 What Were the Specific Roles of Different Social Classes in Technological Advancements?

One significant area of inquiry is the role of various social classes in the development and application of technologies in ancient Rajasthan. While some archaeological findings indicate advanced skills in metallurgy, agriculture, and architecture, the extent to which these technologies were accessible or controlled by different societal groups remains largely unexplored.

Open-ended questions include:

- What were the specific roles of artisans, farmers, and traders in the dissemination and innovation of these technologies?
- How did social stratification impact access to technological knowledge?
- Were there particular classes or castes that specialized in specific technologies, and how did their expertise influence the societal dynamics of ancient Rajasthan?

By investigating these questions, researchers can develop a more nuanced understanding of the socio-economic frameworks that underpinned technological advancements.

19.3.2 How Did Ancient Communities Adapt Their Technologies to Changing Environmental Conditions?

Rajasthan's arid climate and unique topography present challenges for human habitation and agricultural practices. Open-ended questions regarding the adaptability of ancient technologies to environmental changes can provide valuable insights into resilience and sustainability.

Potential inquiries include:

- How did ancient communities modify their agricultural techniques in response to periods of drought or flooding?
- What innovations emerged in response to changes in climate, and how did these adaptations influence settlement patterns?
- To what extent did the availability of resources, such as water and arable land, shape the technological choices of these communities?

Exploring these questions can shed light on the adaptive strategies employed by ancient populations and their relationship with the environment.

19.3.3 What Were the Influences of Trade Networks on

Technological Development?

Trade routes have historically facilitated the exchange of goods, ideas, and technologies across regions. In Rajasthan, the intersection of various trade routes likely influenced local technological practices. Open-ended questions about the impact of trade on technology could include:

- How did the exchange of materials and ideas through trade networks shape local technologies in Rajasthan?
- What specific artifacts or technologies can be traced back to trade interactions with other civilizations?
- How did the influx of external influences modify existing technological practices in the region?

Investigating these questions can enhance the understanding of how trade contributed to the evolution of technological knowledge and practices in Rajasthan.

19.3.4 How Can Modern Technologies Enhance Archaeological Discoveries?

Advancements in technology provide new tools and methodologies for archaeological exploration. Open-ended questions regarding the integration of modern technologies can shape future discoveries in Rajasthan:

- What role can remote sensing, GIS (Geographic Information Systems), and drones play in identifying potential archaeological sites?

- How can molecular analysis and scientific dating methods enhance the understanding of artifacts and sites?

- What are the potential benefits and limitations of using digital modeling and visualization techniques in reconstructing ancient technologies and structures?

By addressing these questions, researchers can leverage contemporary technologies to improve archaeological practices and discover previously overlooked aspects of Rajasthan's historical landscape.

19.3.5 How Do Folklore and Oral Traditions Shape Our Understanding of History?

As discussed in earlier chapters, folklore plays a significant role in preserving historical narratives and guiding archaeological explorations. Open-ended questions regarding the relationship between folklore and historical accuracy can enhance future studies:

- How do local legends and oral histories influence contemporary interpretations of archaeological findings?

- What is the reliability of folklore as a historical source, and how can it be critically assessed in light of archaeological evidence?

- How can archaeologists work with local communities to document and preserve folklore while maintaining scholarly rigor?

Exploring these questions can contribute to a deeper understanding of the intersection between archaeology and cultural narratives, enriching the context of discoveries in Rajasthan.

19.3.6 What Are the Long-Term Impacts of Ancient Technologies on Contemporary Practices?

The legacies of ancient technologies and knowledge systems continue to influence modern practices in Rajasthan. Open-ended questions regarding the connections between past and present can provide valuable insights:

- What aspects of ancient agricultural or metallurgical techniques are still utilized in contemporary practices?

- How have traditional crafts evolved over time, and what role do they play in the local economy and cultural identity?

- What lessons can modern society learn from the sustainable practices of ancient civilizations in Rajasthan?

Addressing these questions can foster a better appreciation for the continuity of knowledge and the relevance of ancient technologies in today's world.

19.3.7 How Can Collaborative Efforts Advance Archaeological Research?

The future of archaeological research in Rajasthan can benefit from collaborative efforts among scholars, local communities, and government agencies. Open-ended questions about collaboration can guide future research strategies:

- What frameworks can be established to promote cooperation between archaeologists and local communities?
- How can interdisciplinary approaches enhance the understanding of ancient technologies and knowledge?
- What role do public engagement and education play in fostering interest and support for archaeological research?

By exploring these questions, researchers can identify ways to strengthen partnerships and promote a collaborative spirit in archaeological endeavors.

CHAPTER TWENTY

The Role of Women in Rajasthan's Archaeological Record

20.1 Representation of Women in Sculptures, Inscriptions, and Relics

The representation of women in the art and archaeological finds of Rajasthan offers a unique insight into the social, cultural, and religious dynamics of historical communities. From intricate sculptures adorning temples to inscriptions chronicling their lives, these artifacts reflect the multifaceted roles women played in ancient society. This chapter explores the various forms of representation of women found in sculptures, inscriptions, and relics, examining their implications for understanding gender dynamics in Rajasthan's history.

20.1.1 Women in Sculptures: Aesthetic and Symbolic Representations

Sculptures in Rajasthan serve as a primary medium for exploring the representation of women in art. From the grandeur of the **Dilwara Temples** to the intricacies of the **Ranakpur Jain Temple**, sculptures depict women in various forms and roles, ranging from deities to everyday figures. The aesthetic beauty of these sculptures often symbolizes idealized femininity, portraying women with delicate features, elaborate hairstyles, and intricate jewelry.

In many cases, these representations reflect religious and cultural ideals. For instance, female deities such as **Durga**, **Lakshmi**, and **Saraswati** are frequently depicted in temple sculptures, embodying attributes such as strength, prosperity, and knowledge. These representations indicate that women were revered not only as nurturers but also as powerful figures within the spiritual framework of society. The depiction of women in sacred spaces emphasizes their integral role in religious practiccs and the broader cultural narratives of the time.

Moreover, sculptures of women engaged in daily activities—such as grinding grain, playing musical instruments, or performing dance—offer glimpses into the lives of women in ancient Rajasthan. These representations highlight their contributions to family and community life, emphasizing the importance of women in maintaining cultural traditions and social structures. Such artifacts challenge monolithic perceptions of gender roles, suggesting a more nuanced understanding of women's agency in historical contexts.

20.1.2 Inscriptions: Chronicling Women's Lives and Contributions

Inscriptions found on temples, monuments, and relics serve as vital records that chronicle the lives and contributions of women throughout Rajasthan's history. These inscriptions often commemorate the deeds of queens, goddesses, and notable female figures, reflecting their significance within the social hierarchy. Notable examples include inscriptions dedicated to queens who played crucial roles in governance, warfare, and cultural patronage.

One significant inscription is the **Rani Padmini inscription** at **Chittorgarh Fort**, which recounts the valor and sacrifices of the legendary queen. Such inscriptions not only celebrate women's achievements but also provide insights into their influence on political and social structures. They illustrate how women were not merely passive figures but active participants in shaping historical narratives.

Additionally, inscriptions often shed light on the familial connections and relationships of women. Many records detail marriages, alliances, and familial lineages, emphasizing the importance of women in forging social ties. These documents challenge traditional narratives that tend to overlook women's contributions, highlighting their roles as matriarchs and key figures in lineage and heritage.

20.1.3 Relics: Everyday Lives and Cultural Practices

Relics, including pottery, jewelry, and household items, provide tangible evidence of women's daily lives and cultural practices. The examination of artifacts associated with women allows researchers to reconstruct aspects of their everyday existence, shedding light on domestic roles, social status, and cultural expressions. For instance, the discovery of terracotta figurines depicting women in various poses reflects not only aesthetic sensibilities but also social practices related to fertility, motherhood, and domestic life.

Jewelry and adornments discovered at archaeological sites reveal insights into the status and wealth of women in ancient society. The intricate designs and materials used in these artifacts reflect regional craftsmanship and cultural influences, showcasing how adornments played a role in expressing identity and status. These relics serve as a testament to the significance of personal adornment in cultural practices, further emphasizing the importance of women in the socio-economic fabric of their communities.

Furthermore, the analysis of pottery and cooking tools offers valuable insights into the culinary practices and daily routines of women. The presence of specific types of vessels associated with cooking or storage provides a glimpse into their roles as caregivers and homemakers. Such artifacts highlight the critical contributions of women in sustaining households and preserving culinary traditions, reinforcing their importance in the domestic sphere.

20.1.4 Cultural and Historical Implications

The representation of women in sculptures, inscriptions, and relics has profound implications for understanding the cultural and historical dynamics of Rajasthan. These artifacts challenge simplistic notions of gender roles, suggesting a more complex interplay of power, agency, and societal expectations. Women in Rajasthan were not confined to domestic roles; they participated actively in religious, political, and cultural life.

Moreover, the depictions of women reflect evolving cultural attitudes toward gender over time. As Rajasthan's history is marked by various influences—from indigenous traditions to the impact of invasions and colonialism—these representations reveal how perceptions of women shifted in response to changing social and political contexts. The study of these artifacts allows scholars to trace the continuity and change in women's status, identity, and representation across centuries.

20.1.5 Challenges in Interpretation

Despite the wealth of information provided by sculptures, inscriptions, and relics, challenges remain in interpreting these representations. The multifaceted nature of art and inscriptions means that meanings can vary significantly based on context, cultural beliefs, and historical periods. Moreover, modern interpretations can be influenced by contemporary gender norms and biases, potentially distorting historical understandings.

Additionally, the preservation of artifacts poses challenges for researchers. Erosion, vandalism, and neglect can lead to the loss of significant representations of women in Rajasthan's archaeological record. Continued efforts are needed to document and protect these artifacts, ensuring that they remain accessible for future generations of scholars and the public.

20.2 Notable Queens and Female Figures in Rajasthan's History

Rajasthan's history is replete with remarkable queens and female figures whose contributions have shaped the region's cultural, political, and social landscapes. From valiant warriors to astute administrators, these women have played crucial roles in the narrative of Rajasthan, often serving as symbols of strength, resilience, and leadership. This chapter delves into the lives and legacies of notable queens and female figures in Rajasthan's history, highlighting their achievements and impact on the state's heritage.

20.2.1 Rani Padmini of Chittorgarh

One of the most iconic figures in Rajasthan's history is **Rani Padmini**, the legendary queen of Chittorgarh. Her story, immortalized in various literary and artistic works, reflects themes of beauty, valor, and sacrifice. According to historical accounts and folklore, Rani Padmini was renowned for her exceptional beauty, which captivated the Sultan of Delhi, Alauddin Khilji.

The most famous narrative surrounding Rani Padmini is her act of **Jauhar** (self-immolation) along with the other women of the fort to avoid capture and dishonor at the hands of Khilji. This act of bravery has made her a symbol of honor and valor, representing the ideals of Rajput women. The tale of Rani Padmini has transcended time, inspiring countless adaptations in literature, dance, and cinema, making her an enduring symbol of Rajput pride.

20.2.2 Rani Durgavati of Gondwana

Another noteworthy queen in Indian history is **Rani Durgavati**, who ruled the Gondwana region of present-day Madhya Pradesh but had significant interactions with the Rajput clans of Rajasthan. Born into the **Tomar dynasty**, she became the queen of Gondwana through her marriage and is celebrated for her remarkable courage and leadership.

Rani Durgavati is best known for her fierce resistance against the Mughal forces led by **Adil Shah** in the 16th century. In a remarkable display of valor, she led her troops into battle, wielding a bow and arrow herself. Despite her eventual defeat, her legacy as a warrior queen has been celebrated in folklore, and she is often remembered as a symbol of women's empowerment in the face of adversity.

20.2.3 Maharani Gayatri Devi of Jaipur

In the modern era, **Maharani Gayatri Devi** stands out as a prominent figure in Rajasthan's history. Born into the royal family of Cooch Behar, she became the third wife of Maharaja **Sawai Man Singh II** of Jaipur. Her grace, beauty, and intelligence made her a beloved figure in Jaipur, and she played a significant role in social reforms and the upliftment of women's status in society.

Maharani Gayatri Devi was not only a fashion icon but also a strong advocate for women's education and empowerment. She founded the **Maharani Gayatri Devi Girls' School** in Jaipur, which aimed to provide quality education to girls in the region. Her contributions to politics were also notable, as she served as a member of the Lok Sabha in the 1960s. Her life and achievements have inspired generations of women in Rajasthan and beyond, showcasing the role of female leaders in shaping society.

20.2.4 Rani Sahiba of Alwar

Rani Sahiba, the queen of Alwar, is another significant figure in Rajasthan's history. Known for her philanthropic efforts and contributions to education, she dedicated her life to improving the conditions of women and children in her kingdom. Under her guidance, several schools and healthcare facilities were established, promoting education and health care for the underprivileged.

Rani Sahiba's legacy is particularly evident in her commitment to social justice and empowerment. Her initiatives laid the foundation for future generations to advocate for women's rights and education, reflecting the importance of royal patronage in promoting societal progress.

20.2.5 Rani Chennabhairadevi of Mandore

Rani Chennabhairadevi, the queen of Mandore, played a pivotal role in the defense of her kingdom during the 13th century. She is celebrated for her exceptional leadership and bravery in the face of adversity. When her husband was killed in battle, she took charge of the forces and fought against invading armies to protect her kingdom.

Rani Chennabhairadevi's resilience and strategic acumen earned her a place in the annals of Rajasthan's history as a fierce warrior queen. Her story exemplifies the qualities of leadership and courage that many Rajput queens embodied, and she is remembered as a symbol of strength and determination.

20.2.6 The Role of Women in Folk Culture and Arts

Apart from the prominent queens, Rajasthan's history is rich with contributions from various female figures in folk culture, art, and crafts. Women in rural Rajasthan have traditionally played vital roles in preserving cultural heritage through folk music, dance, and handicrafts.

The **Ghoomar** dance, for example, is a cultural performance that celebrates femininity and community spirit, often performed by women at festivals and weddings. Similarly, the intricate **bandhani** (tie-dye) and

block printing crafts are often passed down through generations of women, showcasing their artistic skills and creativity.

20.2.7 Contemporary Influences of Historical Queens

The legacies of these queens and female figures continue to influence contemporary Rajasthan. Their stories serve as powerful reminders of women's strength and resilience, inspiring modern movements advocating for gender equality and empowerment.

In recent years, there has been a growing emphasis on highlighting the contributions of women in Rajasthan's history, with initiatives aimed at preserving their stories and promoting gender-sensitive narratives. Educational institutions and cultural organizations are increasingly recognizing the importance of female figures in shaping Rajasthan's history, ensuring that their contributions are acknowledged and celebrated.

20.3 Gender Roles as Reflected in Material Culture

Material culture—the physical objects, resources, and spaces that people use to define their culture—provides invaluable insights into the gender roles prevalent in historical societies. In Rajasthan, the examination of artifacts, tools, and domestic items illuminates the intricate dynamics of gender relations and societal expectations across various historical periods. This chapter explores how material culture reflects the construction and performance of gender roles in Rajasthan, highlighting the interplay between artifacts and the lived experiences of men and women.

20.3.1 Theoretical Framework: Understanding Material Culture and Gender

To comprehend how material culture reflects gender roles, it is essential to establish a theoretical framework. Material culture studies often draw from anthropological and sociological theories that emphasize the relationship between objects and identity. Gender roles are not merely social constructs; they are shaped, reinforced, and contested through material culture. Artifacts serve as tangible manifestations of cultural norms, beliefs, and practices related to gender.

The concept of **gender performativity**, introduced by Judith Butler, posits that gender is not an innate quality but rather a performance enacted through repeated behaviors and practices. Material culture, therefore, plays a crucial role in this performance, providing the tools and contexts through which gender identities are expressed and negotiated. By analyzing artifacts within their historical and cultural contexts, scholars can discern how gender roles have evolved and been redefined over time.

20.3.2 Domestic Artifacts: A Reflection of Women's Roles

The examination of domestic artifacts in Rajasthan reveals significant insights into women's roles within the household. Items such as cooking pots, grinding stones, and weaving tools serve as indicators of women's responsibilities in maintaining the home and family. The prevalence of these artifacts in archaeological sites underscores the importance of women in domestic spheres, suggesting that their contributions were foundational to the social fabric of ancient communities.

For instance, the discovery of **ceramic vessels** in residential areas indicates that women were primarily responsible for food preparation and storage. The design and function of these vessels can also reflect social status and cultural practices. Intricate pottery often associated with ceremonial use may indicate women's involvement in religious and social rituals, further illustrating their multifaceted roles beyond mere domesticity.

Additionally, textiles and weaving tools are central to understanding women's craftsmanship and economic participation. In Rajasthan, the art of weaving is not only a means of producing clothing but also a cultural practice that conveys identity and tradition. The presence of weaving tools in archaeological sites highlights women's contributions to the economic life of their communities, suggesting that they played vital roles in both production and trade.

20.3.3 Tools and Artifacts Associated with Men

While domestic artifacts primarily reflect women's roles, tools and items associated with men provide insights into their societal functions and status. Weapons, agricultural implements, and architectural tools are significant in understanding the roles men played in labor, defense, and governance. These artifacts underscore the gendered division of labor, where men often occupied roles in public life, warfare, and land management.

For example, the presence of **swords and shields** in burial sites indicates the valorization of warrior culture, emphasizing masculinity associated with strength and protection. Such artifacts often carry symbolic meanings, representing not only the physical attributes of masculinity but also the social expectations surrounding male identity. The craftsmanship involved in producing these weapons reflects the cultural values placed on martial prowess and honor.

Similarly, agricultural tools like plows and sickles highlight men's involvement in farming and land cultivation. The significance of agriculture in Rajasthan's economy suggests that men's roles in food production were crucial for the community's survival and prosperity. This division of labor is further reinforced by the way these tools are often found in contexts that signify male activities, such as fields or communal spaces.

20.3.4 Gendered Spaces and Material Culture

The concept of gendered spaces is another critical aspect of material culture that reveals gender roles. Different areas within settlements—such as domestic spaces, communal areas, and religious sites—are often associated with specific gender activities and roles. The spatial organization of these areas can reflect societal norms regarding gender behavior and expectations.

For instance, the segregation of domestic spaces within households—often with women's quarters separate from men's areas—indicates a clear demarcation of gender roles. The layout of these spaces can suggest control over resources, privacy, and the performance of gendered duties. The presence of artifacts like **jewelry and cosmetics** in women's quarters emphasizes their roles in beauty and domesticity, while items found in men's areas may reflect authority and labor.

In religious contexts, the presence of male and female deities in temples often reinforces gender roles. Temples dedicated to female deities, like **Maa Durga**, often feature spaces designed for women's participation in rituals, while male deities are typically associated with power and governance. The architectural design and spatial arrangements within temples can illustrate the cultural significance of gender in religious practices, influencing how men and women engage with the sacred.

20.3.5 Changing Gender Roles and Material Culture

As Rajasthan's history has unfolded, the material culture has also evolved, reflecting changing gender roles and societal dynamics. The impact of colonialism, modernization, and globalization has introduced new materials and technologies that have reshaped gendered labor and identities. For example, the introduction of industrial textiles and mechanized tools has transformed traditional practices, affecting women's roles in weaving and textile production.

Moreover, contemporary movements advocating for gender equality have influenced perceptions of gender roles in material culture. The revival of traditional crafts and the recognition of women artisans in Rajasthan challenge historical narratives that often overlooked women's contributions. By documenting and promoting women's craftsmanship, scholars and activists highlight the importance of preserving gendered knowledge and practices in contemporary society.

CHAPTER TWENTY-ONE

Rajasthan's Underground Architecture: Hidden Secrets

21.1 Exploring Underground Cities, Tunnels, and Stepwell Networks

The arid landscape of Rajasthan is home to a remarkable array of underground cities, tunnels, and stepwell networks that reflect the ingenuity of ancient civilizations in adapting to their environment. These subterranean structures served various purposes, from providing refuge during invasions to ensuring water supply in an arid climate. This chapter delves into the historical significance, architectural features, and cultural implications of these underground sites, highlighting how they illuminate the lives of the people who inhabited this desert region.

21.1.1 Historical Context of Underground Architecture

Rajasthan's harsh climate, characterized by extreme temperatures and scarce water resources, necessitated innovative architectural solutions. The history of underground cities and structures in Rajasthan can be traced back to ancient civilizations, including the **Indus Valley Civilization** and various Rajput kingdoms. As the region faced challenges related to water scarcity and security threats, communities began to construct subterranean structures to meet their needs.

One of the earliest examples of underground architecture in Rajasthan is the **Harappan city of Kalibangan**, where evidence of underground drainage systems has been discovered. These early innovations laid the groundwork for more complex underground networks that would develop over the centuries. As Rajasthan became a crossroads for trade routes and faced invasions from various empires, the need for fortified underground spaces increased, leading to the construction of extensive tunnel systems and underground cities.

21.1.2 Underground Cities: A Testament to Ingenuity

Several sites in Rajasthan showcase the remarkable ingenuity of ancient builders in creating underground cities. One such site is **Bhangarh**, known for its well-preserved ruins and extensive tunnel networks. Legend has it that Bhangarh was cursed, leading to its abandonment, but its underground passages and chambers reveal the complexity of its design. These tunnels likely served as escape routes during conflicts or as means of connecting different parts of the city.

Another notable underground city is **Kumbhalgarh**, famous for its massive fortifications. The fort complex includes hidden chambers and passages that allowed for clandestine movements and served as storage areas for provisions during sieges. The strategic placement of these underground spaces reflects the foresight of the Rajput rulers in safeguarding their territory.

The **underground city of Chand Baori**, a stepwell located in Abhaneri, is one of the most impressive examples of subterranean architecture. Constructed during the 9th century, this stepwell features 3,500 steps and a deep, intricately designed well that provides access to water even during the dry seasons. Chand Baori exemplifies the blend of functionality and artistry, showcasing the sophisticated engineering skills of its creators.

21.1.3 Tunnels: Pathways of History

Tunnels in Rajasthan served various purposes, ranging from military strategies to facilitating trade. The **tunnels of the Mehrangarh Fort** in Jodhpur are a prime example. These tunnels connected different parts of the fort, allowing for quick movements during battles and the transportation of goods. The fort's design illustrates the integration of security and functionality, with tunnels strategically placed to enhance the defense system.

In addition to military uses, tunnels also played a role in trade and commerce. The underground routes allowed traders to transport goods discreetly, shielding them from potential threats. The intricate network of tunnels in cities like **Jaisalmer** reflects the historical significance of trade in the region, connecting Rajasthan with neighboring states and facilitating the exchange of goods and culture.

21.1.4 Stepwells: Engineering Marvels of Water Management

Stepwells are unique architectural features found throughout Rajasthan, designed to provide water access in a region marked by scarcity. These structures not only served practical purposes but also reflected the cultural and social values of the communities that built them. Stepwells were often elaborate, featuring intricate carvings and architectural designs that transformed them into communal spaces.

The **Adalaj Stepwell**, located near Ahmedabad, is a notable example of the architectural grandeur associated with stepwells. Although not located in Rajasthan, its design influenced stepwell architecture in the region. The intricate carvings and multiple levels of the Adalaj Stepwell reflect the artistic sensibilities of the time, showcasing the importance of water management in an arid environment.

In Rajasthan, stepwells like **Panna Meena ka Kund** and **Raniji ki Baori** exemplify the fusion of utility and aesthetics. These structures served as social gathering places, where communities would come together for water access, rituals, and festivities. The architectural details of these stepwells, including ornate pillars and beautifully carved niches, highlight the significance of water in both practical and cultural contexts.

21.1.5 Cultural and Social Implications

The exploration of underground cities, tunnels, and stepwell networks reveals significant cultural and social implications for the people of Rajasthan. These structures served as symbols of resilience and adaptability, reflecting the ways communities navigated the challenges of their environment. The construction of underground spaces also illustrates the collaborative efforts of artisans, engineers, and laborers, fostering a sense of community and shared purpose.

Furthermore, the cultural practices associated with these structures are noteworthy. Stepwells, for example, became integral to religious and social rituals, with many adorned with sculptures of deities and floral motifs. The communal aspect of stepwells transformed them into spaces of interaction, reinforcing social bonds and cultural traditions.

The legacy of these underground structures continues to resonate in contemporary Rajasthan. Many of these sites are now recognized for their historical and architectural significance, attracting tourists and researchers alike. The preservation and promotion of these underground cities and stepwell networks serve not only to honor the ingenuity of ancient builders but also to educate future generations about the rich cultural heritage of Rajasthan.

21.2 Purpose and Significance of Subterranean Structures

Subterranean structures, often referred to as underground architecture, hold a significant place in the architectural heritage of Rajasthan. These constructions, which range from ancient water storage systems to intricate temples and residential spaces, have served various purposes throughout history, deeply intertwining with the region's socio-economic and environmental contexts. Understanding the purpose and significance of these subterranean structures not only sheds light on their functional roles but also reveals insights into the innovative spirit of Rajasthan's inhabitants in adapting to their challenging environment.

21.2.1 Historical Context of Subterranean Structures

Rajasthan's arid climate and scarce water resources necessitated the development of effective methods for water conservation and management. The use of subterranean structures can be traced back to ancient times, when early civilizations faced challenges related to agriculture, drinking water supply, and urban planning. As populations grew, the demand for efficient water management systems became increasingly critical, leading to the construction of various underground facilities.

These structures reflect the ingenuity and adaptability of Rajasthan's inhabitants, who ingeniously utilized the available materials and geographical features to create functional spaces that addressed their needs. From ancient reservoirs (known as **baoris** or **stepwells**) to underground temples, each type of subterranean structure has played a vital role in the region's development.

21.2.2 Water Management: The Backbone of Subterranean Structures

One of the primary purposes of subterranean structures in Rajasthan has been water management. The region's arid conditions often result in seasonal fluctuations in water availability, making the storage and conservation of water crucial for survival.

Stepwells, or **baoris**, are a quintessential example of subterranean water management systems. These multi-storied structures are designed to access groundwater and provide a reliable water supply during dry periods. The architectural ingenuity involved in constructing these wells is remarkable; they typically feature a series of descending steps leading to a water reservoir, allowing for easy access to water.

The significance of stepwells extends beyond mere functionality; they served as social and cultural gathering places. Many stepwells were adorned with intricate carvings and sculptures, making them not only practical facilities but also architectural masterpieces that reflected the artistic sensibilities of the time. The communal aspect of these structures fostered social interactions, particularly among women who often visited them for daily water collection.

21.2.3 Shelter and Habitat: The Role of Subterranean Dwellings

In addition to water management, subterranean structures in Rajasthan also served as shelters and habitats. The extreme temperatures of the region, characterized by scorching summers and chilly winters, made underground dwellings an attractive alternative for comfort and protection from the elements.

Cave dwellings and **underground homes** have been found in various parts of Rajasthan, particularly in the **Aravalli** range. These subterranean residences not only provided thermal comfort but also offered security from external threats. The thick earth cover helped maintain a stable internal climate, making these structures viable living spaces throughout the year.

Moreover, the use of locally sourced materials such as stone and mud in constructing these dwellings exemplifies sustainable architectural practices. The incorporation of natural elements into the design not only ensured the durability of these structures but also minimized the environmental impact of construction.

21.2.4 Religious Significance: Subterranean Temples and Shrines

Subterranean structures also hold immense religious significance in Rajasthan. Various temples and shrines have been constructed underground, often associated with ancient beliefs and practices. These religious sites served as spaces for worship and meditation, reflecting the spiritual dimensions of subterranean architecture.

One notable example is the **Adinath Temple** in **Osian**, which features intricate carvings and sculptures. The temple's subterranean layout not only enhances the mystical experience of worship but also demonstrates the architectural prowess of the artisans who designed and built these sacred spaces. Similarly, underground shrines often provided a serene environment conducive to spiritual reflection, allowing devotees to connect more deeply with their faith.

21.2.5 Cultural and Social Significance

Beyond their practical functions, subterranean structures have profound cultural and social significance. They serve as historical markers, providing insights into the lifestyles, traditions, and values of past societies. The preservation of these structures is essential for understanding Rajasthan's rich cultural heritage.

Subterranean structures often become sites of folklore and mythology, contributing to the region's collective memory. Tales surrounding these sites can enhance local identity and foster a sense of community, as they are often associated with shared histories and narratives. The cultural significance of these structures is further emphasized by the festivals and rituals that take place in and around them, solidifying their role as integral components of social life in Rajasthan.

21.2.6 Modern Relevance and Conservation Efforts

In contemporary times, the significance of subterranean structures extends to environmental conservation and sustainable development. With increasing urbanization and the challenges posed by climate change, there is a renewed interest in traditional water management practices, including the use of stepwells and other underground water storage systems.

Efforts to conserve and restore these structures are vital for preserving Rajasthan's architectural heritage. Various organizations and government initiatives aim to protect these sites from neglect and degradation, recognizing their historical and cultural importance. By promoting awareness and education about the value of subterranean architecture, stakeholders can encourage sustainable practices and community involvement in preservation efforts.

21.3 Hidden Chambers and Secret Passages: Fascination with the Unknown

The allure of hidden chambers and secret passages has captivated the imagination of historians, archaeologists, and adventurers alike. In the context of Rajasthan, a region known for its grand forts, opulent palaces, and intricate architecture, the existence of such enigmatic spaces adds a layer of intrigue to the study of its historical sites. This chapter explores the cultural significance, historical context, and archaeological findings related to hidden chambers and secret passages in Rajasthan, emphasizing how these architectural features reflect the complexities of human experience and the enduring fascination with the unknown.

21.3.1 Historical Context: The Purpose of Hidden Spaces

The architectural designs of Rajasthan's forts and palaces often include hidden chambers and secret passages, reflecting both practical and symbolic purposes. Historically, these features served various functions, including security, escape routes, and spaces for clandestine meetings. The tumultuous history of Rajasthan, characterized by conflicts, invasions, and power struggles, necessitated the incorporation of such elements into the architecture of its forts.

Hidden chambers were often strategically placed to provide refuge during sieges or to facilitate a swift escape for royals and important figures. For instance, the **Chittorgarh Fort**, known for its storied past and numerous sieges, includes several secret pathways and concealed rooms designed for protection. These architectural choices not only reveal the practical needs of the time but also symbolize the constant threat of violence and the need for resilience.

In addition to security, hidden spaces served as venues for intimate gatherings, political discussions, and even clandestine romances. The existence of secret passages within the palatial structures allowed for discreet interactions, underscoring the complexities of court life in Rajasthan. These spaces became repositories of secrets, intrigue, and personal stories that remain partially obscured by time.

21.3.2 Architectural Features: Designs of Secrecy

The design and construction of hidden chambers and secret passages in Rajasthan's forts and palaces demonstrate remarkable ingenuity and craftsmanship. These features are often characterized by intricate carvings, concealed entrances, and clever mechanisms that allow for easy concealment. The architectural style is a blend of practicality and artistry, reflecting the cultural values and aesthetic preferences of the time.

One prominent example is the **Mehrangarh Fort** in Jodhpur, which boasts an array of hidden chambers used by the royal family. The fort's walls are adorned with stunning frescoes and carvings that tell stories of valor and love, while its secret passages reveal the fort's strategic planning. These passages, often designed to blend seamlessly with the surrounding architecture, are a testament to the skills of the artisans who constructed them.

The use of local materials, such as sandstone and marble, adds to the uniqueness of these hidden features. The craftsmanship is evident not only in the structural design but also in the decorative elements that adorn these secret spaces. Carvings of flowers, geometric patterns, and motifs inspired by nature often embellish hidden chambers, creating an ambiance of beauty that contrasts with their secretive purpose.

21.3.3 Archaeological Discoveries: Uncovering the Secrets

Archaeological explorations in Rajasthan have unveiled fascinating discoveries related to hidden chambers and secret passages. Excavations in sites such as **Amber Fort** and **Jaigarh Fort** have revealed previously undiscovered areas, shedding light on the architectural ingenuity of the time. These findings have ignited the imagination of researchers and historians, prompting further investigations into the significance of these hidden spaces.

In **Jaipur**, for instance, the exploration of underground passages has led to the discovery of ancient artifacts, frescoes, and even ceremonial spaces that were long forgotten. These archaeological findings provide a tangible connection to the past, offering insights into the lifestyles and practices of those who once inhabited these grand structures.

Moreover, the restoration efforts of various forts and palaces have revealed hidden chambers that were obscured by time and neglect. The process of uncovering these spaces has not only enhanced our understanding of architectural practices but also highlighted the importance of preserving cultural heritage. Such efforts allow us to appreciate the historical narratives embedded within these hidden features and their significance in shaping Rajasthan's identity.

21.3.4 Cultural Significance: Myths and Legends

The existence of hidden chambers and secret passages in Rajasthan has given rise to numerous myths and legends, contributing to the region's rich folklore. Stories of hidden treasures, ghostly apparitions, and royal secrets abound, further enhancing the allure of these architectural features. Local traditions often intertwine with historical narratives, creating a tapestry of stories that reflect the cultural values and beliefs of the community.

For example, many tales recount the adventures of queens and princesses who navigated secret passages to escape from pursuers or to meet their lovers. These stories not only entertain but also serve to underscore themes of bravery, loyalty, and the challenges faced by women in historical contexts. The legends associated with hidden chambers often reflect broader societal values, illustrating the complex interplay between gender, power, and secrecy.

In addition to personal narratives, the architectural features themselves have become subjects of fascination for tourists and scholars alike. The allure of exploring hidden spaces resonates with those seeking adventure and mystery, transforming visits to Rajasthan's forts into journeys of discovery. This cultural significance reinforces the idea that architecture is not merely functional; it is a canvas for storytelling and the preservation of collective memory.

21.3.5 Contemporary Reflections: Preservation and Interpretation

In contemporary times, the fascination with hidden chambers and secret passages continues to influence how we interpret and preserve Rajasthan's architectural heritage. As awareness of the historical and cultural significance of these features grows, efforts are being made to document and protect them. Conservation initiatives aim to ensure that these hidden spaces remain accessible for future generations, allowing for ongoing exploration and appreciation.

Moreover, the integration of technology in archaeological research, such as ground-penetrating radar and 3D modeling, has enhanced our ability to discover and study hidden chambers without intrusive excavations. These advancements allow researchers to map and analyze the layout of hidden spaces, providing new insights into their functions and significance.

The narrative surrounding hidden chambers also plays a role in tourism, as visitors are drawn to the mysteries of Rajasthan's forts and palaces. Guided tours often highlight these enigmatic features, weaving together history, legend, and architectural beauty. This intersection of tourism and heritage preservation underscores the importance of maintaining the authenticity of these sites while sharing their stories with a broader audience.

CHAPTER TWENTY-TWO

ARTIFACTS OF POWER: ROYAL TREASURES AND SYMBOLISM

22.1 Royal Treasures Unearthed from Palaces and Forts

The rich history of Rajasthan is deeply intertwined with its majestic palaces and formidable forts, which served as symbols of power, wealth, and artistry for the royal families that ruled the region. These structures are not only architectural marvels but also treasure troves of artifacts that provide invaluable insights into the cultural, social, and economic dynamics of the time. This chapter explores the royal treasures unearthed from various palaces and forts in Rajasthan, highlighting their historical significance and the stories they tell about the lives of the nobility.

22.1.1 The Significance of Royal Treasures

Royal treasures encompass a wide array of artifacts, including jewelry, weapons, ceremonial items, manuscripts, and everyday objects that belonged to the elite classes. These treasures are significant for several reasons:

1. **Cultural Heritage:** They represent the artistic and cultural achievements of their time, reflecting the aesthetics, craftsmanship, and technological advancements of the period.

2. **Historical Insight:** The objects provide insights into the political, social, and economic structures of the royal courts, revealing the status, power, and influence of the ruling elite.

3. **Symbolism and Ritual:** Many treasures served symbolic or ritualistic purposes, highlighting the beliefs, practices, and traditions of the royal families and their connections to religious and cultural practices.

4. **Trade and Economy:** The materials and craftsmanship of these artifacts often indicate trade networks and economic interactions with other regions, showcasing the wealth and influence of Rajasthan in historical contexts.

22.1.2 Unearthing Royal Treasures: Archaeological Discoveries

Several archaeological excavations in Rajasthan have unearthed significant royal treasures that shed light on the opulence of the region's past. Notable sites include:

- **Amber Fort:** Excavations at Amber Fort, the former capital of the Kachwaha Rajputs, have revealed a wealth of artifacts, including exquisite jewelry, ornate weaponry, and elaborate textiles. Among the finds are intricately designed gold and silver jewelry pieces, reflecting the craftsmanship of local artisans and the luxurious lifestyles of the royal families.

- **City Palace, Jaipur:** The City Palace complex in Jaipur is renowned for its stunning architecture and historical significance. Recent excavations have uncovered ceremonial items, manuscripts, and decorative objects that illustrate the royal court's daily life and rituals. Notable artifacts include finely crafted weapons adorned with precious stones, showcasing the martial prowess and status of the royal family.

- **Chittorgarh Fort:** This fort, a UNESCO World Heritage site, is associated with tales of valor and sacrifice. Archaeological findings have included royal jewelry and weapons, often linked to the legendary stories of the Rajput queens and kings. The treasures unearthed here reflect the martial heritage and the cultural ethos of the Rajputs, emphasizing their commitment to honor and bravery.

22.1.3 Types of Treasures Discovered

The treasures unearthed from Rajasthan's palaces and forts can be categorized into several types, each offering unique insights into the royal lives:

1. **Jewelry and Ornaments:** Gold, silver, and precious gemstone jewelry adorned the royals, symbolizing wealth and status. Pieces like necklaces, earrings, and armlets often featured intricate designs inspired by nature and mythology. The craftsmanship displayed in these items highlights the skill of artisans and the artistic trends of the time.

2. **Weaponry:** Swords, daggers, and shields are significant components of royal treasures, reflecting the martial culture of Rajasthan. Many weapons were ornately decorated, serving both functional and ceremonial purposes. The designs and inscriptions often tell stories of valor and honor, emphasizing the importance of warfare in royal identity.

3. **Ceremonial Objects:** Items used in religious and royal ceremonies, such as **chariots, thrones, and ceremonial plates**, offer insights into the rituals and practices of the royal court. These objects often feature elaborate craftsmanship and intricate designs, highlighting their significance in royal traditions.

4. **Textiles and Manuscripts:** Fabrics, tapestries, and manuscripts discovered in royal residences provide insights into the daily lives, cultural practices, and artistic expressions of the time. Textiles often displayed vibrant colors and intricate patterns, while manuscripts may contain records of historical events, poetry, and royal decrees.

5. **Pottery and Household Items:** Everyday objects like pottery, utensils, and storage containers reveal the daily routines and lifestyles of the royal families. The quality and design of these items reflect the social hierarchy and the importance of domestic life in royal households.

22.1.4 The Role of Artisans in Crafting Treasures

The creation of royal treasures involved skilled artisans who specialized in various crafts. These artisans played a crucial role in the production of jewelry, textiles, and weaponry, often passing down their knowledge through generations. The collaboration between artisans and the royal families fostered a vibrant cultural milieu, where artistic innovation thrived.

Artisans employed techniques that blended indigenous styles with influences from trade routes and neighboring regions. For example, the intricate inlay work seen in Rajput weaponry reflects the influence of Mughal artistry, resulting from the cultural exchanges that occurred over centuries. This fusion of styles enriched the aesthetic vocabulary of Rajasthan, creating unique treasures that continue to captivate historians and art enthusiasts.

22.1.5 Conservation and Preservation Challenges

While many royal treasures have been unearthed, the preservation of these artifacts poses significant challenges. Factors such as environmental conditions, urban development, and tourism can threaten the integrity of archaeological sites and their treasures. Efforts to conserve these artifacts require collaboration between archaeologists, historians, and government agencies to implement sustainable preservation practices.

Museums and cultural institutions play a vital role in showcasing these treasures, educating the public about their significance, and promoting heritage tourism. Exhibitions that highlight the artistry and historical context of royal treasures not only preserve cultural heritage but also foster a sense of pride and identity among local communities.

22.2 Symbolism in Jewelry, Crowns, and Ceremonial Objects

Jewelry, crowns, and ceremonial objects hold profound cultural significance in Rajasthan, reflecting the region's rich heritage, traditions, and beliefs. These adornments are not merely ornamental; they serve as powerful symbols of identity, status, and spirituality. The intricate craftsmanship and the symbolic meanings embedded in these items provide a fascinating insight into the history and culture of Rajasthan. This chapter explores the diverse forms of jewelry and ceremonial objects, examining their symbolism and the roles they play in Rajasthani society.

22.2.1 The Significance of Jewelry in Rajasthani Culture

Jewelry in Rajasthan is a vital aspect of cultural identity and social status. Traditionally, jewelry is not just an adornment for women; it signifies wealth, prosperity, and familial ties. In many Rajasthani communities, the possession and gifting of jewelry represent social standing and lineage. Different regions and communities within Rajasthan have distinct styles and preferences for jewelry, which reflect their unique cultural narratives.

For instance, **Kundan** and **Meenakari** jewelry are particularly famous in Rajasthan. Kundan, characterized by its intricate gold work and gemstones, represents luxury and sophistication, while Meenakari involves the art of enameling, adding vibrant colors to the jewelry. These styles symbolize the artistic heritage of Rajasthan and the skilled craftsmanship passed down through generations.

22.2.2 Crowns and Their Regal Significance

Crowns are among the most potent symbols of power and authority in Rajasthan. Traditionally worn by rulers and royal family members, crowns (known as **mukut**) embody the sovereignty and divine right to rule. The design of these crowns varies significantly, often incorporating precious stones, intricate carvings, and symbolic motifs that reflect the wearer's status and lineage.

Crowns are often adorned with **lotus flowers**, a symbol of purity and enlightenment, and **peacock feathers**, representing grace and beauty. The combination of these elements in royal crowns conveys not just status but also the spiritual beliefs associated with kingship. The elaborate nature of these crowns signifies the wealth and power of the ruling class and their connection to divine authority.

22.2.3 Ceremonial Objects: Instruments of Ritual and Identity

Ceremonial objects in Rajasthan play a crucial role in various cultural and religious practices. These items are imbued with symbolism and are often used in rituals, celebrations, and rites of passage. Objects such as **kalash** (water pots), **thalis** (plates), and **aarti** (lighted lamps) serve as integral components of religious ceremonies, symbolizing purity, abundance, and the presence of the divine.

The design of these ceremonial objects often incorporates specific motifs and symbols that hold cultural significance. For example, a kalash might feature engravings of **mango leaves** and **coconut**, symbolizing fertility and prosperity. Such objects are not only functional but also convey the beliefs and values of the community, serving as reminders of their cultural heritage.

22.2.4 Symbolism of Materials Used

The materials used in jewelry, crowns, and ceremonial objects also carry symbolic meanings. Gold, considered the most auspicious metal in Indian culture, symbolizes wealth, purity, and prosperity. Silver, on the other hand, is associated with healing and protection. The choice of materials often reflects the values and beliefs of the community, as well as their economic status.

Gemstones used in Rajasthani jewelry also have specific symbolic meanings. For instance, **rubies** symbolize love and passion, while **emeralds** are associated with fertility and rebirth. Each gemstone is believed to possess unique energies that can influence the wearer's life, and their use in jewelry adds another layer of meaning to the adornments.

22.2.5 The Role of Jewelry in Life Cycle Events

In Rajasthan, jewelry is integral to various life cycle events, including births, marriages, and festivals. For instance, during weddings, specific pieces of jewelry are worn by brides, symbolizing auspiciousness and fertility. **Nath** (nose rings), **maang tikka** (forehead jewelry), and **bangles** are essential adornments for brides, each carrying its own significance.

The act of gifting jewelry during these ceremonies reinforces familial bonds and signifies the merging of two families. It is common for family members to present elaborate pieces of jewelry to the bride, symbolizing their love and support. This tradition underscores the importance of jewelry in maintaining cultural continuity and strengthening familial ties.

22.2.6 Influence of Folklore and Mythology

Rajasthani jewelry and ceremonial objects are often inspired by folklore and mythology, which imbue them with deeper meanings. Stories of gods, goddesses, and legendary figures are frequently depicted in the designs of jewelry and ceremonial items, connecting them to the region's rich narrative traditions.

For instance, motifs depicting **Krishna** and **Radha**, symbols of love and devotion, are often incorporated into jewelry designs, reflecting the cultural values of love and companionship. Similarly, designs inspired by the tales of **Rani Padmini** and other historical figures serve to honor their legacies and reinforce the ideals they represent.

22.2.7 Preservation of Craftsmanship and Cultural Heritage

The craftsmanship involved in creating Rajasthani jewelry, crowns, and ceremonial objects is a vital aspect of the region's cultural heritage. Skilled artisans pass down their techniques and knowledge through generations, ensuring that traditional practices continue to thrive.

Efforts to preserve this craftsmanship have gained momentum in recent years, with various initiatives aimed at promoting and supporting local artisans. By recognizing the artistic and cultural value of these creations, communities can safeguard their heritage while also contributing to the local economy.

22.3 Cultural and Political Significance of Royal Artifacts

Royal artifacts serve as invaluable remnants of a bygone era, offering insights into the cultural and political fabric of societies. In the context of Rajasthan, a region steeped in history and tradition, these artifacts encapsulate the grandeur of royal life, the intricacies of political power, and the rich cultural heritage that has shaped its identity. This chapter explores the cultural and political significance of royal artifacts in Rajasthan, highlighting their role in symbolizing authority, artistic expression, and historical continuity.

22.3.1 Defining Royal Artifacts

Royal artifacts encompass a wide array of items associated with the royal families of Rajasthan, including regalia, jewelry, weapons, ceremonial objects, and artistic works. These artifacts not only reflect the opulence of royal lifestyles but also serve as symbols of power and authority. They are often crafted with great attention to detail and artistry, showcasing the skills of artisans who contributed to the rich material culture of the region.

Regalia, such as crowns, scepters, and thrones, are perhaps the most overt symbols of royal power. These items are imbued with political significance, representing the authority of the ruler and the legitimacy of their reign. Jewelry, often made from precious metals and adorned with gemstones, signifies wealth and status, while also playing a role in rituals and ceremonies that reinforce the ruler's position.

22.3.2 Political Significance: Power and Authority

The political significance of royal artifacts extends beyond mere decoration; they embody the very essence of governance and authority. The intricate designs and craftsmanship of these artifacts communicate messages of power and sovereignty, reinforcing the social hierarchy within the kingdom. For instance, the **golden throne** of a king or queen is not merely a seat; it symbolizes the ruler's dominion over their subjects and the divine right to govern.

Artifacts associated with military power, such as swords, shields, and armor, are equally significant. These items not only reflect the martial prowess of the ruler but also serve as tangible manifestations of their authority over warfare and defense. The presence of such artifacts in royal courts emphasizes the ruler's responsibility to protect and lead their people, illustrating the connection between material culture and political obligation.

Moreover, royal artifacts often played a role in diplomatic relations. Gifts exchanged between rulers—such as ornate swords or intricately designed jewelry—served to solidify alliances and signify respect. The value placed on these artifacts underscores the importance of material wealth and artistry in establishing and maintaining political relationships.

22.3.3 Cultural Significance: Artistic Expression and Identity

Royal artifacts also serve as vessels of cultural identity, reflecting the artistic traditions and values of the time. The craftsmanship involved in creating these items often incorporates local materials, techniques, and motifs, contributing to a unique artistic heritage. For instance, the use of **blue pottery** and intricate **miniature paintings** in royal artifacts highlights the artistic innovations that emerged within the context of Rajasthan's cultural landscape.

The symbolism embedded in these artifacts often communicates deeper meanings related to cultural beliefs and practices. For example, motifs depicting deities, animals, and nature not only enhance the aesthetic appeal of artifacts but also serve to convey spiritual and cultural narratives. This interplay between art and culture reinforces the connection between royal power and the values held by the society it governs.

Furthermore, royal artifacts are integral to ceremonies and rituals, which are essential in shaping cultural identity. Coronation ceremonies, weddings, and religious festivals often involve the use of specific artifacts that hold ceremonial significance. The participation of royal families in these events, adorned with their regalia and artifacts, reinforces their status and the cultural traditions that have been passed down through generations.

22.3.4 Continuity and Change: The Legacy of Royal Artifacts

The legacy of royal artifacts extends beyond their immediate historical context. These items serve as important markers of continuity and change in Rajasthan's cultural and political landscape. As dynasties rose and fell, the styles and functions of royal artifacts evolved, reflecting shifting power dynamics and societal values.

For instance, the transition from the **Mughal** to the **Rajput** styles of artistry in royal artifacts highlights the blending of cultures and influences over time. The adaptation of design elements and materials signifies the dynamic nature of royal representation, illustrating how rulers navigated changing political landscapes while maintaining their identity.

Moreover, the preservation and display of royal artifacts in museums and cultural institutions contribute to the ongoing narrative of Rajasthan's history. These artifacts serve as educational tools, allowing contemporary audiences to engage with the past and understand the cultural significance of royal legacies. Exhibitions often highlight the craftsmanship and artistry involved in creating these items, fostering a sense of appreciation for the region's rich heritage.

22.3.5 Modern Implications: Revival and Rediscovery

In contemporary times, there has been a renewed interest in royal artifacts, leading to initiatives aimed at preserving and reviving traditional craftsmanship. Artisans and craftsmen are increasingly recognized for their contributions to cultural heritage, and efforts are being made to promote traditional techniques that produce royal-style artifacts. This revival not only supports local economies but also reinforces cultural pride and identity.

Additionally, the fascination with royal artifacts has sparked interest in heritage tourism, as visitors are drawn to Rajasthan's historical sites and museums to experience the grandeur of royal life. This engagement with the past encourages a deeper understanding of the cultural and political significance of these artifacts, fostering a connection between history and contemporary society.

CHAPTER TWENTY-THREE

ANCIENT WARFARE AND DEFENSE MECHANISMS

23.1 Rajasthan's Geography and its Impact on Military Strategies

Rajasthan, the largest state in India, is known for its arid desert landscapes, rugged mountains, and unique geographical features. Its geography has significantly influenced the military strategies employed by various kingdoms and empires throughout history. From the formidable fortresses perched on hills to the expansive Thar Desert, the geographical diversity of Rajasthan has shaped the tactics, defense mechanisms, and overall military operations of its rulers. This chapter explores how Rajasthan's geography impacted military strategies, detailing its historical context and the evolution of warfare in the region.

23.1.1 The Unique Geography of Rajasthan

Rajasthan's geography can be characterized by several key features that have played crucial roles in shaping its military strategies:

1. **The Thar Desert:** This vast arid region occupies a significant portion of western Rajasthan and poses unique challenges for military operations. The harsh climate and shifting sands can hinder troop movements and logistics, making it difficult for armies to operate effectively. However, the desert also provided natural barriers against invasions, allowing local rulers to develop strategies suited to their environment.

2. **The Aravalli Range:** This ancient mountain range stretches across Rajasthan from northeast to southwest, creating a natural defense line. The rugged terrain offers excellent vantage points for surveillance and defense, enabling armies to spot approaching enemies. The forts built on the hills, such as **Kumbhalgarh** and **Chittorgarh**, leveraged this geographical feature to enhance their defensive capabilities.

3. **Rivers and Water Bodies:** Rivers like the **Banas** and **Chambal** not only provided essential resources for sustaining armies but also served as strategic barriers. Control over these waterways was crucial for securing supplies and facilitating trade, thus impacting military

strategies.

4. **Urban Settlements and Trade Routes:** Rajasthan's cities were strategically located along major trade routes, connecting northern India with the Deccan and beyond. Control of these routes allowed rulers to exert influence over trade, gather resources, and mobilize troops efficiently.

23.1.2 Historical Context of Military Strategies in Rajasthan

The military strategies employed in Rajasthan have evolved over centuries, influenced by the state's unique geographical features. Several significant historical periods demonstrate this evolution:

1. **Ancient Warfare:** During the early periods of Rajasthan's history, various tribes and communities adapted their military strategies to the challenges posed by the Thar Desert and the Aravalli Range. For instance, the **Rajputs**, known for their martial prowess, developed guerrilla warfare tactics, using their knowledge of the terrain to ambush larger armies. They established fortified settlements in the hills, which served as strongholds against invading forces.

2. **Medieval Empires:** With the rise of powerful empires like the **Mughals**, Rajasthan's geographical features continued to influence military strategies. The Mughal

rulers employed large, well-organized armies and established fortifications to secure their territories. The forts of Rajasthan, such as **Amber Fort** and **Jaipur's City Palace**, were constructed with intricate defensive architectures, including walls, moats, and watchtowers, to withstand sieges and protect their realms.

3. **Rajputana's Resistance:** The Rajputs were known for their fierce independence and valor. Their military strategies were heavily influenced by their geography. The Rajputs fortified their forts at strategic locations, utilizing the hilly terrain to their advantage. During battles, they often engaged in hit-and-run tactics, capitalizing on their knowledge of local terrain to launch surprise attacks against larger forces.

23.1.3 Tactical Advantages of Rajasthan's Geography

Rajasthan's geography provided numerous tactical advantages that shaped military strategies:

1. **Defensive Fortifications:** The hills and rugged terrain made it feasible to construct formidable fortifications. The Rajput rulers built massive forts at strategic locations, allowing them to control access to key trade routes and monitor enemy movements. Forts such as **Mehrangarh** and **Chittorgarh** were equipped with thick walls, bastions, and lookout towers, creating formidable barriers against invasion.

2. **Surveillance and Reconnaissance:** The elevated terrain offered natural vantage points for surveillance. Armies could establish watchtowers and signaling systems to communicate over long distances. This ability to monitor enemy movements allowed local rulers to prepare for potential attacks, often deploying troops in advance to strategic locations.

3. **Natural Barriers:** The Thar Desert and rugged mountains served as natural barriers against invasions. Armies from neighboring regions often faced difficulties navigating the harsh landscape, giving local forces a strategic advantage. Rulers could exploit these barriers to launch surprise attacks or to retreat into their fortified strongholds when faced with overwhelming odds.

4. **Water Resource Management:** Control over water sources was vital for sustaining armies. The construction of **stepwells** and tanks facilitated water storage and management, ensuring that troops had access to essential resources during campaigns. This logistical advantage was crucial in an arid region where water scarcity could impact military operations significantly.

23.1.4 Major Battles Influenced by Geography

Several significant battles in Rajasthan's history were directly influenced by the geographical landscape:

1. **Battle of Haldighati (1576):** This famous battle between **Maharana Pratap** of Mewar and **Mughal Emperor Akbar's** forces exemplifies how geography impacted military strategies. The rugged terrain of Haldighati provided a tactical advantage to Maharana Pratap, allowing him to utilize guerrilla warfare tactics effectively. Despite being outnumbered, the Rajput forces used the landscape to their advantage, launching surprise attacks and using their knowledge of the terrain to evade capture.

2. **Siege of Chittorgarh (1568):** The Mughal siege of Chittorgarh was marked by the fort's strategic location and its formidable defenses. The geography of the fort, with its high walls and natural barriers, initially repelled the Mughal forces. However, the eventual fall of Chittorgarh highlights the challenges even the best defensive strategies face against a well-coordinated military campaign.

3. **Battle of Jodhpur (1857):** The geography of Jodhpur, with its imposing fortifications and strategic positioning, played a crucial role during the uprising against British rule. Local rulers employed defensive strategies that capitalized on the rugged terrain to repel British forces for an extended period.

23.1.5 The Evolution of Military Strategies

As Rajasthan underwent political and social changes, military strategies evolved to adapt to new challenges. The introduction of modern warfare tactics and technologies gradually transformed traditional methods:

1. **Integration of Modern Warfare:** With the advent of modern military technologies in the 19th and 20th centuries, traditional strategies began to adapt. The introduction of artillery and firearms necessitated changes in fortifications and battlefield tactics. Forts were redesigned to withstand cannon fire, and armies began to incorporate more structured formations and strategies into their operations.

2. **Use of Intelligence:** The importance of intelligence and reconnaissance became increasingly significant in military strategies. The rugged terrain made it essential to gather information about enemy movements and local geography. Armies began employing scouts and informants to navigate the complex landscape effectively.

3. **Alliances and Diplomacy:** As the political landscape shifted, military strategies increasingly relied on alliances and diplomacy. Local rulers recognized the importance of collaboration in facing external threats, leading to strategic marriages and treaties that bolstered military strength.

23.2 Archaeological Findings Related to Ancient Warfare: Weapons, Armor

Archaeological findings related to ancient warfare provide invaluable insights into the military strategies, technologies, and societal structures of past civilizations. In the context of Rajasthan, a region known for its rich history of martial traditions, these findings reveal a complex tapestry of warfare that shaped its culture, politics, and economy. This chapter delves into the archaeological discoveries of weapons and armor in Rajasthan, examining their significance in understanding the region's military history and the evolution of combat techniques.

23.2.1 The Historical Context of Warfare in Rajasthan

Rajasthan's history is marked by the rise and fall of various kingdoms and empires, each contributing to its legacy of warfare. From the ancient **Mauryan Empire** to the medieval **Rajput kingdoms**, Rajasthan has witnessed numerous battles, conquests, and territorial disputes. The geographical features of the region, characterized by arid deserts and rugged mountains, influenced military tactics and the types of weaponry used.

The archaeological record indicates that warfare was an integral part of Rajasthani society. The discovery of ancient fortifications, weapons, and armor highlights the region's strategic importance and the necessity for defense against invasions. This context lays the foundation for understanding the significance of the weapons and armor unearthed through archaeological excavations.

23.2.2 Weaponry: Types and Technologies

Archaeological findings in Rajasthan have revealed a diverse array of weapons that reflect the technological advancements and martial practices of ancient societies. Among the most prominent weapons discovered are swords, bows and arrows, spears, and daggers, each serving distinct purposes in combat.

Swords were often considered symbols of power and status. Excavations in sites like **Kalibangan** and **Bikaner** have unearthed intricately designed swords made from iron and steel, showcasing advanced metallurgical techniques. These swords were typically double-edged, allowing for effective slashing and thrusting in battle. The presence of ornate hilts and scabbards adorned with precious materials indicates their importance not only as tools of war but also as ceremonial items.

Bows and arrows were fundamental to ancient warfare, providing ranged capabilities that allowed warriors to engage enemies from a distance. Archaeological sites have yielded numerous arrowheads made from stone and metal, demonstrating the evolution of archery techniques. The craftsmanship involved in creating these weapons reflects a deep understanding of materials and aerodynamics, crucial for effective use in warfare.

Spears and **daggers** also played significant roles in close combat. The discovery of spearheads at various archaeological sites suggests that these weapons were commonly used in battles. Their design often featured sharp tips and barbed edges, enhancing their lethality. Similarly, daggers, often intricately designed, were used both as weapons and as status symbols, reflecting the wealth and power of their owners.

23.2.3 Armor: Protection and Status Symbols

The study of armor provides essential insights into the defensive strategies employed by ancient warriors. Armor was not only designed for protection in battle but also served as a representation of social status and identity. Archaeological findings in Rajasthan have uncovered various forms of armor, including helmets, shields, and body armor, crafted from different materials.

Helmets were crucial for protecting the head in combat. Excavations have revealed helmets made from iron, bronze, and even leather, often adorned with decorative elements. The presence of intricate designs and motifs on helmets indicates their significance beyond mere functionality, serving as symbols of bravery and honor.

Shields were vital for defense, providing protection against projectiles and melee attacks. Archaeological evidence suggests that shields were often made from wood, covered with leather or metal, and decorated with vibrant colors and patterns. The designs on shields often carried symbolic meanings, reflecting the cultural identity of the warrior or their clan.

Body armor, including breastplates and chainmail, was essential for providing protection against slashing attacks.

The discovery of metal plates and chain links in archaeological sites indicates the advanced techniques employed in armor-making. Such armor allowed warriors to engage in battle with greater confidence, enhancing their effectiveness on the battlefield.

23.2.4 The Role of Warfare in Society and Politics

Warfare played a crucial role in shaping the political landscape of Rajasthan. The archaeological findings related to weapons and armor reveal the significance of military power in establishing and maintaining authority. Rulers often relied on a strong military to defend their territories and assert dominance over rival kingdoms.

The presence of fortified structures and defensive architecture in Rajasthan underscores the importance of military preparedness. Archaeological sites such as **Chittorgarh Fort** and **Kumbhalgarh Fort** serve as testaments to the strategic significance of these structures in warfare. These forts, equipped with advanced defensive mechanisms, were designed to withstand sieges and protect inhabitants from invading forces.

Moreover, the discovery of weapons and armor in royal tombs suggests that military prowess was a key criterion for status and prestige. Warriors and rulers were often buried with their weapons, reflecting their esteemed positions within society. This practice highlights the cultural reverence for martial skill and the belief in an afterlife where these attributes would continue to hold significance.

23.2.5 Warfare and Cultural Exchange

Warfare in Rajasthan also facilitated cultural exchange and the dissemination of technologies. The interactions between different kingdoms and empires led to the sharing of military techniques, weapon designs, and armor-making skills. For instance, the influence of Persian and Mughal military practices can be observed in the weaponry and armor styles found in Rajasthan.

The incorporation of diverse influences into Rajasthani warfare reflects the region's dynamic history and adaptability. Archaeological findings reveal that warriors were not only skilled in traditional combat techniques but also embraced innovations that enhanced their effectiveness on the battlefield.

23.2.6 Challenges in Archaeological Research

While archaeological findings related to ancient warfare in Rajasthan provide valuable insights, researchers face various challenges in this field. The preservation of artifacts can be hindered by environmental factors, including moisture and temperature fluctuations, which can lead to degradation. Additionally, many sites have been subject to looting and illegal excavations, resulting in the loss of valuable historical information.

Collaboration between archaeologists, historians, and local communities is essential for preserving the archaeological record and promoting awareness of its significance. By engaging local populations in preservation efforts, researchers can foster a sense of ownership and responsibility toward their cultural heritage.

23.3 Battlefields and Their Archaeological Remnants

The battlefields of Rajasthan are not merely landscapes scarred by conflict; they are rich repositories of history, culture, and the human experience. The region's tumultuous past, characterized by numerous battles and power struggles, has left behind archaeological remnants that offer invaluable insights into the military strategies, societal values, and cultural transformations of the time. This chapter delves into the significance of Rajasthan's battlefields, exploring their archaeological remnants, historical context, and the lessons they impart about warfare and society.

23.3.1 Historical Context: A Legacy of Conflict

Rajasthan, often referred to as the land of kings, has a history marked by fierce battles and dynastic rivalries. The region's strategic location, characterized by its deserts and rugged terrain, made it a battleground for various kingdoms, including the Rajputs, Mughals, and Marathas. Prominent battles, such as the **Battle of Haldighati** (1576) and the **Siege of Chittorgarh**, exemplify the valor and sacrifice of warriors in their quest for sovereignty and honor.

The historical context of these battles is essential for understanding the archaeological remnants found at these sites. Many battlefields were the sites of significant military engagements, where tactics, weaponry, and fortifications played crucial roles. The remnants of these conflicts—be they weapons, armor, or fortifications—offer a glimpse into the military strategies employed by the warring factions, reflecting the social and political dynamics of the time.

23.3.2 Archaeological Findings: Unearthing the Past

Archaeological excavations at various battlefields in Rajasthan have yielded a wealth of artifacts that illuminate the region's martial heritage. Items such as swords, shields, arrows, and armor have been unearthed, providing insights into the materials and techniques used in warfare. For instance, the remnants of weapons discovered at the **Haldighati** battlefield showcase the craftsmanship of local artisans and the evolution of weaponry over time.

In addition to weaponry, archaeological investigations have uncovered remnants of fortifications, such as walls and defensive structures, which reveal the strategic planning that went into military engagements. The fortifications at **Chittorgarh Fort**, for instance, not only served as a stronghold during battles but also reflected the architectural prowess of the Rajputs. These remnants underscore the significance of the landscape in shaping military strategies and the resilience of the defending forces.

Moreover, the presence of mass graves and burial sites on some battlefields offers poignant insights into the human cost of conflict. These sites, often marked by memorials and inscriptions, serve as solemn reminders of the sacrifices made by warriors and the impact of warfare on communities. The discovery of burial practices provides valuable information about the cultural attitudes towards death and honor, further enriching our understanding of Rajasthan's martial heritage.

23.3.3 Cultural Significance: Memory and Identity

The archaeological remnants found on Rajasthan's battlefields are not just relics of the past; they are integral to the cultural memory and identity of the region. The stories of valor, sacrifice, and resilience associated with these battlefields are woven into the fabric of local folklore and oral traditions. The narratives surrounding key battles, such as the heroism displayed during the Siege of Chittorgarh, contribute to a collective identity that celebrates bravery and honor.

The cultural significance of battlefields is also reflected in the commemorative practices that have emerged over time. Many battle sites are the focus of local festivals, rituals, and pilgrimages, where communities gather to honor the memory of fallen warriors. These practices not only preserve the historical narratives but also reinforce social cohesion and a sense of belonging among community members.

Furthermore, battlefields serve as a source of inspiration for literature, art, and music, reflecting the enduring legacy of conflict in Rajasthan. The tales of legendary warriors, their triumphs, and tragedies continue to resonate in contemporary cultural expressions, shaping the collective consciousness of the region.

23.3.4 The Impact of Modernity: Conservation and Tourism

In recent years, there has been a growing recognition of the importance of conserving battlefields and their archaeological remnants. As modernization and urbanization encroach upon these historic sites, efforts are being made to protect and preserve the integrity of battlefields. Archaeological organizations and heritage management bodies are collaborating to ensure that these sites are maintained for future generations.

The archaeological significance of these battlefields has also attracted the interest of heritage tourism. Visitors are drawn to the historical narratives associated with the sites, seeking to engage with the past and experience the stories of valor firsthand. Guided tours, reenactments, and educational programs have emerged as means to connect visitors with the historical context of these battlefields, fostering a greater appreciation for the region's martial heritage.

However, the commercialization of battlefields poses challenges to their preservation. Balancing the demands of tourism with the need for conservation requires careful management to ensure that the cultural and historical significance of these sites is not compromised. Strategies such as sustainable tourism practices and community involvement in heritage management are essential to maintaining the integrity of battlefields while providing educational opportunities for visitors.

23.3.5 The Lessons of Conflict: Understanding Warfare and Society

The archaeological remnants of battlefields in Rajasthan provide more than just historical artifacts; they offer valuable lessons about warfare, society, and human resilience. By examining the material culture associated with conflict, we gain insights into the motivations behind warfare, the strategies employed by different factions, and the societal impacts of battle.

For instance, the evolution of weaponry and military tactics over time reflects changing political landscapes and technological advancements. The study of artifacts from various battlefields allows researchers to trace the trajectory of martial practices and understand how societies adapted to shifting circumstances.

Moreover, the exploration of mass graves and burial sites highlights the human cost of conflict, prompting reflections on the ethics of warfare and the importance of preserving human dignity in times of strife. The stories of those who fought and died on these battlefields remind us of the sacrifices made in the name of honor and sovereignty, urging us to consider the broader implications of conflict in our contemporary world.

CHAPTER TWENTY-FOUR

Future Prospects in Archaeological Research

24.1 Modern Techniques in Archaeological Research: Aerial Surveys, Remote Sensing

Archaeological research has undergone a significant transformation over the past few decades, primarily due to advancements in technology. Traditional methods of excavation and analysis have been supplemented, and in some cases replaced, by innovative techniques that allow for more comprehensive, efficient, and less invasive exploration of archaeological sites. Two of the most impactful modern techniques are aerial surveys and remote sensing. These methods have not only enhanced the speed and accuracy of archaeological research but have also expanded the possibilities for discovering and documenting ancient cultures, particularly in regions like

Rajasthan, where the landscape poses unique challenges.

24.1.1 Aerial Surveys: Revolutionizing Archaeological Discovery

Aerial surveys involve capturing images of the Earth's surface from an elevated position, typically using aircraft, drones, or satellites. This method allows archaeologists to gain a broader perspective on landscapes and identify potential sites of interest that may not be easily discernible from the ground.

1. **Identification of Site Locations:** Aerial surveys can reveal patterns in the landscape that indicate the presence of archaeological features. For example, variations in vegetation, soil color, and topography can signal the existence of ancient structures, such as buildings, roads, or fortifications. In Rajasthan, aerial surveys have helped uncover numerous sites hidden beneath the sands of the Thar Desert, offering new insights into past civilizations.

2. **Mapping and Documentation:** Once potential sites are identified, aerial imagery can be used to create detailed maps and documentation. This allows archaeologists to document the spatial relationships between different features, leading to a better understanding of site layout and organization. In Rajasthan, the mapping of forts and urban settlements through aerial surveys has enhanced knowledge about the region's historical architecture and urban planning.

3. **Non-Invasive Exploration:** One of the most significant advantages of aerial surveys is that they allow for non-invasive exploration. Traditional archaeological excavation can be destructive, often damaging or erasing vital information about a site. In contrast, aerial surveys can identify areas of interest without disturbing the ground, preserving the archaeological context for future studies.

4. **Enhanced Data Collection:** With advancements in technology, aerial surveys can now be conducted using high-resolution cameras and sensors. These tools enable archaeologists to capture detailed images and data, facilitating more accurate analysis and interpretation. Drones, in particular, have become increasingly popular in archaeological research due to their ability to navigate difficult terrains and provide high-quality images from multiple angles.

24.1.2 Remote Sensing: Uncovering Hidden Archaeological Features

Remote sensing involves the use of satellite or airborne sensors to detect and monitor physical characteristics of an area without direct contact. This technique can provide valuable information about the Earth's surface and subsurface, making it a powerful tool in archaeological research.

1. Types of Remote Sensing Techniques:

- **LiDAR (Light Detection and Ranging):** LiDAR technology uses laser light to measure distances to the

Earth's surface, creating high-resolution digital elevation models. This method can penetrate dense vegetation, revealing hidden features such as ancient road networks, settlement patterns, and architectural remains. In Rajasthan, LiDAR has been instrumental in mapping archaeological sites obscured by forest cover or debris.

- **Satellite Imagery:** Satellites equipped with various sensors can capture images of large areas, allowing researchers to identify changes in land use, vegetation patterns, and geological features. This data can be analyzed to locate potential archaeological sites, especially in regions that are difficult to access on foot.

- **Geophysical Surveys:** Techniques such as ground-penetrating radar (GPR), magnetometry, and electrical resistivity can provide information about subsurface structures without excavation. These methods help archaeologists detect buried features like walls, foundations, and graves, providing insights into past human activities.

2. Understanding Landscape Dynamics: Remote sensing techniques help archaeologists understand the historical landscape dynamics and environmental changes that influenced human settlement and activity. By analyzing data over time, researchers can track changes in land use, water availability, and climate, shedding light on how ancient civilizations adapted to their surroundings. For instance, in Rajasthan, remote sensing data has been used to study the impact of monsoon patterns on agricultural practices and settlement patterns in ancient times.

3. Data Integration and Analysis: The integration of aerial survey data and remote sensing results allows for a comprehensive analysis of archaeological landscapes. By combining various data sources, archaeologists can develop more nuanced interpretations of human behavior and societal organization. For example, integrating LiDAR data with historical texts and archaeological findings can lead to a deeper understanding of the socio-political dynamics of Rajasthan's past kingdoms.

4. Challenges and Limitations: While modern techniques like aerial surveys and remote sensing have revolutionized archaeological research, they are not without challenges. Data interpretation requires specialized training and expertise, and the effectiveness of these methods can vary depending on environmental conditions, such as vegetation cover and soil types. Additionally, while aerial surveys and remote sensing can identify potential sites, ground truthing through excavation and on-site investigation is often necessary to verify findings and gain a more comprehensive understanding of the archaeological context.

24.1.3 The Future of Archaeological Research in Rajasthan

As technological advancements continue to evolve, the potential for further enhancing archaeological research in Rajasthan is immense. The integration of artificial intelligence (AI) and machine learning into data analysis may streamline the identification and interpretation of archaeological features, allowing for more efficient site assessment and documentation.

Moreover, community involvement and citizen science initiatives are gaining traction, enabling local populations to participate in archaeological projects. Engaging local communities not only fosters a sense of ownership and pride in cultural heritage but also enriches archaeological studies with local knowledge and perspectives.

24.2 Unexplored Sites and Future Excavation Plans

Rajasthan, with its rich historical tapestry and archaeological significance, remains a treasure trove of unexplored sites that hold the potential for significant discoveries. While many important archaeological sites have been excavated, numerous areas still await thorough investigation, promising to enhance our understanding of the region's ancient civilizations. This chapter delves into some of these unexplored sites, their historical significance, and future excavation plans aimed at unveiling the hidden narratives of Rajasthan's past.

24.2.1 The Importance of Unexplored Sites

Unexplored archaeological sites are crucial for expanding our knowledge of ancient civilizations. These sites often preserve artifacts, structures, and cultural remnants that can provide insights into the social, economic, and political dynamics of past societies. In Rajasthan, where a complex interplay of diverse cultures has existed for centuries, the potential for new findings is immense.

Many unexplored sites may contain layers of habitation, reflecting various historical phases and cultural influences. Excavating these sites can reveal how different communities interacted, adapted to environmental changes, and contributed to the region's development over time. Furthermore, these sites can provide valuable information about ancient technologies, trade networks, and belief systems, enriching our understanding of Rajasthan's historical narrative.

24.2.2 Prominent Unexplored Sites in Rajasthan

1. **Sihor Fort**: Nestled in the Aravalli range, Sihor Fort is a lesser-known site that dates back to the 12th century. Its strategic location offers insights into the military architecture of the time. Preliminary surveys suggest the presence of ancient structures and artifacts that could shed light on the fort's role in regional defense and trade. Future excavations may uncover hidden chambers, weaponry, and inscriptions that could enhance our understanding of the site's historical significance.

2. **Bhangarh Fort**: Famous for its haunting legends, Bhangarh Fort is often overlooked for its archaeological potential. The fort, built in the 17th century, contains

ruins that hint at its historical importance as a bustling town. Future excavations could uncover residential areas, temples, and marketplaces, providing a glimpse into the daily lives of its inhabitants and the socio-economic dynamics of the time.

3. **Mandore**: Located near Jodhpur, Mandore is known for its historical significance as the former capital of the Marwar region. While some areas have been excavated, many sections remain unexplored. The presence of ancient temples, cenotaphs, and burial sites suggests a rich cultural heritage. Targeted excavations could reveal artifacts that illustrate the artistic styles, religious practices, and political history of the region.

4. **Osian**: Often referred to as the "Khajuraho of Rajasthan," Osian is home to numerous temples and ruins. However, much of the surrounding area remains unexplored. Excavations could uncover additional temples, inscriptions, and artifacts that provide insights into the religious practices and architectural styles of ancient Rajasthan, as well as the influence of trade routes in the region.

5. **Narlai**: Narlai is a small village that holds the potential for significant archaeological discoveries. Historical records indicate that it was once an important trade center. Preliminary surveys have identified ancient structures and artifacts that suggest a bustling settlement. Future excavations could reveal trade routes, residential patterns, and the socio-economic structure of the area during its peak.

24.2.3 Future Excavation Plans

To tap into the archaeological potential of unexplored sites, comprehensive excavation plans are necessary. Collaborations between local governments, archaeological departments, and academic institutions can facilitate systematic exploration. Here are some proposed strategies for future excavations:

1. **Survey and Mapping**: Conducting detailed surveys and mapping of unexplored sites is essential to identify areas of interest. Utilizing modern technology, such as ground-penetrating radar (GPR) and aerial photography, can provide insights into subsurface structures without extensive excavation.

2. **Interdisciplinary Research**: Collaborating with historians, geologists, and environmental scientists can enrich the excavation process. Understanding the geographical and environmental context can help identify factors that influenced settlement patterns, trade routes, and resource management in ancient Rajasthan.

3. **Community Engagement**: Involving local communities in excavation efforts fosters a sense of ownership and responsibility for cultural heritage. Community-led initiatives can help identify potential sites and ensure that archaeological findings are preserved for future

generations.

4. **Preservation of Artifacts**: Developing plans for the preservation and conservation of artifacts uncovered during excavations is vital. Establishing local museums and conservation centers can facilitate the study and display of findings, promoting public interest and awareness of Rajasthan's archaeological heritage.

5. **Educational Programs**: Implementing educational programs that emphasize the importance of archaeology can inspire future generations to engage with their cultural heritage. Workshops, seminars, and field schools can raise awareness about the significance of preserving unexplored sites and the stories they hold.

24.2.4 Challenges in Excavation

While the prospects of exploring new archaeological sites in Rajasthan are exciting, several challenges must be addressed. Funding limitations, bureaucratic hurdles, and the need for specialized expertise can hinder excavation efforts. Additionally, the preservation of sites in the face of urban development and environmental degradation is a significant concern.

To overcome these challenges, collaboration between governmental agencies, non-profit organizations, and academic institutions is crucial. Securing funding from various sources, including grants and public-private partnerships, can facilitate the neccssary research and excavation activities. Moreover, raising public awareness about the importance of archaeological heritage can garner community support and foster a collective effort to protect and preserve these sites.

24.3 Importance of Technology in Preserving Rajasthan's Heritage

Rajasthan, known for its rich cultural heritage, historical monuments, and vibrant traditions, faces significant challenges in preserving its heritage amidst rapid modernization, urbanization, and climate change. Technology plays a crucial role in addressing these challenges, offering innovative solutions for the documentation, conservation, and promotion of Rajasthan's diverse cultural assets. This chapter explores the importance of technology in preserving Rajasthan's heritage, highlighting various technological advancements, their applications, and their impact on heritage conservation.

24.3.1 Digitization of Heritage: A New Era of Documentation

One of the most significant technological advancements in heritage preservation is digitization. This process involves converting physical artifacts, manuscripts, and structures into digital formats, allowing for their documentation and analysis. In Rajasthan, numerous initiatives have been undertaken to digitize cultural heritage, enabling greater accessibility and preserving valuable information for future generations.

For instance, organizations like the **Rajasthan Heritage Walk** project utilize digital platforms to document historical sites, providing virtual tours and detailed information about monuments. By creating 3D models of temples, forts, and palaces, researchers and tourists can explore these sites from anywhere in the world. This not only enhances awareness of Rajasthan's rich heritage but also serves as a vital educational tool for students, researchers, and the general public.

Furthermore, digitization enables the preservation of fragile manuscripts and texts. Initiatives such as the **National Manuscripts Mission** focus on cataloging and digitizing ancient texts, ensuring that invaluable knowledge is not lost to decay or damage. By creating digital archives, scholars can access and study these texts without risking their physical deterioration.

24.3.2 Geographic Information Systems (GIS): Mapping Heritage Sites

Geographic Information Systems (GIS) are essential tools for heritage conservation in Rajasthan, enabling researchers to map and analyze cultural heritage sites. GIS technology allows for the visualization of spatial data, facilitating the identification of patterns and relationships among heritage sites, landscapes, and surrounding communities.

In Rajasthan, GIS has been employed to create detailed maps of heritage sites, helping conservationists understand the geographical context of these locations. For example, mapping the locations of forts, palaces, and temples across the state provides insights into historical trade routes, military strategies, and cultural exchanges. This spatial analysis is crucial for effective heritage management, as it aids in prioritizing conservation efforts and resource allocation.

Moreover, GIS can assist in monitoring changes to heritage sites over time. By integrating satellite imagery and remote sensing data, researchers can track the impact of urbanization, climate change, and natural disasters on cultural heritage. This information is invaluable for developing strategies to mitigate risks and enhance the resilience of heritage sites.

24.3.3 3D Scanning and Modeling: Preserving Physical Structures

The application of 3D scanning and modeling technology has revolutionized the preservation of physical structures in Rajasthan. This technology enables the creation of accurate digital representations of monuments, allowing for detailed analysis and restoration planning.

For instance, the **3D scanning of the Hawa Mahal** in Jaipur provides architects and conservationists with precise data on the structure's dimensions and conditions. This information is crucial for developing restoration plans that respect the original architectural integrity while addressing any structural issues. Additionally, 3D models can be used for educational purposes, allowing students and researchers to interact with heritage structures in a virtual environment.

Furthermore, 3D printing technology has emerged as a valuable tool in heritage preservation. Replicas of artifacts and architectural elements can be created to replace damaged or missing components without compromising the integrity of the original structure. This approach not only facilitates restoration efforts but also allows for the display of artifacts in museums and educational institutions, providing visitors with a tangible connection to Rajasthan's cultural heritage.

24.3.4 Conservation Technologies: Innovative Approaches to Preservation

Advancements in conservation technologies have enhanced the methods used to preserve Rajasthan's heritage. Techniques such as non-invasive imaging, chemical analysis, and materials science are increasingly employed to assess the condition of artifacts and structures.

For example, **infrared imaging** and **ultrasonic testing** are non-invasive methods that can reveal hidden structural issues in monuments without causing damage. These techniques are particularly valuable for assessing the condition of ancient structures like forts and palaces, allowing for informed conservation decisions.

Chemical analysis plays a crucial role in understanding the materials used in historical artifacts. By analyzing the composition of paints, pigments, and building materials, conservators can develop appropriate conservation strategies that respect the original materials while addressing degradation and deterioration.

24.3.5 Community Engagement: Leveraging Social Media and Online Platforms

Technology also plays a vital role in engaging local communities and raising awareness about heritage preservation efforts. Social media and online platforms provide opportunities for heritage organizations to connect with the public, fostering a sense of ownership and responsibility for cultural heritage.

In Rajasthan, various NGOs and cultural organizations utilize social media to share stories, photographs, and information about heritage sites. Campaigns that encourage community involvement in conservation activities, such as cleanup drives and awareness programs, have gained traction through these platforms. By harnessing the power of social media, heritage organizations can mobilize support and advocate for the protection of Rajasthan's cultural assets.

Moreover, online platforms offer avenues for crowdsourcing information and resources. Initiatives that invite individuals to contribute their knowledge, photographs, and experiences related to heritage sites enhance the collective understanding of Rajasthan's rich cultural tapestry.

Conclusion

The exploration of Rajasthan's archaeological heritage reveals a complex historical narrative shaped by the region's unique geography and diverse civilizations. From the Stone Age to the grandeur of Rajput forts, the archaeological record uncovers a rich tapestry of human adaptation, innovation, and cultural exchange. This journey through the various stages of civilization in Rajasthan highlights how ancient societies responded to the challenges posed by their environment, particularly in the arid expanses of the Thar Desert.

Modern techniques such as aerial surveys and remote sensing have significantly transformed archaeological research in Rajasthan. These technologies empower researchers to uncover hidden sites and gather invaluable data without intrusive excavation. Aerial surveys provide a broader perspective of the landscape, while remote sensing techniques enable detailed analysis of subsurface features, enhancing our understanding of historical settlement patterns and architectural development. This fusion of traditional methodologies with cutting-edge technology offers a more holistic view of Rajasthan's archaeological landscape, enriching comprehension of ancient societies.

Furthermore, the findings discussed emphasize the importance of interdisciplinary approaches in archaeology. By integrating historical texts, folklore, and environmental studies, researchers can construct more nuanced interpretations of past cultures. The role of local communities in archaeological research is also vital, highlighting the need for collaborative efforts that draw on indigenous knowledge and heritage.

The significance of Rajasthan's archaeological explorations lies in understanding the intricate relationships between geography, culture, and technology throughout history. As ongoing advancements in technology continue to shape the future of archaeological research, the insights gained from studying Rajasthan's past will undoubtedly inform and inspire future generations. The commitment to preserving and studying this rich archaeological heritage ensures that the stories of Rajasthan's ancient civilizations remain vibrant and accessible, fostering a deeper appreciation for the complexities of human history.

www.ingramcontent.com/pod-product-compliance
Ingram Content Group UK Ltd.
Pitfield, Milton Keynes, MK11 3LW, UK
UKHW062305290726
14090UKWH00018B/889

9 798886 674880